THE DIMENSIONS OF PARKING

FOURTH EDITION

Urban Land Institute

About ULI—the Urban Land Institute

ULI–the Urban Land Institute is a nonprofit education and research institute that is supported and directed by its members. Its mission is to provide responsible leadership in the use of land in order to enhance the total environment.

ULI sponsors education programs and forums to encourage an open international exchange of ideas and sharing of experiences; initiates research that anticipates emerging land use trends and issues and proposes creative solutions based on that research; provides advisory services; and publishes a wide variety of materials to disseminate information on land use and development. Established in 1936, the Institute today has more than 15,000 members and associates from more than 50 countries representing the entire spectrum of the land use and development disciplines.

Richard M. Rosan
President

Editorial and Production Staff

Rachelle L. Levitt
Senior Vice President, Policy and Practice
Publisher

Gayle Berens
Vice President, Real Estate Development Practice

Robert T. Dunphy
Senior Resident Fellow, Transportation
ULI Project Director

Christian R. Luz
Senior Vice President, HNTB
NPA Project Director

Nancy H. Stewart
Director, Book Program
Managing Editor

Carol E. Soble
Manuscript Editor

Betsy Van Buskirk
Art Director
Book and Cover Design

Martha Loomis
Desktop Publishing Specialist

Diann Stanley-Austin
Director, Publishing Operations

About NPA–the National Parking Association

The National Parking Association (NPA), founded in 1951, is an international network of more than 1,100 parking professionals from across the United States and around the world —the trade association for the parking industry. Members include private commercial parking operators; suppliers of equipment or services to the industry; parking administrators for colleges and universities, hospitals, municipalities, airports, and public authorities; engineers and architects; and developers. The Parking Consultants Council is a special professional group within the NPA, composed primarily of engineers and architects who produce a broad range of technical publications on the design, construction, and layout of parking facilities as well as recommended guidelines for zoning ordinances, use of handicapped spaces, lighting, and other issues of importance to traffic engineers, state and municipal officials, and parking professionals. The NPA acts as a clearinghouse for parking industry information, provides special services for its members, tracks federal legislation of interest to parking, sponsors an annual international convention and trade exposition, and publishes a magazine ten times a year.

Martin L. Stein
Executive Director

Recommended bibliographic listing:
ULI–the Urban Land Institute and NPA–the National Parking Association. *The Dimensions of Parking*. Fourth Edition. Washington, D.C.: ULI–the Urban Land Institute, 2000.

ULI Catalog Number: D85
International Standard Book Number: 0-87420-827-0
Library of Congress Catalog Card Number: 00-100594

Copyright 2000 by ULI–the Urban Land Institute
1025 Thomas Jefferson Street, N.W.
Suite 500 West
Washington, D.C. 20007-5201

Third Printing, 2005

PACKNOWLEDGMENTS

This publication is the latest product of a partnership between the Urban Land Institute and the National Parking Association that goes back over 25 years. It presents the expert judgment of the NPA's Parking Consultants Council on 24 parking topics. Providing leadership to this group was Chris Luz of HNTB, who chaired the effort, facilitated the review, brokered disagreements, and assisted in all phases of the manuscript preparation. HNTB also provided artwork for the cover design as well as photos. We owe special thanks for the organization of the book to Dick Beebe of Consulting Engineers Group, John Burgan of HNTB, Dewey Hemba of Graef, Anhalt, Schloemer and Associates, and especially Rick Choate, Choate Parking Consultants, the current chair of the Parking Consultants Council. Former NPA staff member Bart Ecker assisted in the committee review of the manuscript and in providing access to NPA's photo resources. Professor Robert Cervero of the University of California at Berkeley, a ULI fellow, also reviewed the manuscript. The project has enjoyed strong commitment from Rachelle Levitt, ULI's senior vice president, policy and practice, and Gayle Berens, vice president, real estate development practice, who directed the product design and development.

Finally, I would like to thank the ULI staff members instrumental in production, led by Nancy Stewart, Martha Loomis, and Ronnie Van Alstyne, who helped maintain contact with the many different participants and assisted in the compilation of the manuscript.

Robert T. Dunphy
Senior Resident Fellow, Transportation
Project Director

ABOUT THE AUTHORS

Richard S. Beebe, director of parking and transportation, Consulting Engineers Group, Mount Prospect, Illinois.

Larry Church, project manager, Walker Parking Consultants/Engineers, Inc., Elgin, Illinois.

Thomas J. D'Arcy, president, CEG-TX, Consulting Engineers Group, San Antonio, Texas.

Larry Donoghue, president, Larry Donoghue Associates. Inc., Park Ridge, Illinois.

Thomas Feagins, Jr., vice president, Walter P. Moore & Associates, Inc., Houston, Texas.

Norman L. Goldman, senior vice president, Desman Associates, West Hartford, Connecticut.

Abraham Gutman, president, Lev Zetlin Associates, New York, New York.

Mark Hoffman, THP Limited, Cincinnati, Ohio.

Robert P. Jurasin, PE, senior vice president, Wilbur Smith Associates, New Haven, Connecticut.

Jean M. Keneipp, senior consultant, Kimley-Horn Associates, Inc., Chicago, Illinois.

Kenneth Kowall, vice president, Consulting Engineers Group, Mount Prospect, Illinois.

I. Paul Lew, senior vice president/principal, Lev Zetlin Associates, New York, New York.

Christian R. Luz, PE, AICP, senior vice president, HNTB Corporation, East Lansing, Michigan.

Donald R. Monahan, CPFM, principal, Walker Parking Consultants/Engineers, Inc., Englewood, Colorado.

Stephen J. Rebora, RA, vice president, Desman Associates, Chicago, Illinois.

Richard C. Rich, principal, Rich + Associates, Inc., Southfield, Michigan.

Gerald Salzman, principal associate, Kimley-Horn Associates, Inc., Chicago, Illinois.

Michael P. Schaefer, principal, Parking Finance Associates, Inver Grove Heights, Minnesota.

Stephen J. Shannon, director of parking services, Cagley Harman & Associates, King of Prussia, Pennsylvania.

Mary S. Smith, senior vice president, Walker Parking Consultants/Engineers, Inc., Indianapolis, Indiana.

James E. Staif, president, Carl Walker, Inc., Dallas, Texas.

William Surna, senior parking planner, Graef, Anhalt, Schloemer & Associates, Inc., Milwaukee, Wisconsin.

H. Carl Walker, CEO, Carl Walker, Inc., Kalamazoo, Michigan.

CONTENTS

FOREWORD

The parking industry continues to be a vital force in the American economy. The availability of parking is central to the successful development of the nation's urban centers and businesses. Thousands of men and women are employed by companies that design and build parking facilities, manage them, or manufacture equipment used in the parking industry.

It is said that there is no such thing as a free lunch. There is also no such thing as free parking. Construction costs, maintenance costs, operating costs —all must be paid. Although the end-user may not pay, someone does— merchants seeking to increase patronage, employers striving to retain employees, municipalities providing a public service. Those who pay for parking expect it to be constructed, operated, and maintained safely, efficiently, and economically. Builders and managers alike must be aware of and able to use or respond to advances in technology, changes in customer preferences, the requirements of the Americans with Disability Act (ADA), zoning ordinances, financing options, tax law, and a host of other considerations.

The Parking Consultants Council of the National Parking Association was formed in 1972 in an effort to consolidate the best current knowledge in the field of parking design and management and to provide a mechanism for making this information available to the public. Composed of experts, the council is concerned with economic analysis, functional and structural design, financial counseling, research, analysis, and maintenance of off-street parking facilities. The training and experience of council members make them uniquely qualified to examine every aspect of parking.

The first edition of *The Dimensions of Parking* was published in 1979 and quickly became an overwhelming success. In response to continuing demand

and changing conditions, a second edition was published in 1983 and a third edition in 1993. Now, the industry has witnessed many major developments in parking, including increasing computerization and automation and changes in ADA requirements and transportation demand management regulations. We believe that this updated fourth edition of *The Dimensions of Parking* will continue to fill an important need for timely information on the parking industry. We extend our thanks to the Urban Land Institute for its cooperation and assistance in this joint venture.

Martin L. Stein
Executive Director
The National Parking Association

PREFACE

The Dimensions of Parking, Fourth Edition, is the result of a continuing joint effort between the National Parking Association and the Urban Land Institute. The first edition was published in 1979, the result of a joint involvement that extended over five years. That edition covered 14 topics related to parking. In 1983, the second edition was expanded to 18 chapters with substantial appendix material. With this edition, the book has been expanded to 24 chapters and includes new topics on intermodal and automated parking.

Previous topics have been revised, updated, and expanded where appropriate. The result is a guide to best practice in the field of parking.

Since the original edition was published, the dimensions of parking have gone through a full cycle, from accommodating some of the big gas guzzlers of the 1970s to the smaller cars of the 1980s. Recent trends have seen the popularity of the light truck and sports utility and larger vehicles.

This change in the dimensions of the vehicle fleet requires a fresh approach to assure that parking facilities are properly sized, constructed, and operated.

ULI's principal objective is to improve the quality of land use and development. Parking drives development as a significant component of built space. The space required for parking is a critical element in site design, constraining designers' options for the size and location of buildings. Moreover, structured parking is costly, often making public sector participation in its financing key to the feasibility of a downtown revitalization project.

An underlying principle of this publication is that adequate parking can be provided in a cost-effective manner. This will be an increasingly important concern as a profusion of free parking, once a commonly accepted assumption, is challenged on traffic congestion and air quality grounds.

This book gives due space to structured parking because such facilities minimize the amount of land needed to accommodate cars. Emphasis is also given to the fact that ill-conceived facility designs that lack the flexibility to respond to change can damage the present and future economic viability of the land use they are intended to serve. The parking consultant and the parking operator will play increasingly important roles on the development team to assure that parking is adequate but not excessive, and that it is well located, properly maintained, and efficiently operated.

It is hoped that the guidance provided in this publication will be of value to those needing current information on parking. In a field of rapid changes, each project should be addressed with the best information at hand. This edition continues to keep pace with the changes seen since the first *Dimensions of Parking* was conceived a quarter century ago.

Robert T. Dunphy
Senior Resident Fellow, Transportation
ULI Project Director

CHAPTER 1
INTRODUCTION

James E. Staif

STEVEN DUNWELL

Parking as we know it today had its birth in the 1920s. Before that time, early forms of mass transit provided the means of delivering workers to their employment destinations and shoppers to retail destinations. But it was during the 1920s, when the downtown area (central business district or CBD) of all large cities was the major hub of activity, that the concept of the parking garage began to develop. The garage's primary purpose was to protect a vehicle's oil-paint finish from the elements. Getting vehicles off the roadway was not a major concern.

With the potential dangers of carbon monoxide then unknown, garages were typically enclosed. Moreover, automobiles of this era were difficult to start in cold weather; as a result, many parking structures, especially in northern climates, were heated. The importance of mechanical ventilation was not yet a consideration.

In addition, the notion of self-parking had not been conceived. Instead, attendants parked the vehicles of garage patrons. Chauffeurs were not uncommon. Attendant parking required a large drop-off area at the garage entrance, allowing customers to leave their vehicle until an attendant was available to park it. Early garages also sold gasoline and provided other services, such as lubrication, washing, and mechanical repair.

Early parking structures were built with short-span construction; the technology of clear-span construction had yet to be developed. Short-span structures dictated column intrusions with two or three parking stalls between columns; the typical parking stall was seven feet wide. The advent of the large-car versus small-car space was not yet a factor in facility design. Designers of

1

automobiles apparently assumed that future vehicles would not exceed five to six feet in width.

The early boom in parking garage construction flourished until the Great Depression and did not resume until after World War II. Land values decreased significantly as a result of these two events, leading to a proliferation of surface parking lots in the nation's CBDs. During the same period, technological advances saw the emergence of enamel as an automobile paint finish. No longer did vehicles have to be parked indoors to protect their finish.

At the same time, recognition of the often irregular size and dimensions of surface parking areas led to the evolution of parking consulting as a profession. The challenge was to park as many vehicles as possible on any given site. Another important development was the emergence of suburban surface parking.

Parking as we know it today evolved from 1945 to 1965. The early years of the post–World War II era were still characterized by parking garages constructed with short-span structural systems. Yet, the economy was changing and large downtown developments became common. Street congestion underscored the need for more off-street parking facilities.

In the 1950s, attention to garage design came to the forefront. Internal traffic flow patterns became an important consideration. Vehicle battery technology had developed significantly, eliminating the need for enclosed garages to ensure that vehicles would start readily in cold weather.

Self-parking has required changes in parking facility design.

Older parking structures were designed for narrower parking stalls.

Ramp systems were designed to accommodate the rapid entry and exit of vehicles. Enclosed parking garages became a thing of the past. The elimination of exterior enclosing walls meant substantial cost savings. And one benefit of eliminating walls was natural ventilation. Thus, the concept of the open parking structure was born.

During the 1950s and 1960s, the notion of "bigger is better" in vehicle design made its impact on parking design. The five-foot-wide vehicle went the way of horse-drawn vehicles. New vehicles were six and one-half feet wide and 19 feet long—or more. As a result, traditional short-span construction could not accommodate newer vehicles. The existing column grids that determined the area available for parking spaces effectively reduced garage capacity by one-third to one-half.

The mid-1950s brought two important changes in the parking industry. The first was the development of clear-span construction technology, which allows longer spans and eliminates the interference of columns with parking space layouts. The second change was the introduction of self-parking. Drivers' preference for parking their own vehicles and the opportunity for major labor savings led to shifts in the parking facility design profession. A complete rethinking of design concepts and dimensional standards evolved, and innovation in parking design to meet the needs of self-parking brought many changes.

Another aspect of the self-park evolution was the development of head-in parking. In earlier decades, an attendant backed the vehicle into its parking space to facilitate its rapid retrieval. In contrast, head-in parking at angles ranging from 45 to 90 degrees better accommodates patrons who park their own vehicle.

With self-parking came the introduction of gently sloping and continuous floor systems. The elimination of steep ramps allowed park-on ramps with slopes of 5 percent or less and meant that efficient designs could use the park-on ramps for the vertical circulation of vehicles. Other concepts that evolved at this time for the benefit of the parking patron included a focus on lighting, signage, drainage, and safety throughout the structure. Gone were the manlifts used by attendants to retrieve a patron's vehicle. Pedestrian elevators expedited patron travel to and from the parked vehicle.

The development and acceptance of prestressed concrete afforded designers the ability to achieve long spans at a more economic cost. The use of precast, prestressed concrete and cast-in-place, post-tensioned concrete allowed designers to achieve clear spans of 60 feet or more. These structural innovations are still used in the construction of most parking structures. In fact, clear-span construction became an important element of general building construction in response to ever-increasing land and construction costs.

From the beginning and up to the mid-1960s, parking garages were usually built by, owned by, or associated with large retail department stores and large office buildings located within the central business district. However, the continued development of both CBDs and suburban business districts has had a profound impact on parking garage construction in terms of facility users and the parking demand generated by development. Today, parking facilities are constructed for a variety of user categories such as hospitals, colleges and universities, office buildings, hotels, municipalities, airports, sports stadiums, and even places of worship.

Each of the above user categories requires special garage design features to ensure facility efficiency and effectiveness. Meeting the parking needs of the user and responding to land constraints often translate into the construction of freestanding multilevel parking. It also is not uncommon for a parking structure to be completely integrated with the building that it serves.

With the advent of self-parking and the design of parking facilities for different user types, the need for the development of garage operating control equipment soon became apparent. The concept of a professional parking operator was beginning to take hold as a means of developing and managing garage operations and providing resources for constructing new parking facilities. The benefit of collecting fees for parking became an opportunity to create a steady stream of income. Obviously, parking more vehicles on a given site would increase total revenue. Initial operations

were a true "cigar-box" method of collection. But the introduction of the ticket dispenser and the increased size of facilities changed all that, and today's parking operator began to emerge. Equipment such as the ticket dispenser, vehicle presence detectors, differential counters, and card-controlled access gates were undergoing development. Operating control equipment was designed to facilitate the movement of vehicle traffic into and out of parking facilities, to reduce operating costs, and to ensure the collection of parking revenue. Pay parking became a vital element in the successful development of many projects, allowing for a revenue stream to offset the expenses of the facility.

Today, parking access and revenue control systems (PARCS) are a major factor in both the design of many new parking facilities and the retrofit of existing facilities. Operational components such as pay-and-display, central cashiering, exit cashiering, pay-on-foot, and credit card use are all part of the design considerations for new facilities. Technology such as Automatic Vehicle Identification (AVI), License Plate Inventory (LPI), and License Plate Recognition (LPR) has enhanced parking facilities' overall operations and revenue control capabilities.

A major factor in the suburbanization of retailing in the 1950s and 1960s and of office space in the 1960s and 1970s was the proliferation of free parking for all users. Given that suburban land was inexpensive, developers did not pay careful attention to estimates of demand and efficient park-

Improved signage and elevators are necessary to support self-parking.

ing design, both of which typified the development of paid garages in the nation's CBDs. Parking studies, at least in urban areas, that considered the characteristics of tenants or owners, the availability of alternative modes of transportation, and competition from other parking facilities were typically replaced with generic local parking codes imposed by suburban governments. Moreover, the codes have remained remarkably consistent across different cities despite varying economic levels, population size, and density. One consequence is that suburban parking facilities are sometimes oversized, leading to unproductive use of land and excess drainage and pollution from runoff.

Two other events had a significant impact on the design of parking facilities. First, the 1970s saw an increase in the number of foreign-made vehicles sold in the United States. Second, the gasoline shortage of the early and late 1970s spurred demand for smaller cars. Designers were faced with the challenge of implementing smaller-width parking stalls; widths decreased from nine feet to eight feet to seven and one-half feet.

Designing specifically for small cars increased overall facility capacity by 15 to 20 percent. However, small-car use was not universal across the country; as a result, location and site-specific use trends became design factors. More important was how to control facilities that accommodate both large- and small-car parking stalls. The dilemma was how to ensure that drivers of small vehicles would not park in large-

Parking facility developed behind restored retail shops has helped revitalize South Beach in Miami.

The mix of different sized vehicles determines the stall dimensions.

car spaces and vice versa, thus causing a potential loss of total available parking spaces in a given parking facility.

The impact of small cars on the parking industry was enormous. The 1980s saw almost 50 percent of all vehicles sold in the United States classified as small cars. One significant influence on small-car production was growing concern over clean air. Many West Coast cities reported as much as a 75 percent increase in the small-car population.

Concerns over air quality, especially ozone, have led some communities to focus on parking as a means of limiting driving. For example, in the 1970s, Massachusetts capped the number of commercial parking spaces in downtown Boston. Just as the use of simple parking codes in the suburbs has resulted in some overdesigned parking facilities, public policies that limit parking below market demand can stifle development, particularly given that a downtown is typically the area with the highest level of transit use, car pooling, multiple trips, and thus automobile use within a metropolitan region. In the same way that suburban parking policies have attracted businesses to the suburbs, city parking policies should not drive businesses to the suburbs, especially if doing so undermines environmental goals.

In the late 1990s and early 2000s, the bigger is better attitude resurfaced. It is apparent that the nation will always have a mixed population of large and small vehicles; however, the proportion of large vehicles, including trucks and

Modern garage integrated into development served by a shuttle bus.

sport utility vehicles, is increasing and must be considered a major design factor.

We must remain cognizant of the challenges to be addressed in the design of parking facilities. Ingenuity, creativity, and experience will be major components in successful parking projects. Clean air, the electric car, and adaptive use are some of the many challenges we face in the new millennium.

The evolution of parking facilities from the early 1920s to today has brought about significant adaptation to reduced site size and availability as well as new materials, construction technologies, parking patterns, user needs, and vehicle sizes. The chapters in this volume discuss many of the parking industry's latest technologies and strategies. Owners and developers are encouraged to use this material when proposing or constructing parking facilities.

CHAPTER 2
PARKING STUDIES

Mary S. Smith

Automobile parking is essential to most land uses. The adequacy of parking influences economic return on public and private sector investments and affects property values. On a broad scale, decisions about parking influence travel behavior and choice of travel mode as well as land use and development patterns. The development, operation, and maintenance of parking facilities can represent a significant expense. Thus, adequate, convenient, and affordable parking is of concern to nearly everyone who uses an automobile or is affected by the use of automobiles.

To plan, design, construct, operate, and regulate parking requires a wide range of expertise and usually reflects some degree of both public and private sector involvement. Public involvement can range from the typical permitting and regulatory responsibilities to full responsibility for development and operation of parking facilities. Most parking, however, is developed and operated by the private sector. Regardless of how responsibilities are allocated, parking poses a multitude of challenges. The best means of addressing these challenges is largely a matter of experienced judgment based on proper data collection and analysis of site-specific circumstances. The complexity of the associated issues has made parking planning a highly specialized technical art.

The intricacies of parking warrant careful analysis and coordinated decision making. As a result, parking consultants are now typically involved in all aspects of parking facility development and operation. Parking consultants perform services that assist public agencies, hospitals, institutions, businesses, developers, and investors. The parking consultant's role is to provide experienced technical assistance to individuals in decision-making positions.

FIGURE 2-1

KEY STEPS IN FINANCIAL FEASIBILITY ANALYSIS

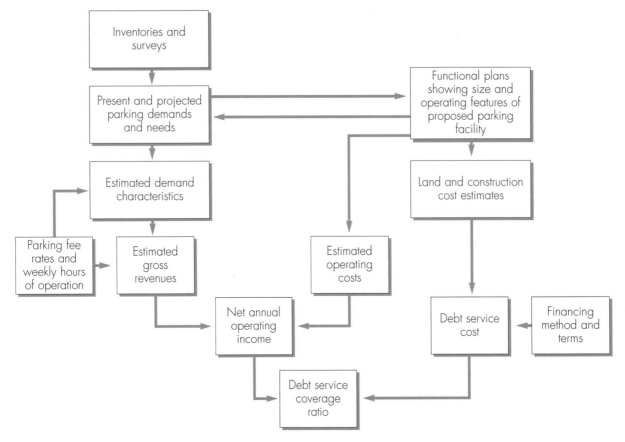

Source: Robert A. Weant and Herbert S. Levinson, *Parking* (Westport, Conn.: Eno Foundation for Transportation, Inc., 1990).

Some parking consultants offer a limited but highly specialized scope of services. Others may command the capabilities and resources to provide a comprehensive range of consulting services, including

- planning and site studies;
- traffic studies/engineering reports;
- design;
- construction management;
- operations consulting; and
- repair and maintenance programs.

Given the usual complexity of parking problems, the first step toward a solution is the parking feasibility study. Whether the problem is how to meet current or future needs, how to improve current operations, or how to determine the extent of facility repair or maintenance, the parking study quantifies a parking problem and its causes, analyzes alternative solutions, and recommends actions based on site-specific evidence and circumstances. When appropriate, the parking consultant identifies opportunities for coordinated actions, details the probable ramifications of implementing those actions, and provides an estimate of financial and other related costs.

A parking feasibility study should be no more voluminous than necessary, highlighting the most salient statistics and making recommendations based on data collection and analysis. It should communicate in a way that is easily understood by nonspecialists, thereby enabling the client to use the data to arrive at the same conclusions as the professionals who performed the study.

There are as many types of parking studies as there are parking problems to be solved. In some cases, the parking study may have multiple tasks. In general, though, a traditional parking feasibility study includes each of the following three components:

- parking supply/demand analysis;
- site alternatives analysis; and
- financial feasibility analysis.

Some parking feasibility studies consist of only one of the above components; others include additional components, such as an analysis of traffic impacts or management/operations issues.

The menu of analysis that might form parts of a parking study includes the following:

- *Parking supply/demand analysis.* Determines current and future parking supply and demand.

- *Market study.* Identifies how many users a facility will capture on a particular site given demand, competitive climate, and prevailing parking rates.
- *Shared parking.* Determines the need for parking in mixed-use/multiuse development areas in view of variations in individual-use needs by time of day, day of week, and season and the relationship of needs among planned land uses.
- *Site alternatives.* Involves selection and comparison of sites for the parking improvements that will be required to resolve documented parking shortages.
- *Schematic design.* Involves developing the functional design for a proposed parking facility to a level of detail sufficient to obtain concurrence of the interested parties. Design documents normally constitute the first phase of a design contract, but they may be nec-

essary during the feasibility study phase to provide the background information needed to obtain consensus and proceed with design and funding.
- *Traffic impact analysis (TIA).* Applies standardized traffic engineering analysis to determine current and/or future traffic conditions and to recommend improvements. Although the TIA generally focuses on determining the effect of a proposed parking facility on traffic conditions, it sometimes needs to address existing traffic problems that should be considered simultaneously with parking needs.
- *Financial feasibility.* Involves an analysis of what and how much various parties should pay for the parking facility (see chapter 18). In most cases, a client already knows how a parking project or improvement program will be financed. For example, a city plans to use

FIGURE 2-2

PARKING STUDY AREA MAP

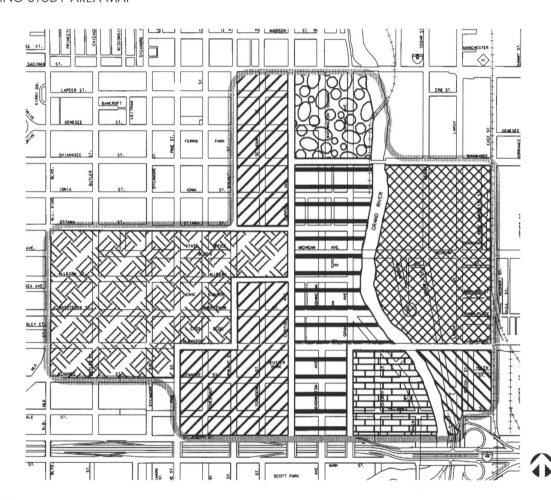

LEGEND

- Central Business District
- Entertainment
- Office
- Institutional
- Historic
- Commercial/Light Industrial
- Government

Source: HNTB, *Downtown Lansing Parking Study* (Lansing, Mich.: City of Lansing, 2000).

A parking facility evaluation determines the extent of deterioration and cost of repair.

general obligation bonds and has financial experts in-house or on retainer who will provide information on the interest rates and terms of the financing instruments under consideration (see Figure 2-1). The financial analysis may address some or all of the following considerations:

- development costs;
- estimates of use and rates;
- revenue and operating expense projections;
- financing costs, interest rate, and term;
- standalone feasibility of a parking facility; and
- feasibility of adding a new facility to an existing system.

- *Financing method.* Involves a detailed study of the available financing methods and their legal ramifications as well as a determination of the interest rate, term, insurance, debt reserves, and other requirements (see chapter 19). The options for consideration may include public/private partnerships, federal/state/local financing programs, private ownership and financing, and sources of creative funding.
- *Parking management.* Addresses the broad issues of parking problems that are attributable to or correctable by changes in management and operating strategies, decisions, and/or policies.
- *Organization and administration review.* Involves detailed study of the administration and operation of the parking system as a whole. It considers issues such as allocation and use of resources, staffing needs, assignment of responsibility for functions, and the general organization chart for all functions. The review is often needed to establish a parking authority or other operating agency that will run an entire parking system.
- *Parking revenue controls and operations study.* Calls for a review of current revenue collection systems and other policies and procedures to ensure

that revenue is maximized and that theft, fraud, and evasion are minimized.

- *Parking equipment acquisition.* Involves a review of current and future operations and recommendations with respect to control equipment and the appropriate type and number of access and egress lanes. The feasibility study phase usually includes cost estimates and outline specifications; detailed construction documents are developed later.

The growth in the size and complexity of large-scale parking systems, such as those at airports, medical centers, and urban complexes, has created the need for highly sophisticated revenue control and parking management systems. These systems report on parking activity levels, fee collections, and revenue and facility management related to levels of use by user type, duration, frequency, and status. Systems that include state-of-the-art hardware, software, and management functions are now available for customization by each owner in accordance with site-specific conditions. For example, Minneapolis–St. Paul International Airport and Los Angeles World Airport are now installing comprehensive revenue control systems for 17,000 and 31,000 parking spaces, respectively. Both projects are scheduled for completion in spring 2001.

- *Parking facility evaluation.* Determines the extent of deterioration in a parking structure floor and frame, along with appropriate repair and cost estimates. Construction documents for repairs are not part of a feasibility study.

Maintenance of parking structures is essential to preserving a facility's function and service and to maintaining its revenue stream. When operators fail to follow routine maintenance practices, they may face serious deterioration problems that result in costly repair/renovation programs or, in the most serious cases, facility closure. Those responsible for facility maintenance (public agencies, private owners, and professional operators) should review physical conditions annually and undertake corrective actions as required. In 1999, the city of Milwaukee completed the renovation of the 490-space garage at 2nd and Plankinton streets in the downtown core. Deterioration had advanced to a point that parking spaces were removed from use because of falling concrete. Neighborhood businesses that rely on the facility developed a phased repair program that closed only two floors of the seven-story garage at a time so that parking operations could continue during reconstruction. Such an approach ensures the success of rehabilitation projects and the continued economic feasibility of parking improvements.

CHAPTER 3
PARKING DEMAND

Gerald Salzman and Jean M. Keneipp

The estimation of parking demand is a critical step in the evolution of a successful parking facility. Unfortunately, parking demand estimation is complex, time-consuming, expensive, and misunderstood and therefore often approached incorrectly. It frequently lends itself to shortcuts that yield erroneous results.

The time and resources spent in estimating parking demand should be consistent with the purpose for developing the estimate. If the estimate is intended to provide only a general idea of how many patrons might use a facility, a broad range is acceptable; in fact, that range may be determined by using a factor available in a published table. On the other hand, if the estimate is to be used to help establish the size of a proposed garage or to support a financial pro forma, the best possible estimate is justified.

Demand estimates may be made for a single land use, such as an office building, or a large mixed-use development, such as a shopping center or a central business district. Sometimes, the demand estimate may include the possible impact of shared parking.

Parking demand is generated by land use, but it can be expressed either in terms of total users for the entire land development project or total users for a given facility. For example, an office building might generate a peak demand of 600 employee parkers and 75 visitor parkers. On the other hand, a proposed garage intended to serve the parking needs of the same building might have an estimated peak occupancy of only 500 employee and 50 visitor parkers; the other parkers destined for the building may park elsewhere.

The reason that parking demand is difficult to determine accurately is that it can be influenced by many conditions. To begin, a given land use can attract many person-trips during a 24-hour period. The number and types of trips in turn depend on the size of the land use, its nature, and the characteristics of the persons who will be attracted to it. If analysts isolate these variables accurately for a representative land use, they can estimate parking demand with great precision. However, analysts rarely develop such data because of the requirement for extensive field surveys and analytic work.

A common shortcut is to select a parking generation ratio or factor from a published source and to modify it to represent estimated conditions. Yet, no simple set of factors can be developed to support an accurate estimate of parking demand. No one factor can be used to estimate the parking demand for a retail establishment located in a suburban area of California, in a small community in the Midwest, or in the heart of an older, large city in the Northeast. Even if a magic factor with a high degree of accuracy could be derived for current conditions, it would become obsolete in a few years as the inevitable changes in shopping habits, transportation characteristics, regulatory policies, and environmental constraints unfold. Further, a table of factors usually does not specify the assumed percent of transit riders or the average number of persons per automobile.

An example of how parking factors can shift over the years is provided by the factor used to determine space requirements for regional shopping centers. In 1965, the shopping center industry standard was 5.5 parking spaces per 1,000 square feet of gross leasable area (GLA), according to the findings of a 1965 Urban Land Institute study (*Parking Requirements for Shopping Centers*, Technical Bulletin 53). Twelve years later, on the basis of research reported in the May 1977 issue of *Urban Land*, "5.0 parking spaces per 1,000 square feet of gross leasable area would be, in general, a valid national maximum as a basis for planning regional shopping centers that have, or will have, a GLA greater than 800,000 square feet." A 1982 study sponsored by ULI concluded that the then-current shopping center generation rate was slightly less than 5.0 and even lower for smaller centers. ULI repeated the study in a 1999 report, *Parking Requirements for Shopping Centers*, Second Edition. This new study shows that shopping center parking rates have declined again, as evidenced by the following findings:

- 4.0 spaces per 1,000 square feet of GLA for centers containing between 25,000 and 400,000 square feet;
- a sliding scale of 4.0 to 4.5 spaces per 1,000 square feet for centers containing between 400,000 and 600,000 square feet; and
- 4.5 spaces per 1,000 square feet for centers containing more than 600,000 square feet.

Adjustments are recommended for shopping centers with significant amounts of floor space used for restaurants, entertainment, and/or cinemas.

Demand Parameters

Three fundamental characteristics or parameters control the parking demand of a given land use: the nature of the building or development that creates the demand; site-specific factors that may constrain parking demand; and time frame factors.

Basic Demand

The first three characteristics below provide the basis for estimating the unrestrained number of person-trips to be made to the proposed development. The other factors can act as a restraint on demand.

- *Type of land use or building use (size, special conditions).* Examples include a freestanding general office building of 200,000 square feet in a suburban setting, a 500-room hotel with 5,000 square feet of restaurant space, or a conference facility with a 200-seat capacity.
- *Socioeconomic characteristics of the persons expected to visit the development.* An example includes a shopping center in a suburb with high levels of automobile ownership. The basic parking demand of the site, building, or area under evaluation can be modified by the nature of the site itself, its trade area, or even the metropolitan area.
- *The proportion of multiple-use trips.* Parking demand at a restaurant, many of whose customers work nearby, is lower because patrons walk to the restaurant, leaving their cars in the work-related parking location.
- *Traffic accessibility of the site.* A proposed garage location could be more or less convenient to its approach streets compared with nearby competitive parking facilities.
- *Parking facility efficiency and attractiveness.* If exiting from a given garage requires excessive time, that garage may lose patronage when better alternatives are available.
- *Cost of parking.* Other factors being equal, if a garage charges high fees, it will experience less-than-ideal patronage compared with competing facilities that charge lower rates.
- *Alternative modes.* If the parking site is well served by transit and an active program encourages or even subsidizes employee transit passes, parking demand will be diminished. An active carpool program can also reduce parking demand.
- *Local policy and codes.* A city may impose a parking tax in certain locations on certain types of parkers, or it may require a specified number of spaces to be held vacant until 10:00 a.m. to accommodate repeat parkers.

FIGURE 3-1

PARKING DEMAND ESTIMATION PROCESS

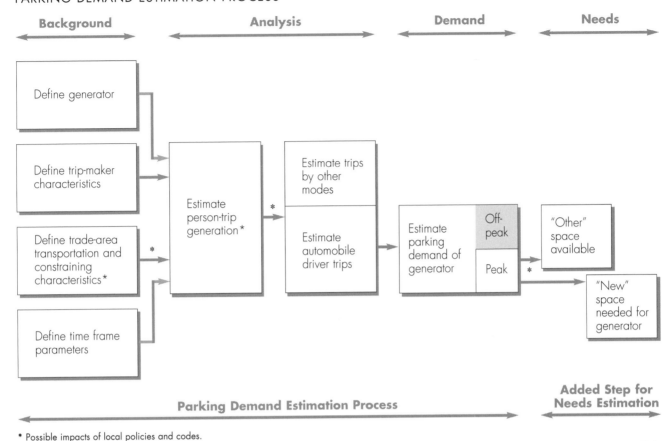

* Possible impacts of local policies and codes.

- *Time frame factors.* Daily trips and parking demand are assigned to the appropriate peak hours to size a parking facility and estimate its revenues.
- *Peak-to-daily relationships.* What proportion of day-long parking occurs during the daily peak on week-days and Saturdays? How does the proportion vary by type of parker—employee, visitor, and so on?
- *Periodic factors (daily, monthly, seasonal).* In most places, retail parking demand is at a maximum in December and typically low in February or July, although current trends suggest increasingly uniform parking demand throughout the year.
- *Nonperiodic factors (long-term changes, abrupt changes).* A downtown may experience a long-term upward or downward trend in economic activity, or a major retail store may leave the CBD.

Figure 3-1 illustrates how the above considerations are used in demand estimation.

Estimating Demand

Despite the problems and cautions already noted, reliable demand estimates can be prepared if the analyst is willing to take time. The best approach is to start with reliable factors and calibrate them to reflect local conditions. Such an

approach assumes that the purpose of the demand estimate justifies the work involved. A four-step approach is outlined as follows:

- Use the best factors available.
- Obtain a reliable definition of the land uses that will generate parking demand.
- Calibrate and/or adjust the factors to replicate local conditions.
- Prepare the estimates of parking demand.

First, the analyst needs to select factors from a reliable source and try to understand all underlying assumptions, such as the number of persons per car, the percent of transit users, and the percent of "captive" patrons or multipurpose trips.

As a guide, Figure 3-2 provides ranges of parking generation for typical situations; generators include retail, office, medical, industrial, and residential uses. Four Urban Land Institute publications—*Industrial Development Handbook, Shopping Center Development Handbook, Residential Development Handbook,* and *Parking Requirements for Shopping Centers,* Second Edition—offer additional insights into parking demand.

After selecting the parking generation factor or factors, the analyst should obtain a reliable accounting of the land

FIGURE 3-2

RANGES OF GENERATION FACTORS

Land Use	Peak Space Factor	Unit	Short-Term Percent
Shopping Center >600,000 sq. ft.	4.5 spaces	Per 1,000 square feet GLA	80
Shopping Center <600,000 sq. ft.	4.0–4.5 spaces	Per 1,000 square feet GLA	80
Office	0.50–3.00 spaces	Per 1,000 square feet GLA	10
Office	0.10–0.75 space	Per employee	10
Medical Center	0.75–4.50 spaces	Per bed	33
Medical Center	0.10–0.75 space	Per employee	33
Industrial	0.67–3.50 spaces	Per 1,000 square feet GLA	10
Industrial	0.36–1.60 spaces	Per employee	10
University/College	0.10–0.50 space	Per student	NA
	0.80 space	Per staff person	NA
Cinema	10–85 spaces	Per screen	100
Hotel	0.20–1.50 spaces	Per room	NA
Restaurant	5–25 spaces	Per 1,000 square feet GLA	90
Residential	0.20–2.00 spaces	Per unit	NA

Sources: ULI–the Urban Land Institute and ICSC, *Parking Requirements for Shopping Centers*, Second Edition (Washington, D.C.: ULI, 1999); ULI–the Urban Land Institute, *Shared Parking* (Washington, D.C.: ULI, 1983); and Barton-Aschman Associates, Inc., for survey data.

uses that will generate parking demand. Land uses should be defined in terms of square footage and/or number of employees by type of use (retail, restaurant, private office, government office, medical facility, hotel, special generator, or other). Units of measurement include seats, rooms, and other units.

The most difficult yet most important step is to calibrate the raw factors to reflect local conditions. First, the analyst should conduct a field count of peak parking occupancy for the representative land use or uses—one building or one area. Next, the analyst uses the unadjusted parking generation factors to estimate peak parking occupancy by multiplying each factor by the appropriate quantified land use. For example, the retail factor (parkers per 1,000 square feet) is multiplied by the number of thousands of square feet of retail. Finally, the analyst compares the two results—counts and estimates. The first comparison is likely to show a difference. If so, the analyst performs a series of iterations to adjust the factors until the results agree, that is, until the estimates match the field counts. The process is easier and more accurate if employees and visitors can be stratified as long- and short-term parkers. When the calibration is completed, the analyst can use the resulting factors or model to estimate parking demand.

Tips on Estimating Demand

If a project involves more than one land use with integrated parking facilities, the analyst should consider adjustments for

shared parking. Substantial parking space reductions may result when variation in peak demand by time of day and season is taken into account. It should be noted, however, that the concept of shared parking applies only if parking is fully integrated into a multiuse project and a significant number of spaces are not reserved.

The most accurate projection of parking demand derives from a thorough understanding of the development program and/or existing conditions, the availability of sound data, and the accurate identification of local factors. To this end, a parking demand study should be conducted at a comparable site or sites and include a detailed parking occupancy survey that determines the availability of existing parking. It may also be helpful to survey patrons or employees at comparable facilities to determine travel patterns, automobile occupancy, and length of stay.

The use of a computer spreadsheet to assist in calculating parking demand permits a greater emphasis on sensitivity analysis. A computerized analysis makes it easy to answer the "what if" questions: What if automobile occupancy changes, or transit use increases, or shared parking is expanded? But, as with most computer applications, good software is not a substitute for reliable data.

How Do I Begin?

Probably the most important question related to a parking demand study is the nature of the information that must be collected. The answer to this question varies by type of project, level of detail needed, and location; however, all studies share certain data needs.

- *An analysis of existing conditions in the study area.* The inventory and occupancy of existing spaces and information on current parking fees can be obtained from public agencies or collected by field survey. At a minimum, the data should be collected for peak hours, which may vary with land uses. Before collecting any data, the analyst must determine the appropriate peak hour and peak day, especially weekdays versus weekends. In some locations, the analyst may need to collect data hourly to determine the peak hour. The analyst might also find it useful to ascertain parking demand at similar developments.

- *An accurate understanding of the proposed project.* To determine parking demand accurately, the analyst must develop a full understanding of the proposed project by identifying any existing use of the property as either a development or a parking facility. If the site is currently used for parking, will such parking be displaced, or will parking continue to be accommodated on site? It is also essential to understand the nature of the proposed development. Will it include multiple land uses, and will parking be isolated or shared? Answers to these questions provide a strong foundation on which to base projections.

- *A detailed list of project constraints and legal requirements.* Legal and other constraints may have a profound effect on parking demand. It is wise to determine any limit at a project's outset. For example, a local zoning ordinance may not permit a reduction due to shared parking. Similarly, a hotel operator in a mixed-use project may insist on segregated and reserved parking for hotel guests. Either of these constraints would increase total parking demand.

- *Parking demand ratios for comparable facilities.* The preferred method for determining parking demand is to survey existing facilities that serve a similar mix and size of land uses and demonstrate similar automobile use and occupancy. Ideally, the study should be conducted on a design day—a day that represents the maximum parking demand that needs to be accommodated during a year. The design day may not be the peak day of the year, but it is usually within the top 10 percent. If possible, an analysis of sales data (for commercial developments) or employment levels (for office or industrial developments) should be used to determine the design day.

- *Unusual site factors.* A brief overview of unusual site factors that may affect parking demand yields the last type of information required for demand estimation. For example, a site plan might show the subject building set far back from the roadway such that transit use would be extremely low. Conversely, a site's inability to provide adequate parking might increase transit use. Parking demand is also influenced by a perception of security and by several other factors.

Armed with basic data, developers and designers can prepare realistic demand estimates.

CHAPTER 4
TRAFFIC IMPACT AND SITE ACCESS

Robert P. Jurasin, PE

S ite access is an important element in the proper planning and design of a parking facility. Safe and efficient entry into, exit from, and circulation within a parking facility contribute significantly to the facility's successful operation.

Site access, which involves the roadway or driveway connections between a parking facility and the public roadway system, requires a thorough evaluation to ensure safe, efficient, and convenient access to and within the facility and to maintain safe and efficient traffic operations on the public roadway system. In many cases, a parking facility may require off-site transportation improvements to facilitate proper traffic flow associated with the facility. The improper placement or design of driveways can create congestion and unsafe operations within the facility itself, at the intersections of driveways and the adjacent roadway system, and even at other major intersections within the larger street system. The result can be an unsuccessful parking garage and therefore an unsuccessful land use served by the facility.

One of the first steps in designing proper site access is to estimate parking demand. A parking facility is not by itself a traffic generator but rather supports the demand for nearby land uses. Such land uses could include

- downtown business centers;
- intermodal transportation facilities;
- shopping centers;
- office and other commercial centers;
- industrial parks;
- major residential complexes;
- mixed-use developments;

- airports, railway stations, and other transportation centers;
- universities and medical centers;
- major recreational facilities; and
- major events and activities (civic centers, convention centers, sports events).

The size and location of parking facilities serving various land uses as well as the size, density, and location of the land uses themselves are critical factors in determining the demand for parking and the resultant traffic generated by the facility (see Figure 4-1). Therefore, traffic impact and access studies and the associated site design for a facility should be part of the planning and design process for parking facilities.

The complexity and extent of a traffic impact and access study depends on the size of the parking facility, the land use(s) served by the facility, the facility's location (urban versus suburban), and the adjacent public roadway system. In addition to determining the traffic served by the facility, the study needs to address the method of access control under consideration for the facility. Whether the parking facility will offer free access or rely on a ticket/cashier system or a card-activated gate system influences the time requirements for vehicles entering and/or exiting from the facility and thus the number of driveways and number of lanes at each driveway.

The potential variation in the considerations noted above makes it difficult to set a standard for the complexity and extent of a traffic impact and access study. Nonetheless, this chapter guides the reader through a traffic impact and access study.

Project Initiation

During the early stages of planning a parking facility, the site for the facility may already have been determined, or there may be opportunities for locating the facility at alternative sites. In either event, the traffic impact and access study is a critical component in identifying preferred locations. The optimal site should be capable of accommodating the required number of on-site parking spaces in proximity to the designated land use(s) that the proposed facility is to support.

The size and location of the parking facility, the land uses to be served, and the local public roadway system all help define the area of influence or the study area. Sometimes the study area encompasses only the roadway adjacent to the parking facility; at other times it may extend to major highways/expressways. Traffic engineers should work with the project team to develop the extent of the traffic impact and access study. The project consists of the proposed development as a whole such as a new office building plus the supporting parking facility. The project team typically comprises the owner, developer, designers, and planners as well as the public review agencies responsible for ultimately approving the project.

Once the project study area has been identified, the traffic and impact access study can be initiated by undertaking the following tasks:
- field investigations and observations of the transportation system and traffic characteristics;
- data collection;
- determination of traffic generation by land uses supported by the parking facility;
- assignment of project site traffic to the transportation system;
- projection of future traffic volumes;
- off-site traffic analysis;
- review of on-site traffic circulation;
- development of a site access plan;
- preparation of recommendations for the on- and off-site transportation system; and
- ensuring compliance with local ordinances, regulations, and approval procedures.

Field Investigation and Data Collection

In this task, the study area is reviewed through field visits to ascertain the physical and operational characteristics of the transportation system and traffic. The field visits should note roadway and intersection geometry and locations and types of signal operation and traffic control devices. Traffic-counting programs should also be undertaken. The data can be summarized into three categories: physical transportation features, operating conditions, and traffic volume activity. Figure 4-1 lists the information often needed for a traffic impact and access study.

Typically, some of the required information is available from municipal, regional, and/or state government agencies and their traffic, planning, and engineering departments. Some data, however, may need to be collected directly through field surveys and traffic-counting efforts. Available data should be categorized, summarized, tabulated, and presented in a clear and concise way for presentation to the client.

Allocation of Traffic Generation to the Land Uses Associated with the Parking Facility

As mentioned, the relative traffic impact of a parking facility is contingent on the land use(s) supported by the facility. Some examples of typical land uses requiring traffic impact and access studies are a shopping center, medical center, office facility, mixed-use development, airport, intermodal transportation center, and special-event facility such as a convention center or sports arena.

Trip Generation, 6th Edition, published by the Institute of Transportation Engineers (ITE), is the most commonly recognized resource document used by traffic engineers to determine the volume and characteristics of traffic generated

FIGURE 4-1

TYPICAL DATA COLLECTED

Physical Transportation Features

Number and width of travel lanes

Directional flow by lane

Roadway and median treatments

Direction of street systems (one-way versus two-way)

Horizontal and vertical geometry of the roadway

Shoulder, curb, and drainage features

Roadway right-of-way widths

Signs and pavement markings and their conditions

Pavement conditions

On-street parking regulations

Posted speed limits

Pedestrian facilities

Traffic control features at intersections (traffic signals, stop, yield)

Bus and transit facilities

Truck loading facilities

Railroad crossings

Above- and below-ground utility services

Other adjacent fixed features (fences, stone walls, bridges, overpasses/underpasses, landscaping)

Adjacent land uses and driveways

Operating Conditions and Features

Traffic flow and turning movement operations

On-street bus activity (frequency and duration), including public transit and school buses

Pedestrian activity

Operating speeds on the roadway system

Sight distances at key intersections and/or site driveways

Effectiveness/condition of traffic control devices

Activity at adjacent driveways

Accident frequency and types of accidents

On-street parking activity

Truck loading and unloading activity

Traffic Volume

Daily and/or peak traffic volume on the roadway system for a typical weekday and, depending on the use of the parking facility, during a typical weekend day

Directional traffic volumes during anticipated peak hours associated with the parking facility and the land use(s) it serves

Vehicle classification (automobile, truck, bus)

Peak-volume characteristics

Other Available Data

Previous traffic impact studies

Transportation improvement programs

Traffic accident records for the most recent three-year period

Overall land use activity

Master plan for the area

Future traffic projections

Transportation use by mode

Ordinances and regulations associated with driveway requirements, including construction and operations

Plans for other major traffic generators and associated roadway improvements

by a land use served by a parking facility. *Trip Generation* provides trip rates expressed as the number of trips generated per employee, acre, or number of square feet for a given land use. It reports trip rates for different land uses during critical peak hours (typically the peak commuter hours) for adjacent roadways and during the peak activity of the land use generator. It also provides estimates of projected daily traffic by land use type.

Seasonal factors should also be considered in developing critical traffic flows entering and exiting from a facility. Seasonal activities typically relate more to retail/shopping centers and recreational activities than to other types of developments. Figure 4-2 illustrates typical peak periods for selected land uses while Figure 4-3 illustrates typical trip generation rates during critical peak hours along the adjacent roadway system for selected land uses.

In most cases, ITE's *Trip Generation* can be used to estimate the traffic to be generated by a development. Occasionally, local governments apply their own trip generation rates and peak-hour traffic volumes associated with various land uses. In the case of special-event activities or specialized land uses, more thorough field studies may be required to estimate traffic generation. In mixed-use settings and downtown business centers, a high level of coordination with the affected municipality may be needed to understand and develop potential traffic flows into and out of a parking facility.

In any event, generally accepted statistical trip generation rates and standardized peak-hour traffic volumes associated with a particular land use and thus with a projected parking facility should be adjusted to reflect local conditions. Some factors that could affect traffic adjustments include the following:

- modal splits (bus versus automobile travel);
- pass-by traffic (drivers already on the road who would be expected to patronize a development);
- carpooling/vanpooling programs;
- pedestrian and bicycle access;
- localized working hours and associated staggered/flexible working hours; and
- special events.

The product of the traffic generation exercise is a detailed representation of traffic volumes projected to enter and exit from the facility during the identified peak hours. At times, it may be appropriate to undertake an analysis of the traffic flow characteristics and associated site access and traffic impacts of a fully discharging parking facility during a peak hour. Such an analysis may be required for evaluating response time in the event of an emergency or for marketing adjacent land use(s).

Assignment of Project Traffic to the Roadway System

The distribution of site traffic during the peak hours of facility operation is essential for understanding the relative impact

FIGURE 4-2

TYPICAL PEAK PERIODS FOR SELECTED LAND USES

Land Use	Peak Periods
Office	7:00 a.m.–9:00 a.m. weekdays
	4:00 p.m.–6:00 p.m. weekdays
Retail	4:00 p.m.–6:00 p.m. weekdays
	7:00 p.m.–9:00 p.m. weekdays
	12:30 p.m.–3:30 p.m. Saturdays seasonal
Special Events (conventions/sports events)	Varies with activity
Hospitals/Medical Centers	7:00 a.m.–9:00 a.m. weekdays
	2:30 p.m.–3:00 p.m. weekdays

Source: Institute of Transportation Engineers, *Trip Generation* (Washington, D.C.: ITE, 1997).

of the parking facility on the adjacent roadway system. Factors for consideration in traffic distribution include the following:

- the existing roadway system serving the local area and routes leading to major highways/expressways within the study area;
- the geometrics and operation of the roadway system (one-way versus two-way, roadway and intersection geometrics, and traffic control devices);

- socioeconomic and demographic information that can help determine the directional distribution of trips to and from the parking facility; and
- overall travel characteristics of the transportation system.

Site traffic is assigned to the roadway system in accordance with expected traffic patterns within the study area. Distribution patterns are usually represented as a percent of the total project-generated traffic to/from major access points in the study area. It is important to consider planned and programmed future transportation improvements and thus account for any impacts on existing travel patterns with respect to current traffic volumes and traffic generated by the proposed project.

Traffic flow diagrams indicating the routing of site traffic entering and exiting from the facility should be prepared. The diagrams should be developed for each of the critical hours of operation associated with both the parking facility and the land use(s) served by the facility.

Projection of Future Traffic Volumes

Existing traffic volumes (referred to as base traffic volume) for each critical peak hour of analysis should be projected to a specified future year of operation. The future year can be the first year of operation of the proposed parking facility and/or project or, in some cases, five years after operation, ten years after operation, and/or 20 years after operation depending on review agency requirements, procedures, and policies.

For projects that involve various phases of development, an analysis of each phase is suggested. Off-site roadway improvements can then be staged to correspond to the relative traffic impact of each development phase. Therefore, the capital expenditure required for all off-site roadway improvements for a phased project would not be required in the initial years of operation.

FIGURE 4-3

TYPICAL TRIP GENERATION RATES BY SELECTED LAND USES

Land Use	Trip Unit	Morning Peak Highway Hour	Evening Peak Highway Hour
Office	1,000 square feet GFA[1]	1.56 trips per unit 88% in/12% out	1.49 trips per unit 17% in/83% out
Retail	1,000 square feet GLA[2]	1.03 trips per unit 61% in/39% out	3.74 trips per unit 48% in/52% out
Hospital	Beds	1.07 trips per unit 72% in/28% out	1.22 trips per unit 34% in/66% out

[1]Square feet of gross floor area.
[2]Square feet of gross leasable area.
Source: Institute of Transportation Engineers, *Trip Generation* (Washington, D.C.: ITE, 1997).

Direct access to the air cargo facility from adjacent streets at Miami International Airport.

Future traffic volumes can be projected by either applying a single traffic growth rate per year through the design year of analysis or employing highly sophisticated transportation and land use forecast models based on future or build-out conditions for the study area.

In addition, anticipated traffic volumes associated with other approved but not yet constructed land uses should be added to the transportation system if not already accounted for in the growth rate or travel forecast model. Volume might include traffic generated by a proposed retail center adjacent to the proposed project.

Projected peak-hour traffic volumes associated with the proposed parking facility should be superimposed on and combined with the base traffic volume projections for the roadway system. The result is a traffic volume projection for each of the peak hours of analysis for each of the critical future years of development. Typically, an analysis is performed both with and without the site-related traffic to evaluate the impact of proposed new development on the transportation system.

Off-Site Traffic Analyses and Development of Off-Site Traffic Improvements

A detailed analysis should be undertaken for each of the critical roadway segments and intersections in the study area. In particular, a capacity analysis that follows the procedures and methodologies included in the *Highway Capacity Manual* published by the Transportation Research Board is important in determining the ability of a specific roadway link or intersection to accommodate traffic under various levels of service. Level of service is a quantitative measure describing driver satisfaction with several factors that influence the degree of traffic congestion as measured by delay in seconds, including speed and travel time, traffic interrup-

tion, freedom of maneuverability, safety, driving comfort, and convenience.

The level of service for each intersection in the study area, as determined through a capacity study, is the basis for understanding roadway and intersection deficiencies. Once deficiencies are recognized, transportation improvement strategies can be developed and evaluated to ascertain their relative ability to achieve a desired level of service. Improvements for consideration include but are not limited to the following (see Figure 4-4):

- the addition of through travel lanes;
- the addition of turn lanes;
- the installation of new or upgraded traffic signals and/or traffic control devices;
- the addition of traffic-calming techniques such as roundabouts;
- modifying traffic operations such as from one-way to two-way travel;
- prohibiting turns;
- restrictions on on-street parking;
- improvements to pavement-related deficiencies;
- the addition of informational and directional signage systems;
- the addition of safety-related improvements;
- the addition of pedestrian- and/or bicycle-related improvements;
- the addition of access management strategies; and

FIGURE 4-4

SUGGESTED TRAFFIC FLOW IMPROVEMENTS NEW PARKING GARAGE

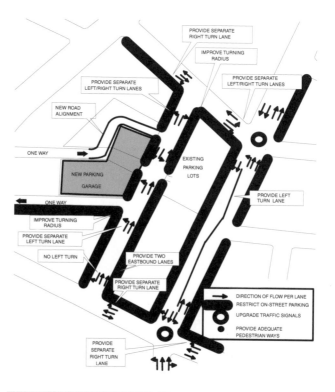

- modification of other localized geometric and traffic operations.

Depending on the volume of traffic associated with a land use and the impact on overall roadway system adequacy, other more cost-intensive improvements may be required, such as construction of new roadways and modified expressways. In addition, the number and location of site driveways to the parking facility may influence the level of improvements needed to provide safe and efficient operation. Therefore, different access locations should be evaluated so that site traffic is efficiently accommodated.

Other types of analyses that may be required are vehicle queuing analyses, accident analyses, and traffic signal warrant studies. Vehicle queuing analyses determine the need for and length of turn lanes such that the vehicle stacking area is sufficient to provide storage for turning vehicles outside the through vehicle lanes. Accident analyses relate to the development of safety-related improvements. Traffic signal warrant studies determine if intersections meet federal and state requirements for installation of traffic signals. Figure 4-4 illustrates suggested off-site roadway and traffic control improvements associated with a new parking garage serving a downtown redevelopment site.

Review of On-Site Traffic Circulation

The site driveway is the connection between the external or off-site roadway system and the parking facility's internal circulation system. The traffic impact and access study should be prepared with input from the parking facility and project planners to ensure that access is adequately and safely located. Some factors that influence traffic flow within a garage include the following:

- the number of parking spaces to be served per driveway;
- the traffic flow into and out of the parking facility at each driveway;
- traffic flow within the parking facility (one-way versus two-way circulation);
- internal ramp systems and their operations; and
- the method of parking facility control such as free access, a ticket/cashier system, or card-activated access.

Sloped floors with parking, speed ramps, and other types of interflow ramp connections affect a facility's ability to accommodate entering and exiting vehicles. Other factors associated with the adequacy of the parking facility include the following:

- service vehicle requirements;
- bus service requirements;
- pedestrian connectivity within the facility and to adjacent land uses; and
- assigned or priority parking within the facility.

LEVEL OF SERVICE

A detailed analysis should be undertaken for each of the critical roadway segments and intersections in the study area. A capacity analysis that follows the procedures and methodologies included in the *Highway Capacity Manual* published by the Transportation Research Board is important in determining the ability of a specific roadway link or intersection to accommodate traffic under various levels of service. (Level of service is a quantitative measure describing driver satisfaction with several factors that influence the degree of traffic congestion as measured by the delay in seconds, including speed and travel time, traffic interruption, freedom of maneuverability, safety, driving comfort, and convenience.)

There are six levels of service describing flow conditions. The highest, Level of Service A, describes a condition of free flow, with low volumes and high speeds and little or no restriction on maneuverability due to the presence of other vehicles; drivers can maintain speeds with little or no delay. Level of Service B represents a stable traffic flow with traffic conditions that begin to influence operating speeds, although drivers still have reasonable freedom to select their speed and lane operations. Level of Service C, which is normally used for design purposes, describes a stable condition of traffic operation. It involves moderately restricted movements due to higher traffic volumes, but traffic conditions are not objectionable to motorists.

Level of Service D, acceptable for traffic operation in most urban environments and during peak hours of traffic flow, reflects a condition of still more restrictive movement. Queues and delays may occur during short peaks, but lower demand occurs often enough to permit clearance of developing queues, thus preventing excessive backup. At Level of Service D, the influence of congestion becomes more noticeable and longer delays may result from unfavorable vehicle progression.

Level of Service E is defined as the actual capacity of the roadway or intersection and involves delay for all motorists due to congestion. High delay values generally indicate poor vehicle progression and represent the limit of acceptable delay. The lowest, Level of Service F, is described as forced flow characterized by volumes greater than the theoretical roadway capacity. Complete congestion occurs and, in extreme cases, the volume passing a given point drops to zero. Level of Service F is generally considered unacceptable.

Development of a Site Access Plan

As discussed previously, the external transportation system and proposed operation of the parking facility will be affected by the connection between the two through site access strategies. The determination of site access is an iterative process that results in the development of a site access plan.

Site access plans should consider the following factors:

- number and location of the site driveways serving the facility (for example, it is important to locate a new

Site access is a critical element in the location and design of a parking facility.

site driveway away from an adjacent intersection or other driveway);

- number of inbound and outbound lanes at each site drive;
- opportunities for reversible lanes within the driveway of the parking facility (such as inbound in the morning peak period and outbound in the evening peak period);
- sufficiently wide lanes and adequate turning radii;
- appropriate vehicle storage areas for each inbound and outbound lane;
- landscaping and sight distance requirements;
- traffic control at the site driveways;
- pedestrian and bicycle access;
- accommodation for special vehicles such as buses and trucks; and
- appropriate signage and pavement markings and other controls to facilitate safe, convenient, and efficient access into and out of the parking facility.

One overall design objective should be to minimize the number of access points while ensuring safe and expeditious movement to and from the street system. Shared or joint-access driveways with other land uses may be advisable but may require legal agreements that create joint-access easements and define maintenance responsibilities.

A variety of traffic, nontraffic-related, and land use factors may influence the site access plan. Therefore, a set of acceptable site access plan alternatives may need to be developed for consideration. A matrix system that compares measures of effectiveness for each alternative should be prepared and evaluated to permit reasonable selection of the preferred site access plan.

Compliance with Local Ordinances, Regulations, and Approval Procedures

The traffic impact and access study should be undertaken in accordance with the governing jurisdiction's review and approval procedures and in compliance with accepted traffic engineering prinicples. Specific requirements such as traffic data collection, traffic analyses, identification of the area of influence, report format, and site access plan documentation may vary among jurisdictions and therefore should be clearly understood.

Summary

The site access plan and related off-site transportation system improvements should be well documented to demonstrate the need for both on- and off-site roadway improvements. It is not unusual for a land developer/owner to accept responsibility for financing off-site access improvements that benefit both the development and the community in general. Nor is it unusual for governments to encourage local development by cooperating with land developers to produce acceptable traffic access and circulation systems. Yet, off-site traffic improvements may be the financial responsibility of the developer when such improvements benefit only the project. Financial participation by others—the city, state, or other private interests—is possible if benefits are to be gained by other participants and funds are available.

A cost-benefit analysis may be required to identify the financial commitments associated with mitigating the traffic impacts generated by a parking facility. The results of the analysis may point to the need to implement transportation demand management strategies or to reduce the size of the development and perhaps the parking facility. If the impact on the transportation system is difficult or impossible to mitigate, the land use intensity may need to be reduced to lessen traffic.

The result of a traffic impact and access study is a report that presents a transportation improvement plan that satisfies the transportation needs of the project (in this case, a parking facility), minimizes adverse traffic impacts on the adjacent roadway system, and meets all government requirements such that the expeditious grant of approvals and permits advances the project to completion.

References

Institute of Transportation Engineers. *Traffic Access and Impact Studies for Site Development*. Washington, D.C.: ITE, 1991.

Institute of Transportation Engineers. *Trip Generation,* 6th Edition. Washington, D.C.: ITE, 1997.

Transportation Research Board, National Research Council. *Highway Capacity Manual*, 3rd Edition. Special Report 209. Washington, D.C.: TRB, 1997.

Weant, Robert A., and Herbert S. Levinson, *Parking*. Washington, D.C.: Eno Foundation for Transportation, 1990.

CHAPTER 5
ZONING REQUIREMENTS

Mary S. Smith

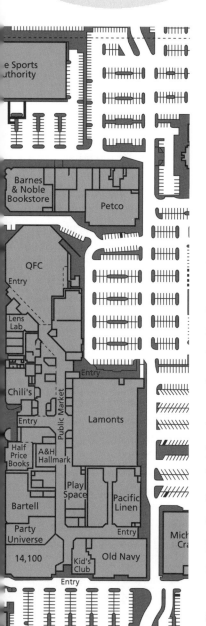

e Sports
Authority

Barnes
& Noble
Bookstore

Petco

QFC
Entry

Lens
Lab

Entry

Chili's

Entry

Public Market

Lamonts

Half
Price
Books

A&H
Hallmark

Play
Space

Pacific
Linen

Bartell

Party
Universe

Entry

Mich
Cra

14,100

Kid's
Club

Old Navy

Entry

N.E. 8th Street

Zoning is the regulatory means by which cities ensure that a new development or redevelopment of an existing property meets community standards. Zoning has been described as "a preventive approach for achieving planned and orderly development."[1]

With respect to parking, zoning standards typically embody formulas for determining how many parking spaces must be provided for specific types of land uses. Parking-related zoning provisions also commonly address street rights-of-way, setbacks, development densities, and traffic flow and access controls and often specify design standards. Most frequently, zoning ordinances prescribe the layout of parking, particularly the size of parking spaces and aisles, although many ordinances also deal with lighting requirements, surface treatments, and landscaping standards. Generally, the latter provisions apply only to surface parking lots, which are not covered by building codes that otherwise set forth standards for the design of enclosed or open parking structures.

Land use concentrations give rise to both traffic and parking considerations. It is instructive to note that many land uses require as much or more paved parking area as building space. For example, a shopping center providing five parking spaces per 1,000 square feet of gross leasable area (GLA) of retail space has approximately 1,500 square feet of paved parking area for each 1,000 square feet of GLA. An office building may have a 1:1 ratio of parking area to leasable space. Thus, parking requirements have a major impact on land use planning.

Most local governments require property owners to provide sufficient off-street parking spaces without overflow onto public streets or adjacent private property. At the same time, zoning policies should not require an excessive amount of parking space and/or waste resources through inappropriate design standards. While a necessary component of development, land and/or resources devoted to parking reduce the amount of development a particular site can support. Dollars spent on excessive parking can usually be better spent on project amenities. Further, excessive paved parking areas are undesirable from both an aesthetic and environmental perspective.

This chapter deals with considerations for establishing reasonable zoning provisions for parking. The Parking Consultants Council (PCC) of the National Parking Association has published a document that suggests a format for developing such provisions. Local governments can modify the format in accordance with some of the considerations discussed here. The document is available from a variety of sources, including the Urban Land Institute, the National Parking Association, and the American Planning Association.[2]

Parking Demand Considerations

Parking demand varies widely from one location to another as well as among cities of similar size. The variations reflect differences in development density, the relative availability of public transportation, local land use policies, the price of parking, and local economic vitality. In areas with a mix of land uses, such as the central business district (CBD), parking demand is often reduced by the interdependence of like activities. Parking demand also varies over time with changes in employment densities and rates of automobile ownership. For example, at hospitals and medical centers, standards for determining the number of parking spaces have historically been based on the number of beds and/or the number of employees per bed. But, with the expansion in outpatient treatment services, the demand for parking continues to grow despite no increase—and sometimes even a decrease—in beds. Therefore, no single national standard for parking space requirements is appropriate for every community. Moreover, no one set of standards, with the exception of off-street parking for industrial use, is recommended.

The underlying assumptions used in drafting local regulations are often unknown and may not be transferable from one locality to another. The best approach, of course, is to develop off-street parking requirements based on local parking and traffic studies and the characteristics of the affected zoning districts. In fact, wholesale adoption of another community's ordinance provisions is inadvisable. In *Flexible Parking Requirements*, the American Planning Association recommended the following steps in revising a local zoning ordinance:[3]

1. Determine generic development characteristics (land use, employment densities, mode of travel, cost of parking, and so on).
2. Review parking experiences (studies, literature, and zoning ordinances) elsewhere.

3. Survey parking demand and problems at existing uses that may be similar to the proposed facility.
4. Establish parking policy governing the level of service to be provided.
5. Determine zoning requirements.
6. Monitor parking standards.

A sensible approach to developing a local ordinance is to start with a national standard that assumes a modal split of 100 percent personal automobile use, then adjust for patterns of local automobile use as determined in step 1, and, finally, develop a preliminary model to be ultimately incorporated into an ordinance. The model should be tested with occupancy studies at existing land uses in the community. The approach used by the APA is an effective method as well as the most reliable procedure for determining the optimal parking need for a given land use or for land use categories within the zoning ordinance. This method, however, is labor-intensive and is more often neglected by municipalities in favor of "borrowing" codes from other zoning ordinances.

Flexibility in Requirements

A predetermined parking formula is unlikely to address all situations for each land use category in all communities. Some of the variables that distinguish one community from another are building size, the nature of tenancies, access and distance to public transit, quality of public transit, ridesharing patterns, shared parking, and zoning districts. The traditional means of accommodating such variables include different requirements in different zoning districts, planned unit development (PUD) permits, and special/conditional use permits (SUP), all of which have proven ineffective. These strategies have produced at best a heavy caseload of variance requests at the zoning board of appeals or city council and at worst inequities in the requirements imposed by the community on specific developments. Some communities have reacted by simply refusing to issue parking variances, taking the position that if requirements impose hardships, the zoning ordinance should be amended.

In *Flexible Parking Requirements*, the APA urges more communities to build flexibility into their zoning ordinances, pointing out specific zoning ordinances that provide mechanisms for adjusting parking requirements. However, the initial impetus behind these mechanisms was to achieve specific land use and traffic management objectives rather than to provide flexibility in meeting local variations. Nevertheless, the built-in or preapproved adjustments provide a means for eliminating the adversarial nature of zoning variance procedures. Some of the provisions that cities use to build flexibility into their parking requirements include shared parking, fees-in-lieu of building parking, off-site parking, credits for ridesharing programs, and credits for public transportation access.

According to *Flexible Parking Requirements*, among the chief stumbling blocks to implementing flexible requirements are local governments' administrative procedures. How does the developer accurately project variations in parking demand before a project is completed? How does the city know whether the developer's plan will succeed? What happens if the project is sold and the new owner terminates the ride-sharing program or reserves half the parking spaces for a specific tenant? What happens if a new tenant of the same use changes operations in a way that affects demand? Some cities have tried to circumvent these issues by setting rigid formulas for shared parking, ridesharing, and public transit credits. Those efforts, however, do not enhance flexibility but rather represent another way of calculating the number of required spaces.

In *Recommended Zoning Ordinance Provisions*, the PCC addresses the issue of flexibility in parking requirements from its own experiences and develops a model ordinance that protects the city's interests while building in a measure of flexibility that addresses the most common circumstances that influence parking demand. In addition to providing language addressing ownership and land use change issues, the PCC recommends the use of a specified credit that developers can routinely apply to handle certain adjustments to parking requirements. At some time, though, the PCC's recommendation calls for a qualified parking or traffic consultant to project demand. Further, the use adjustment requires the developer to pledge to provide additional parking up to the unadjusted standard if the city later finds that the projected demand has been exceeded.

The use adjustment is called the "land bank" provision because it requires the developer to provide a plan detailing how the additional spaces would later be provided in either surface lots or structures that comply with all other requirements of the ordinance. When a developer chooses the land bank approach, the parking plan must undergo review and approval first at the administrative level and then as part of the standard site plan review process. The developer who does not accept the land bank condition is automatically subject to the variance procedure—usually before the zoning board of appeals and/or the city council—and therefore must request a permanent, irrevocable reduction in the prescribed parking requirements.

The following discussion describes in greater detail some of the circumstances in which flexibility in requirements may be appropriate.

Shared parking. The principles of shared parking recognize that different land uses routinely experience peak parking accumulations at different times of the day, week, or season and that parking spaces not occupied by one use can accommodate other uses located near the parking facility. In addition, the interrelationship between adjacent land uses can increase the vitality of businesses by reducing overall parking demand since customers can park once and visit several businesses. A good example is a combination of restaurant and office uses. The restaurant's noon business is

Adequate off-street parking avoids overflow onto adjacent streets or private property.

enhanced by the office building; many lunch patrons are also office employees who are already factored into the demand for office parking. In the evening, when the demand for restaurant parking is at its highest level, diners use the office parking that has been substantially vacated by daytime users. Until publication of ULI's *Shared Parking*, it was difficult to develop a reliable and widely accepted means for projecting shared demand without resorting to an inflexible formula.[4]

It is important to note that a reduction in the number of spaces requires the physical capacity to share parking. That is, parking for particular land uses cannot be reserved for specific users. Moreover, the parking supply for shared parking does not have to be under single ownership. Many cities have unknowingly experimented and succeeded with shared parking by providing municipal parking facilities in their central business districts.

Captive market. In the example of shared parking, office employees represent a captive market for the restaurant during mid-day. The captive market effect is a component of shared parking, although it does not depend on shared parking to achieve reduced demand. Instead, it often occurs among land uses that are not self-contained within a development. Indeed, the captive market effect is one of the most significant determinants of parking demand in central business districts. Therefore, *Shared Parking* allows parking requirements to be adjusted for captive market effects independent of shared parking effects.

Fees-in-lieu. It is usually in the best interest of a city to develop parking in a densely developed business district rather than require each property owner to provide sufficient parking facilities for each building. However, given the high cost of constructing parking and the competing demands on cities' resources, several cities have requested developers who directly benefit from parking to reimburse the city for some or all of the public cost of developing municipal parking facilities. Though the most promising solution to date has been the fee-in-lieu approach, it has met with limited success. Under this approach, the developer may build the required parking within a project or contribute a preset amount per space to a city fund for spaces not provided by the developer.

A significant problem arises with the fee-in-lieu approach when development is slow, small-scale, or random: money dribbles into the fund in increments insufficient to develop parking cost effectively in reasonable proximity to each development. The developer who has paid fees-in-lieu from $8,000 to $12,000 per space does not want the funds to sit idle in the city coffers for several years as officials wait for more money to accrue. Nor does the same developer want to rely on a parking facility located six blocks from a planned project. Success is much more likely when rapid development is expected in a defined area. Further, developers should agree to in-lieu fees only when an off-street parking facility is or will be available on a definite schedule and within acceptable proximity of the planned projects.

Off-site parking. Many cities have added clauses to their zoning ordinances to permit off-site parking to be substituted for on-site parking. Such provisions increase the administrative duties of zoning officials, requiring them to evaluate facility convenience and location, user types, and guarantees that the parking will be available and maintained for as long as the building use exists.

Ridesharing programs. Ridesharing generally refers to various forms of carpooling, vanpooling, subscription bus service, and the like and is usually associated with employees' trips to and from work. It is a fact that properly formulated ridesharing programs can significantly reduce both traffic and parking demand. Zoning credits for ridesharing are a particularly effective means of achieving a community's transportation management goals. It should be noted that the PCC endorses the use of ridesharing credits to adjust parking requirements for any land use that operates a dedicated shuttle. The most common application involves hotels that cater to guests who demand convenient access to an airport. Other land uses may also operate shuttles and may merit reduced parking requirements.

Transit. Smaller communities may have certain areas that are well served by public transit. Allowing a reasonable reduction in parking requirements when a land use is located within a certain distance of a regularly scheduled transit stop recognizes variations in levels of transit service in a community.

Setting Parking Space Formulas

A property owner, the community, and the city staff charged with administering zoning policies all benefit from a zoning ordinance that carefully and clearly spells out the number of required parking spaces. The relevant provisions must be simple enough to leave little to interpretation yet comprehensive enough to cover most circumstances that can rea-

sonably be expected. The provisions must prevent the development of inadequate parking without requiring excessive parking. As a generally accepted matter, a formula should relate parking spaces to a quantitative measure of the associated land use. The following sections discuss a variety of issues that affect the specific formulas used for determining parking requirements.

Units. Parking requirements are generally stated as a ratio of x spaces per y units, with the unit an appropriate measure for a particular land use. The unit in the vast majority of cases is square footage of building area. Other units include dwelling units, hotel rooms, seats, or persons. Units should be measurable at the time of a project's zoning approval. In general, demand ratios based on numbers of employees, which are often highly variable over time, should be avoided. However, certain land uses—specifically, hospitals, schools, and other institutions—represent such highly variable levels of employees or users that allotments per employee, student, and/or patient are the only reasonable basis for parking requirements. In some cases, particularly assembly space such as auditoriums, the capacity in persons that is licensed or posted by a local government provides the basis for parking requirements.

In the past, parking ratios tended to be stated as one space for each y square feet. However, industry groups now prefer to use a ratio stated as x spaces per 1,000 square feet. It is easier for the average person to multiply than divide. For example, consider ratios of one space for every 200 and 250 square feet, which equal, respectively, five and four spaces per 1,000 square feet. The average person can more easily comprehend the magnitude of a requirement expressed as spaces per 1,000 square feet. Therefore, the more recent studies of parking requirements, such as *Parking Generation* published by the Institute of Transportation Engineers (ITE)[5] and *Shared Parking* published by the Urban Land Institute, rely on the convention of spaces per 1,000 square feet of associated use.

Another aspect of ratios based on square footage is the method by which square footage is calculated. Given the wide variation in how national standards and zoning ordinances treat the calculation, the terms gross, net, leasable, and rentable are frequently used to clarify square footage. ULI provides the following definitions with respect to square footage:

- Gross floor area (GFA). Total or gross floor area, including exterior building walls, of all floors of a building or structure.
- Gross leasable area (GLA). Gross floor area available for leasing to a tenant.
- Net floor area (NFA). Total floor area, excluding exterior building walls.
- Net rentable area (NRA). The net floor area available for leasing to a tenant, also called net leasable area (NLA).

Thus, GFA is calculated "out-to-out" and NFA "in-to-in" of exterior walls. For purposes of calculating parking requirements, parking and loading areas as well as the floor area occupied by HVAC, mechanical, electrical, communications, and security equipment are all deducted from either GFA or NFA because the associated areas do not contribute to parking demand. While older ordinances tended to use NFA, most of today's industry standards (ULI, ITE, NPA) use GFA.

With the trend toward large multiple-tenant building developments, the use of leasable or rentable adjustments has gained importance. Generally, GLA totals GFA minus the floor area associated with elevator shafts and stair towers, public restrooms, permanently designated corridors, public lobbies, and common mall areas. Merely accounting for the space connecting tenant spaces does not add to parking demand. For example, if GLA is the same as GFA, the common mall areas of enclosed shopping centers, excluding small retail kiosks or similar customer generators, do not generate any more demand than either a shopping center with open-air courtyards or a strip center whose stores all open to the parking lot. Likewise, the connection between the lobbies of a pair of office towers with an atrium does not generate additional parking demand; thus, the atrium should be excluded from parking demand calculations. In smaller buildings, the difference between GLA and GFA is negligible.

Design day. A critical issue in any discussion of parking demand is the level of parking activity that recurs frequently enough to justify the provision of parking spaces. Within the industry, the level of parking activity that determines the number of spaces is often called the design day. Designing for the activity level in an average day should not translate into an insufficient supply of parking for 50 percent of the days of the year. Conversely, it is inappropriate to design for the peak accumulation that would conceivably never occur. Further, that unusual peak may last only for an hour or so. Neighbors of an office building, hospital, or university will probably not complain if parking spills out into the neighborhood "once in a blue moon," but they will not tolerate overflow parking on a regular basis. *Shared Parking, Parking Generation*, and other references suggest setting parking requirements in accordance with a design day at the 85th percentile of the parking accumulations presented therein. Figure 5-1 demonstrates the 85th percentile by documenting the cumulative distribution of parking generation rates in the ITE database for office buildings.[6]

Effective supply. An important concept in the analysis of parking adequacy is effective supply. A parking system, which includes the total parking supply, operates at optimum efficiency when the system is at somewhat less than full capacity. The occupancy at which a facility achieves optimum efficiency generally ranges from 85 to 95 percent. A key determinant is size of the system. The provision of excess spaces reduces the need to search an entire system

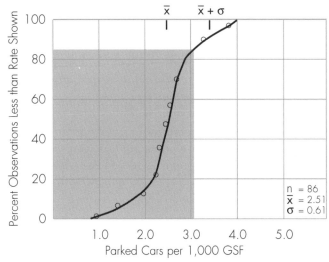

FIGURE 5-1

CUMULATIVE DISTRIBUTION OF PARKING GENERATION

For a General Office Building of 100,000 to 299,999 Gross Square Feet

n = 86
$\bar{x}$ = 2.51
σ = 0.61

85th percentile

Source: Special tabulations of data from Institute of Transportation Engineers, *Parking Generation*, 2nd Edition (Washington, D.C.: ITE, 1987).

for the last available spaces. It also allows for operating fluctuations, vehicle maneuvers, and vacancies created by reserving spaces for certain users and makes up for losses attributable to misparked vehicles, snow cover, and so on.

A system's effective supply also provides for unusual peaks in demand. On peak-demand days, the parking system may not operate as efficiently as desired, although it can still absorb periodically higher demand. When determining the adequacy of a parking system, a parking consultant usually assigns effective supply factors to each of the different parking facilities in a given area and thereby determines overall effective supply. The consultant then compares the supply factors with design day demand. Because it is impractical to require a comparative analysis for every development project, zoning ordinances should specify an effective supply factor of 5 to 10 percent over the projected peak accumulation of parked vehicles on the design day. The NPA's *Recommended Zoning Ordinance Provisions* includes such a factor, but ITE's *Parking Generation* specifies accumulations of vehicles that should be factored up to estimates of the number of parking spaces and thus converted to zoning standards. For smaller or single-tenant buildings, a 5 to 10 percent factor is appropriate; in larger multitenant developments, a 5 percent factor is acceptable.

Size. The size of a development project influences more than just the effective supply factor. The peak accumulation of vehicles at a large multitenant building is much more likely to fit a national standard for the design day than is the peak accumulation of vehicles in a small, single-tenant building within the same land use category. For example, a tenant in a large, general office building may regularly count an unusually high concentration of employees and/or visitors on site while a high proportion of another tenant's employees may be out "on the road." It is a case of probability. For example, among 50 small office buildings, some will register demand high enough to justify a 3.6/1,000 zoning requirement. If the tenants of those 50 buildings move into one large building, the accumulation of vehicles will average out and a 3/1,000 supply may be sufficient. Therefore, it is entirely appropriate for a community to require a higher ratio for smaller concentrations of a specific land use than for larger buildings.

Accessory uses. Accessory uses are areas within a specific land use that are not the principal activity generator but are necessary to the successful tenancy of that land use. Examples include storage, stock, office, and kitchen spaces. Some developers occasionally argue that the floor area associated with accessory uses should be calculated at different parking rates than the primary use. It is therefore important that a zoning ordinance spell out the standard for calculating parking space requirements for accessory uses. Given that most national standards are based on studies that consider accessory uses as part of the floor area used in calculating parking ratios, it is usually appropriate to include accessory areas in the floor area calculations for the primary use.

Complementary uses. A complementary use is a space that is used or leased by a different land use but designed to serve or enhance the primary land use. Although the complementary use normally involves substantially different parking characteristics from those of the primary land use, the interrelationship with the primary use results in reduced parking demand largely through captive market effects. For example, a delicatessen or sandwich shop that might otherwise require a specified number of parking spaces can be permitted in a strip shopping center or office building without increasing the parking ratio of the primary activity generator. ULI's *Parking Requirements for Shopping Centers* specifically addresses this issue and finds that small concentrations of complementary uses do not change the parking requirements from those of the primary land uses. It should be noted that the full GLA, that is, the sum of the primary and complementary uses, should be multiplied by the ratio for the primary use.

Zoning ordinances should limit the percent of leasable space occupied by complementary uses. From the above example, a single strip center should not be allowed to lease more than 40 percent of its space to restaurants without meeting the parking requirements for restaurants. It is often not possible at the time of zoning approvals to project what tenants will occupy given spaces, but a city can identify potential violations through the building permit process. The PCC recommends that zoning ordinances allow up to 10 percent of the GLA to be occupied by complementary uses.

Parking Space Design Requirements

Perhaps no section in zoning ordinances varies more from one locality to another than the geometric standards for parking space design. The early 1970s saw reasonable uniformity among standards, most of which were based on a 1971 study by the Highway Research Board (now the Transportation Research Board).[7] In 1970, however, sharp increases in gasoline prices triggered a significant downsizing of the American automobile and a dramatic increase in the import of smaller foreign cars. The trend continued for about 20 years as small cars became a major factor in parking space geometric design. In response, parking facilities of all types and sizes provided small-car-only parking spaces while retaining standard-size spaces for larger vehicles. Different-sized spaces, however, have given rise to two problems: difficulties in identifying "small cars" within the overall vehicle population and widespread violations of small-car spaces by larger vehicles. Such violations impede traffic circulation and parking space access in many facilities.

During the past five or six years, the rapid increase in the popularity of vans and sport utility vehicles and the trend toward pick-up trucks to replace the conventional family car have led to a significant increase in the size (width and length) of passenger vehicles. Larger numbers of larger vehicles have dramatically reduced the need for small-car-only spaces such that parking facility functional design practices now reflect current vehicle registration figures.

A more practical approach, and one recommended by the PCC and other industry groups, is the use of one-size-fits-all geometry. The single-size stall philosophy assumes that any vehicle can use any parking space and, accordingly, simplifies the definitions of geometric details for facility layout. Only in a limited number of design situations are small-car spaces provided at the end of rows of parking stalls or in end areas of parking lots.

Chapter 8 addresses the PCC's rational approach to parking space design. Suffice it to say, however, that communities need to consider parking dimensions that reasonably serve the needs of users—before geometric standards are codified in local zoning ordinances.

Notes

1   Robert A. Weant and Herbert S. Levinson, *Parking* (Westport, Conn: Eno Foundation for Transportation, Inc., 1990).

2   Parking Consultants Council, *Recommended Zoning Ordinance Provisions for Parking and Off-Street Loading Spaces* (Washington, D.C.: National Parking Association, 1991).

3   T.P. Smith, *Flexible Parking Requirements*, Planning Advisory Service Report No. 377 (Chicago: American Planning Association, 1983).

4 ULI–the Urban Land Institute, *Shared Parking* (Washington, D.C.: ULI, 1983).

5 Institute of Transportation Engineers, *Parking Generation*, 2nd Edition (Washington, D.C.: ITE, 1987).

6 ITE Technical Council Committee 6F-44, "Using the ITE *Parking Generation* Report," *ITE Journal*, July 1990.

7 Highway Research Board, *Parking Principles*, Special Report 125 (Washington, D.C.: HRB, 1971).

CHAPTER 6
INTERMODAL ASPECTS

I. Paul Lew and Abraham Gutman

The intermodal aspect of transportation involves the transfer to and from one mode of transportation to another. In this case, the focus is on movement to and from public transportation. Intermodal facilities succeed when they are convenient and cost effective. In fact, they have become a part of the public policy debate because they reduce traffic, congestion, and pollution. And intermodalism that reduces traffic congestion reduces society's need to expand its road infrastructure. As a result, public financing is available to develop intermodal facilities as an integral part of the public transportation system.

A major element of an intermodal facility is parking, but its significance is traditionally understated as a component of the entire transportation system. In particular, the park-and-ride facility, which is a terminus at the community end of a trip, is the intermodal feature of interest. It has special importance in the user's transition from local resident to commuter.

Intermodal Systems

The system of transfer to public transportation depends on the density of the population at the point of transfer. A series of intermodal movements can occur as discussed below.

Transfer to Rail

Rail transit is best suited to efficiently transferring large numbers of passengers where the density of passengers at the transfer point of the intermodal trip warrants. Rail transit's appeal lies in the speed of the trip on dedicated rail lines unhindered by car, truck, or bus congestion. As a result, rail transit

Bus terminal.

permits rapid, unimpeded movement into the central business district. Nonetheless, the high initial cost of rail infrastructure and the purchase of the associated rights-of-way must be justified. In fact, rail transit's high initial cost means that most commuter rail is operated along existing railroad rights-of-way.

Population density in the vicinity of the intermodal terminal determines if the associated parking component takes the form of a surface lot or parking structure. Most commuters prefer parking lots unless the walking distance to the terminal becomes too great. Parking structures, however, may not be economically feasible unless land costs offer no alternative but to build vertically. To mitigate the cost of a parking structure, today's multiuse parking facilities frequently offer real estate development opportunities such as office space above and/or retail space at grade, particularly when land in a suburban town center is scarce and valuable. In

---

FIGURE 6-1

PROXIMITY RELATIONSHIP TRIANGLE
INTERMODAL PARKING

Pedestrian Sector
Pick-Up
Drop-Off
Bicycles and Walkers
Short-Term (Off-Peak) Parking
Long-Term (Off-Peak) Parking
Parking Sector
Accessible Parking

Intermodal
Facility

Train

Bus

Taxi

Public Sector

---

fact, real estate value may result in part from the convenience of mass transit.

Transfer to Express Bus

Where rail service may not be practical, express buses are the next best option. Intermodal facilities for express buses are typically located along or near expressways, preferably in conjunction with HOV (high-occupancy vehicles) lanes. HOV lanes provide a partially dedicated right-of-way similar to a rail line.

The transit planner should select locations for express bus facilities that best serve transit patrons. The following factors guide site selection for express bus facilities as well as for railway stations:

- site availability, access, and visibility;
- present and future demand;
- access to HOV lanes;
- development and operating costs;
- security considerations;
- environmental constraints, public policy considerations, and land use and local acceptance;
- development and multiuse potential as well as expansion potential; and
- potential for joint use.

Each factor must be considered in terms of its advantages and disadvantages to determine whether an intermodal facility should be located at a particular site.

Local Bus Service

Where express bus service is not cost-effective, local bus service that operates on local streets may be feasible; perhaps it could be supported by a limited type of intermodal facility. Typically, such a facility is a small lot with less than 100 parking spaces or a dedicated area located within a larger parking facility, such as a shopping center, park, or parking lot for a house of worship. As an intermediate form of intermodal facility, small parking lots can support a local bus feeder system that connects with rapid-transit or express bus service to the major intermodal center.

Site Access

Site access is one of the most important aspects in planning an intermodal facility. First, the facility must be located along a major transportation route—whether that route is a commuter rail line or a commuter bus route accessible to primary arterials or expressways. Second, it is critical to the success of the intermodal facility that site access not depend on secondary or residential streets. Commuter traffic is a major source of irritation for local communities, particularly if commuters originate from outside the local area. Third, access to parking at the facility should be provided by an internal circulation road or, where unavoidable, by local streets.

Basic to the design of an intermodal facility is the concept of proximity. Figure 6-1 presents a proximity triangle of suggested priority relationships among users. The most frequent modes of transfer are given priority at the facility. For example, buses have a higher priority and therefore are assigned a location closer to the intermodal facility than are taxis.

Vehicular Access

Express buses can be given direct access to the terminal. The different transportation modes—buses, cars, taxis, pedestrians —should be separated for ease of circulation and safety. Bus riders create the densest transfer of passengers; therefore, local bus service should receive highest priority in terms of proximity to facility users. Taxis require proximity to the station and typically position themselves at the outgoing side of the facility where passengers leave public transit.

The highest priority associated with personal vehicles is accommodation of passenger pick-up and drop-off (or kiss and ride), which requires a vehicular waiting area as well as relatively easy egress without excessive conflicts with other transportation modes. Given that drop-off activities require little standing time, they normally are located closer to the loading area than are pick-up areas, which require longer waiting time. Pick-up areas should have appropriate signage to discourage abuse; a 15-minute maximum waiting time is typical.

As a general matter, access to a site is greatly enhanced by circulation loops and culs-de-sac, particularly if circulation is counterclockwise. Counterclockwise circulation affords passengers curbside entry and exit and permits right-hand turns to and from local roads at entrances and exits. Therefore, counterclockwise, one-way circulation is greatly preferred in an intermodal center. Loop roadways should be designed to allow transit vehicles to pass stopped vehicles.

Parking Access

Short-term parking is parking provided for less than the full work day. It is essential for off-peak passengers who make use of underused transit capacity during nonrush hours. Traditionally, it is located as close as possible to the transfer point.

By far the most prevalent form of parking at an intermodal facility is long-term parking that accommodates commuters for the full work day. Long-term parking is typified by peak entry activity during the morning rush hours and an even more intensive peak exit during the evening rush hours. Evening rush hours are compounded by the influx of large groups of commuters exiting from the train or bus in a matter of seconds, thus creating a pulsing effect. The result is often long queues and waiting periods at the facility exit point. For this reason, it is critical to provide adequate capacity at entry and exit points to and from the facility.

In accordance with the guidelines of the Americans with Disabilities Act (ADA) or (as appropriate) more stringent local laws, intermodal facilities must provide accessible parking spaces and accessible pedestrian paths of travel for per-

Bus aisle layout requires different dimensions than automobile aisle layout.

sons with disabilities. In general, ADA-required parking must be located as close as possible to the terminal.

Bicycles and Pedestrians. Given that public policy encourages bicycle use, parking space for bicycles must be reserved near the station. In addition, pedestrians must have a safe path to the transit loading area, and that path should meet the criteria for an accessible route under the ADA guidelines. The number of pedestrians patronizing an intermodal facility is determined by the type of community in which the facility is located and the availability of on-site parking and bus service.

Entry and Exit Systems. Commuter parking generates high entry and exit volumes over short peak-hour periods. Between 60 and 70 percent of vehicle trips enter the intermodal facility in the peak hours during the morning and exit in the peak hours during the evening. The only opposing traffic is generally kiss-and-ride vehicles. As noted, the concentration of activity is further aggravated during the evening peak by large numbers of commuters leaving the train or bus in a matter of minutes. Studies of revenue control systems indicate that the service rate of ungated entries and exits is about double that of gated entries. As a result, ungated entries and exits are the norm in intermodal facilities.

One key to successful entry into and exit from an intermodal facility is multiple, well-spaced access points. As noted, a loop or perimeter road with counterclockwise traffic is advisable. Culs-de-sac off the loop road can accommodate various intermodal activities. Individual parking lots should have their own internal loop circulation system, normally with cars parked along the perimeter to increase efficiency.

Parking Facilities

In intermodal facilities, convenience is the goal. The time spent transferring from personal transit to public transit is at a premium. Thus, a key quantifiable measure of an intermodal facility's convenience is the time required for the transfer.

Parking Planning

Within individual parking lots, aisles should be oriented toward the station so that pedestrians do not have to walk between cars and conflicts between pedestrians and vehicles can be minimized. One caveat applies to lot shape. If lot dimensions result in a long, narrow configuration, aisle orientation should be in the long direction.

Right-angle parking provides the greatest flexibility for the driver but may not permit all parking bays to be double-loaded (i.e., cars parked on both sides of the aisle) on a given site. In this case, angle parking (less than a 90-degree angle) may be more efficient. In fact, in any lot, angle parking may offer greater efficiency by accommodating interlocked parking spaces, which may not be feasible in ramped parking structures. Given that commuter parking is subject to tidal flows in the morning and evening, it is important to recognize that angle parking is one-directional while right-angle parking is two-directional. In other words, right-angle parking allows all aisles to be used for entering or exiting maneuvers on ramps while angle parking does not.

Circulation roadways within the parking lot may also accommodate parking. Internal perimeter circulation roads with no parking, although conceptually appealing, rarely work because drivers park along the roads despite admonitions not to do so, particularly when such spaces are close to the station or otherwise in short supply. In addition, "parking the perimeter" is an axiom for efficient parking planning.

Parking Structures

Where land is at a premium or walking distances from parking spaces to the transfer point are too great (usually in excess of 1,000 feet), then parking structures are preferable. Even though parking structures can cost more than five times as much per space as surface parking, another workable option may not present itself. As a result, the premium for a parking structure may be justifiable based on user preferences for convenient access to transit and overall societal benefits. Benefits include not building additional roads, not paying prohibitive land costs, and providing the community

Intermodal facility in Chicago serves rail, bus, and automobiles.

with a parking structure that potentially serves other adjacent destinations.

Bus Circulation. Buses should be separated from other vehicular traffic, particularly when bus activity is frequent. In addition, buses may require layover space. Buses need a large turning radius and, if part of an intermodal center, may require back-out room to negotiate loading bays. Where bus volume is limited, buses can use the circulation road, but a pull-in curb space should be provided. A bus shelter and a concrete pad are also essential.

Multiuse Parking Facilities

A multiuse intermodal facility may be appropriate in cases of premium land values and a desire on the part of planners and developers to place the intermodal facility in a community context.

Ground-Level Retail and Alternative Roof-Top Uses. The desire for a functional streetscape may dictate retail or commercial spaces along the curb faces of the intermodal facility. The likely success of retail depends on the particular circumstances. Newsstands and coffee shops typically flourish. Tire stores and automobile supply stores also have succeeded. Government offices, particularly public safety and police stations, likewise succeed because they act as crime deterrents. In some cases, village and town offices are built into the intermodal facility as well.

Where market conditions warrant, office towers have been sited atop parking structures. If space allows, a separate intermodal facility with an adjoining office tower can be more economical than a stacked office and parking facility. In fact, the costs of an intermodal parking facility can be mitigated by the benefits derived from a mixed-use development. Whether the benefits, including community benefits, outweigh additional costs is a matter of public policy that demands close examination.

Circulation in a multiuse parking structure is another matter that requires careful scrutiny. First, the design of the structure must address the issue of ramping from grade. In larger intermodal facilities, express ramps to the first above-grade self-parking level are advisable to allow the ground level to serve the high degree of intermodal activity associated with buses, taxis, and pick-up and drop-off. Second, express ramps allow easier segregation of users by level, with short-term parkers relegated to one level, long-term commuter parkers to other levels, and alternative parkers to the remaining levels. The disadvantage of the express ramp system is its added cost, but that cost may be only one factor in the cost-benefit analysis depending on the scale of the intermodal facility and its operating issues.

Revenue Control

Revenue control performs several functions beyond the collection of money. It assists in policing and managing the facility while enhancing security.

Permits. The simplest form of revenue control for a park-and-ride facility is a permit that can be purchased yearly, semiannually, quarterly, or monthly. Typically, permit charges are not excessive and are used primarily to restrict parking to community residents. Permits can be hang tags but more typically are stickers that cannot be transferred between vehicles. Permits require enforcement to be effective.

Meters. Parking meters offer an alternative means of collecting revenue. Until recently, individual or double-headed meters were a common means of revenue control in intermodal facilities. Individual meters are convenient for the user and easy to police in the case of a violation. Against these advantages, meters incur costs for maintenance and revenue collection and are subject to vandalism, damage, and pilferage. Meters with armored housings or coin vaults are available for heightened security.

Given the shortcomings of individual meters, multispace meters have made inroads into commuter parking. Two multispace meter systems are prevalent: pay and display and pay per space. The pay-and-display system requires the customer to purchase a display voucher at a master meter and display the voucher on the vehicle dashboard. With the pay-per-space system, every parking space is individually numbered. The commuter pays for a specific space at a central location. All spaces that are not paid for can be listed and easily policed for violation. Pay-per-space systems generally provide one master meter for every 50 to 100 spaces to minimize queuing by commuters. When more than one multispace meter is required, the meters must be networked to coordinate data on space use.

The advantage of permit and meter systems is unrestricted access to and from the parking facility, thereby greatly relieving congestion and saving patrons time.

Gates and Booths. For reasons already noted, gates and cashier booths are not frequently installed in intermodal parking. If, however, gated entry and exit lanes are required for each transaction (usually for purposes of security), lane capacity should be based on one lane for each 250 spaces. Where pass cards or AVI (Automatic Vehicle Identification) tags are used, the ratio can double. In general, the concept of pay-on-foot units (precashiering by the patron before returning to the vehicle) offers significant advantages, as described in chapter 23.

Facility Management

Traditionally, parking facilities are part of a larger public or private parking system or a local government's public works system. Whether a facility operates as a profit center is a matter of public policy.

Surface intermodal parking lots, particularly lots with lower capital costs, can earn a profit even when the amortization of capital costs is considered. To amortize a facility's capital costs, however, parking fees must approach commuter rail fares. Clearly, such fees are unacceptable to the

Forest Hills intermodal facility.

general public. Instead, costs may be amortized by the higher costs of public transportation, with parking fees then set to cover maintenance and operations costs. Further, given that a parking structure offers sheltered parking and, in most cases, is located near the intermodal facility, premium demand for parking may be translated into higher fees.

The four main ways to manage intermodal parking facilities are through

- a public transit or transportation authority;
- a local community, by either ownership or a transit authority lease to the community;
- a vendor selected by the transit authority or local community (through the public bidding process) to operate the facility; or
- a private owner and operator.

In many cases, the local community maintains the facility, although the issue of nonresident parking is a potential drawback to such an arrangement. Therefore, when a local public agency does not want to assume responsibility for ongoing costs and operations, it typically selects a contract operator. Many other issues are involved in who will manage a parking facility. Public perception, for example, may be a consideration with respect to public versus private management of parking. In any case, a final decision on the means of facility management should be based on local circumstances.

Community Context

Intermodal facilities built adjacent to railway stations are normally located in a community's traditional town center. In many cases, the railway station is a historic structure that needs to be preserved as a symbol of community identity. Sometimes, the area around the station has deteriorated, and the intermodal facility is seen as a catalyst for revitalization. In other cases, the intermodal center offers access to convenient public transportation that serves the city center and beyond. Whatever the case, the facility can trigger new development as well as support the development of a reverse commute, particularly given that advances in electronic communication have enabled many office operations to move out of the city while remaining close to rapid-transit service. In some instances, corporate headquarters have relocated out of the city center. Although attracting corporate relocation to intermodal centers is not a goal of facility development, it may nonetheless be a desirable byproduct.

Security Issues

Essential to the success of any intermodal facility is security. Nothing is as important as patrolling and monitoring a facility, but attention to the following operational aspects of intermodal parking can help ensure patrons' security:

- Activity during off-peak hours is not a usual occurrence and therefore must be carefully monitored.
- Cars that cruise parking areas and pass up open spaces should be considered suspect.
- Teenagers should not be permitted to congregate in parking lots during school hours.
- Poor maintenance is an invitation to crime because it signals a lack of interest and supervision.

For a further discussion on security, see chapter 16.

Conclusion

An intermodal transfer center is a unique parking facility that is an important component of an overall transportation system. Principles of design can reinforce various elements of the public transportation system. The guidelines in this chapter enumerate the design principles that need to be considered in the design of an intermodal facility.

CHAPTER 7
AUTOMATED PARKING STRUCTURES

Richard S. Beebe

PARKING MAGAZINE

Henry Ford has generally been credited with the development of the motor car as we know it. He may also be credited with the development of the parking space shortage. The history of early 20th century urban planning and transportation management indicates that major parking problems began to emerge even before World War I and grew rapidly thereafter. The increasing volume of vehicles in the prosperous postwar years created a demand for parking that soon moved from the curbside to vacant lots to structures of many types.

During the 1920s, the provision of off-street parking space was initially considered an "in-house" or customer service function and not a public enterprise. Thus, each building owner was more or less "on his or her own" to provide needed parking. In particular, freight elevator systems designed to accommodate parking inside large buildings gained popularity either as a retrofit item or a principal structural component of new construction. In fact, the use of elevators in multilevel garages predated ramps, which require larger building footprints and more ingenious structural formats. One response was early mechanical parking structures that used various elevator or lifting mechanisms.

In 1921, the Detroit Electric Company built a freestanding garage to serve its office complex. By 1928, the profit generation potential of parking had become apparent as evidenced by construction of the 1,000-space elevator-operated Kent Garage—an independent facility—in New York City. In 1931, a pigeonhole facility was built as an integral part of the 34-story Carew Tower mixed-use facility in downtown Cincinnati. That garage provided more than

Given the increasing difficulties associated with assembling adequate land area for garage construction, particularly in urban centers with high land values, mechanical parking has gained new importance around the world.

400 spaces on 16 levels of a core tower reached via an eight-lane entry/exit elevator plaza located in the building's basement. The garage operated every day until 1978 when sections of the building complex underwent renovation. As recently as 1984, replacement of the original elevator parking system was under consideration pending an analysis of both cost and the tower's structural frame capability.

Early elevator parking systems such as the Speed-Park system shifted vehicles from the ground to a building's upper levels where rolling frames or platforms moved the automobile onto upper floors or into individual parking spaces or "slots." The Bowser garages employed an attendant who drove the automobile onto an elevator, operated the elevator from the driver's seat, and parked the car in a designated stall on an upper floor. Other systems used a center-core elevator system to carry automobiles to available upper-level spaces that were arranged in a circular or pie-pan configuration. A pioneer in mechanical system design was the P&H Harnischfeger Corporation of Milwaukee. A major manufacturer of heavy construction cranes and lifting equipment, P&H patented an automobile elevator system in 1934. The elevator garage solved a major space problem: how to park several automobiles on a constricted site that would not otherwise permit the construction of a conventional garage.

Following World War II, the nation again experienced a dramatic increase in vehicle production and the concentration of automobiles in central cities. And, once again, the need to use restricted spaces for parking led to a renewed interest in mechanical parking in the United States, not to mention Europe and Asia. Some of the prewar systems such as Bowser and Pigeon-Hole were upgraded to reflect then-recognized levels of technology. In addition, several new systems appeared around the world during the 1950s and 1960s.

Bowser constructed a mechanical garage in Des Moines in 1951 and went on to build dozens of others, including three garages in Chicago: LaSalle Street (erected 1954), 375 spaces; Wacker Drive (erected 1955), 718 spaces; and Rush Street (erected 1955), 420 spaces. All three have since been demolished to make way for higher-use buildings. Two early Bowser garages, however, remain in operation today in New York City. Among some of the other more noticeable mechanicals built in the postwar boom were Park-O-Mat in Washington, D.C. (erected in 1951), 72 spaces; Pigeon-Hole in Toronto (erected in 1957), 396 spaces; and Speed-Park in New York City (erected in 1961), 270 spaces.

Overseas, mechanical garages were constructed in Germany by Krupp, among others, beginning in the mid-1950s. Designs included vertical, horizontal, and universal or multidirectional systems that responded to requirements for locating either freestanding or integrated garage space in the core area of larger buildings. Krupp later developed the 849-space mechanical garage for the Hotel Lotte in Seoul. In Japan, several large industrial corporations such as Mitsubishi developed mechanical garage designs that took advantage of parking space possibilities in existing buildings. Other tower-type, freestanding units were built by Tshikawajima-Harina Heavy Industries. These units could be constructed above or below ground as part of a larger building's structural frame or as freestanding structures.

More recently, several other systems have emerged to capture some part of the international market for mechanical parking. Some of these systems have progressed to actual construction; others never left the drawing board.

Given the increasing difficulties associated with assembling adequate land area for garage construction, particularly in large urban centers with high land values, mechanical parking has gained new importance around the world. Per-space land surface requirements for the construction of mechanical parking facilities are about one-half those for conventional garages. Other advantages of automated structures include significant reductions in staffing costs and substantial increases in vehicle protection and security.

During the past few years, technologies that rely on computer-controlled vehicle movement and integrated electronic components operating in a solid-state/real-time environment have come to represent the new era in automated facility development. These new systems are characterized by

- faster operating times—in/out vehicle movement in a matter of seconds depending on facility capacity;
- elimination of hydraulic components and thus the associated problems of slower speeds and lengthy repair time;
- greater system reliability;
- total hands-off, automatic operation, eliminating the need for staffing in most instances;
- remote monitoring of all operating systems, including built-in diagnostics;
- patron-only control of access to parking; and
- vehicle and patron security, a principal consideration in many areas.

From a technological standpoint, today's systems are readily available to solve parking space problems in any location where an unmet need exists. These systems provide rapid and easy access for monthly (card) or transient (ticket) parkers, imaging systems that warn of any person remaining in a vehicle, and extensive self-diagnostic alert functions to indicate potential operating problems. Facilities can be located on small parcels as independent structures or inside larger buildings as part of a mixed-use development that might combine parking with residential, office, commercial, institu-

In the United States, several firms now offer one type or another of state-of-the-art mechanical parking systems.

tional, government, or recreational uses. Other key considerations are the short delivery time of vehicles to the street and the location of roadway entry/exit points to best accommodate flow patterns of garage traffic. In most instances, costs for the development of a mechanical parking facility are equal to those associated with conventional garage construction when long-range facility development, operations, and maintenance costs are considered, including differential land value equations.

In the United States, several firms now offer one type or another of state-of-the-art mechanical parking systems, and several potential U.S. garage owners and operators—both public and private—have been seriously considering the development of automated projects. Yet, many U.S. entities are reluctant to construct new-era facilities—probably because the facilities are not traditional systems and therefore may be perceived by the public as highly suspect. The technology, however, has been amply demonstrated in the automobile industry, which uses the same transfer systems to store and then automatically send bodies to the assembly line.

The city of Hoboken, New Jersey, has awarded a contract for construction of a 324-space automated garage on a vacant parcel at 916 Garden Street. The facility will provide parking in a high-density (20,000 persons per square mile) residential area that needs several thousand parking spaces. The site contains approximately 11,000 square feet, less than half that needed to build a conventional parking structure.

The cost of the Hoboken facility is a function of limited experience with automated garages in recent years and a highly restrictive set of project specifications. Some of the cost factors associated with the Hoboken project will decline with the development of additional facilities. Even so, the cost of the project is still lower than the total cost of assembling land and then constructing a conventional facility that meets extremely stringent development requirements. Among the design specifications for the Hoboken facility is replication of the façade of adjacent multilevel residential buildings, particularly the installation of Plexiglas windows and trim in brick exterior cladding panels.

From a development perspective, the major difference between Hoboken's automated facility and a conventional facility lies in the availability and cost of land. The Hoboken site cost $2.1 million (or $160 per square foot), whereas the acquisition of land needed for construction of a conventional structure would have added at least $5 to $6 million to the land cost. A summary of the cost comparison for an automated facility and a conventional facility can be found in Figure 7-1.

The cost per space of the two garages would approach equality only if the conventional facility were enlarged to accommodate at least 600 spaces. Clearly, then, automated parking structures are most financially advantageous in either of two situations: in areas with high land values or in loca-

tions with highly constricted sites.

Among the other significant advantages are reduced annual operations and maintenance costs. In addition, a full-scale cost analysis of all operations and maintenance functions often points to a major life-cycle cost benefit for automated structures. Principal savings relate to personnel, personnel support costs, cleaning, and security and damage claims.

Where do we go from here? Work in Europe conducted by a number of experts, including Dr. Ivo Lozic at the University of Split, reveals that the need for central-city parking is increasing continuously. The development problems caused by new construction are often magnified by the lack of adequate sites for conventional garage construction. Thus, the automated structure may offer the most reasonable solution to parking problems in most large cities.

To spur further interest in and development of automated parking, manufacturers need to

- increase awareness among public agencies and developer/contractor organizations of the benefits of automated parking facilities as freestanding or internal units; and
- reduce per-space construction costs to a level reasonably competitive with conventional construction. Such costs almost always relate to land availability and cost and the complexities of site design and construction access. Project costs also affect parking rates, which must generate sufficient revenue to warrant development and operation of a facility.

The development of standardized construction formats and operating characteristics will help facilitate public agency review and approval of new projects. Standardized information will also help potential owners as well as local code officials understand the various aspects of automated parking, thus providing the basic data necessary to evaluate the feasibility of such structures.

CHAPTER 8
PARKING GEOMETRICS

Christian R. Luz and Mary S. Smith

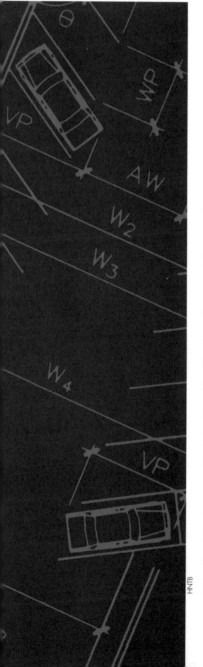

Historically, parking space design has varied with vehicle size. Parking space widths increased from 8 feet, 4 inches in the late 1950s and early 1960s to as wide as ten feet in the late 1960s. By the early 1970s, however, standard stall widths had declined to 8 feet, 6 inches. As the downsizing of vehicles became more widely accepted, many facilities began to design up to 50 percent of their capacity as small-car-only stalls (7 feet, 6 inches wide). In the 1980s, more than two-thirds of the new-car market closely clustered around the overlap between small- and large-vehicle widths. (The definition of a small vehicle is based on the square footage occupied by the vehicle. Classes 5–7 are considered small; classes 8–11 are large.[1]) Further pressure to reduce parking bay modules (a drive aisle plus two rows of parking spaces) resulted from the downsizing of large vehicles, although many experts began to question the prudence of small-vehicle-only parking spaces. In the 1990s and now into 2000, the pendulum has started to swing back toward larger vehicles. The significant increase in the use of light trucks, vans, and sport utility vehicles (LTVU) for daily transportation has once again raised questions about appropriate parking space dimensions. Figure 8-1 presents the percent of vehicles termed "small" since the tracking of LTVU sales began in 1987.

The obvious reason for adjusting parking dimensions to vehicle size is economics. The measure of efficiency in a parking design is the square footage of the lot or floor area per parking space. Thirty years ago, the rule of thumb for an efficient design was approximately 325 to 350 square feet per parking space. As downsized parking dimensions and small-vehicle-only

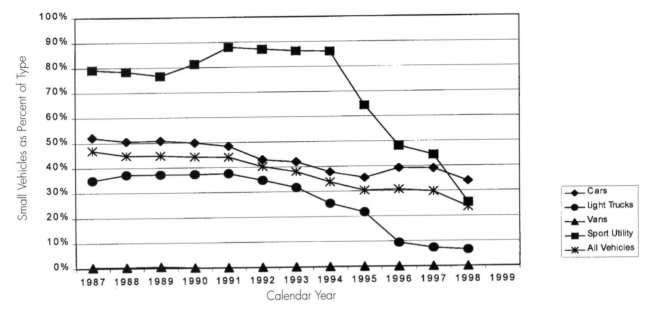

FIGURE 8-1

SALES OF SMALL VEHICLES BY TYPE

Source: Walker Parking Consultants, compiled from *Automotive News Market Data Books* (Detroit: Crane Communications, 1987–1998).

parking space layouts came into common practice, 300 square feet per parking space became a realistic goal, and some designs with a large share of small-vehicle-only parking spaces achieved efficiencies of 270 square feet per space or better. Economics is not the only reason, however, for tailoring parking space sizes to vehicle sizes. With most commercial land uses, as much or more square footage of land is devoted to parking as to the building itself.

Definition of Design Vehicle

Parking designers have found it helpful to select a theoretical vehicle size and then determine the parking space and aisle dimensions that accommodate the needs of the "design vehicle." One approach[2] to selecting the design vehicle is to use the dimensions of the 85th percentile vehicle in the range of vehicles from smallest (zero percentile) to largest (100th percentile). The use of the 85th percentile vehicle parallels the design principle of traffic engineering in which roadways are designed for the 85th percentile of peak-hour traffic volume.

In 1983, parking designers used R.L. Polk statistical data for all passenger-type vehicles registered in the United States to determine the design vehicle. Since that time, the design vehicle has been based on annual sales of small vehicles (Classes 5–7), large vehicles (Classes 8–11), and all vehicles. Since 1987, the design vehicles for light trucks and sport utility vehicles (LTVU) have been monitored by *Automotive News*, Crane Communications, Detroit (see Figure 8-2 for selected years).

The "all car" design vehicle has remained relatively stable since the early 1990s. However, the combined impact of small-car and LTVU sales as an increasing percent of the total market and significant changes in the design vehicle for each LTVU market segment has resulted in a significant change in the overall design vehicle.

In fact, the design vehicle increased by a width of three inches in 1998. Industry forecasts project that the trend toward oversized sport utility vehicles such as the Ford Expedition and Excursion has already peaked. While sales of those vehicles will remain stable, new growth will occur in the hottest new segment: sport utility wagons. These vehicles are built on medium-size car platforms epitomized by the 1999 Lexus 350, which as of this writing is outselling all Lexus models. There is no indication that there will be any further increase in the design vehicle in the foreseeable future (which, in the automobile industry, is less than five years). To remain feasible through the foreseeable future, the design vehicle used to calculate parking dimensions herein has increased in width by four inches to 6 feet, 7 inches but not in length as compared with the 1987 composite vehicle.

The precipitous decline in the sales of small vehicles renders dead the debate over small-vehicle-only parking. Many municipalities are dropping the provisions that encouraged small spaces in new construction; however, they are struggling with how to handle older facilities that depend on small stalls to meet parking needs. The adoption of moderate but rational one-size-fits-all parking space dimensions

FIGURE 8-2

DESIGN VEHICLES

	On the Road 1983 Smith: 1985	1987 Sales PCC: 1989	1993 Sales	1998 Sales	
Small Cars	5'7" x 14'8"	5'8" x 14'8"	5'8" x 14'9"	5'8 x 15'2"	Suburu Legacy
Large Cars	6'7" x 18'4"	6'6" x 18'0"	6'2" x 17'0"	6'3" x 16'9"	Dodge Intrepid
All Cars	6'3" x 17'2"	6'2" x 17'0"	6'1" x 16'8"	6'1" x 16'8"	Mercury Sable
% Small	36.0%	52.1%	42.0%	33.9%	
Trucks		6'7" x 17'6"	Ford F250	6'8" x 18'9	Dodge Ram (long bed)
Vans		6'8" x 17'8"	Ford Econoline	6'8" x 18'3"	Chevy Express
Sport Utility		6'7" x 15'4"	Ford Bronco	6'7" x 17'1"	Ford Expedition
% Small		41.9%		12.1%	
Composite (Cars + LTVU)		6'4" x 17'0"		6'7" x 17'1"	Ford Expedition
% Small		48.8%		23.5%	

Source: Walker Parking Consultants, compiled from *Automotive News Market Data Books* (Detroit: Crane Communications, 1987–1998).

will significantly help in the transition away from small-vehicle-only parking spaces.

Parking Geometrics Guidelines

The critical elements of parking space dimensions are the width of the parking space relative to the width of the vehicle and the ease of maneuvering the vehicle into and out of the parking space. The interrelationship between aisle and parking space width is such that, within reasonable limits, a wider aisle can permit a narrower parking space and vice versa and still offer the same degree of comfort in the turning movement.

A downsized but uniform parking stall accommodates all spaces except those required to serve users with disabilities.

More important, parking dimensions should be customized to the needs of projected users. For example, spaces with high turnover rates, as in the case of convenience stores, should have greater clearances than parking spaces with low turnover rates. Similarly, where there is likely to be a large number of elderly people and/or individuals under stress, such as at hospitals, a more generous design may be appropriate. A self-park structure in a downtown location in a large city can be designed with less generous dimensions than a structure in an upscale suburban mall or in a smaller, rural community. It is also important to note that vehicle sizes no longer vary by region and locality. Sport utility vehicles are just as popular in California and Hawaii as in the rural areas and the Snowbelt.

FIGURE 8-3

RECOMMENDED MINIMUM PARKING STALL WIDTHS

Typical Parking Characteristics	Parking Space Width
Low turnover for employees, students, and so forth	8'6"
Low- to moderate-turnover visitor spaces (offices, regional center retail, long-term parking at airports, and so forth)	8'6" to 8'9"
Moderate- to higher-turnover visitor parking: community retail, medical visitors	8'9" to 9'0"

Source: Parking Consultants Council.

There is a growing disparity between the size of passenger vehicles and light trucks.

Determining Parking Space Dimensions

A parking space that is wide enough for comfortable door opening clearance will be acceptable for vehicle maneuvering if the associated aisle is properly sized. As a result, parking space widths have generally been based on required door opening clearances (the distance between vehicles). Door opening clearances should range from 20 inches for vehicles in low-turnover facilities to 24 to 27 inches for vehicles in high-turnover facilities.[3] Combining these dimensions with the width of the composite design vehicle results in parking space widths that range from 8 feet, 3 inches to nine feet. Figure 8-3 presents recommendations for adjusting stall widths based on turnover. In summary, the ease of maneuverability into and out of spaces and the degree of comfort afforded the motorist and passengers should be related to the local environment.

The turnover rate or user type does not affect the length of the parking space. The average distance between vehicles

and a restraint, such as a curb stop, is generally about nine inches. Combining this dimension with design vehicle length results in a recommended parking space length of 18 feet. It should also be noted that experienced parking and traffic consultants have long recommended that parking space and aisle geometry for parking facilities should be based on rotation of the design vehicle to the desired angle rather than on rotation of the parking space dimensions. The available drive aisle is the width left between two vehicles parked directly opposite each other. The controlling factors for design of the drive aisle are determined by the design criteria for curbs, walls, or other parking space constraints that protrude into spaces and/or the drive aisle.

FIGURE 8-4

RECOMMENDED MINIMUM MODULE DIMENSIONS*

Parking Module Width for One-Way Traffic and Double-Loaded Aisles

Parking Angle (in degrees)	Module	Vehicle Projection	Aisle
45	48'0"	17'8"	12'8"
50	49'9"	18'3"	13'3"
55	51'0"	18'8"	13'8"
60	52'6"	19'0"	14'6"
65	53'9"	19'2"	15'5"
70	55'0"	19'3"	16'6"
75	56'0"	19'1"	17'10"
90	60'0"	18'0"	24'0"

*Design vehicle = 6'7" x 17'0".

FIGURE 8-5

COMMON PARKING DIMENSIONS FOR 8'6" STALLS

Angle	Base Module W1	Single Loaded W2	Wall to Interlock W3	Interlock to Interlock W4	Curb to Curb W5	Overhang o	Interlock i	Stall Width Projection WP
45	48'0"	30'4"	45'0"	42'0"	44'6"	1'9"	3'0"	12'0"
50	49'9"	31'6"	47'0"	44'3"	45'11"	1'11"	2'9"	11'1"
55	51'0"	32'4"	48'7"	46'2"	46'10"	2'1"	2'5"	10'5"
60	52'6"	33'6"	50'4"	48'2"	48'2"	2'2"	2'2"	9'10"
65	53'9"	34'7"	51'11"	50'1"	49'3"	2'3"	1'10"	9'5"
70	55'0"	35'9"	53'7"	52'2"	50'4"	2'4"	1'5"	9'1"
75	56'0"	36'11"	54'11"	53'10"	51'2"	2'5"	1'1"	8'10"
90	60'0"	42'0"	60'0"	60'0"	55'0"	2'6"	0'0"	8'6"

Dimensions have been rounded to nearest inch.

*Design vehicle = 6'7" x 17'0".

FIGURE 8-6

COMMON PARKING DIMENSIONS

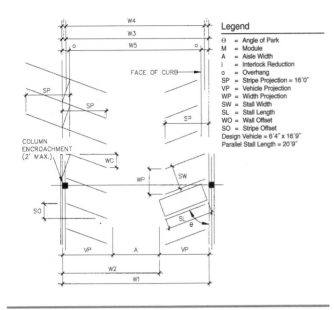

Legend

Θ	=	Angle of Park
M	=	Module
A	=	Aisle Width
i	=	Interlock Reduction
o	=	Overhang
SP	=	Stripe Projection = 16'0"
VP	=	Vehicle Projection
WP	=	Width Projection
SW	=	Stall Width
SL	=	Stall Length
WO	=	Wall Offset
SO	=	Stripe Offset

Design Vehicle = 6'4" x 16'9"
Parallel Stall Length = 20'9"

Determining Aisle and Module Dimensions

Parking designers use the term module for the combined dimension of two parked vehicles and the aisle between. Trial and error originally determined parking modules. However, Edmund Ricker, an early pioneer in the field of parking design geometrics, developed a series of equations that modeled the movement of a vehicle into a parking space. Over the years, the equations have undergone refinement and now better simulate the aisle/parking space relationship. The combination of these equations and practical experience has resulted in the development of a set of module dimensions that provide an acceptable minimum level of comfort for the turning movement as seen in Figure 8-4.

When designing basic parking space geometry for a particular parking facility (surface lot or structured parking), the designer should account for fundamental parking criteria, some of which include site location, site dimensions, site constraints (trees, power poles, buildings, and so forth), surrounding streets, traffic flow, parking demand generators, local zoning and landscaping mandates, surface conditions, and parking user categories. Each criterion can be unique to each parking location, thereby creating circumstances where the parking geometry must be carefully considered and adjusted on a case-by-case basis to allow for the location's maximized potential.

Most of these criteria are "givens," allowing for little flexibility. However, user characteristics may mandate some flexibility in parking space geometry to maximize the efficiencies of the parking facility. We have previously discussed recommended stall widths for low-turnover, medium-turnover, and

high-turnover parking. By holding to the above modules and adjusting the stall width, the designer can ensure comfortable parking dimensions.

It is important to note that the dimensions provided in this chapter list recommended minimums. It may be appropriate and prudent to provide wider spaces in accordance with the location-based criteria discussed above. Consultants have found that increasing stall width and decreasing aisle width is a preferred method of maintaining an overall minimum level of comfort while maximizing user acceptance. An adjustment of three inches less per module for each one inch in additional stall width is recommended.[4]

Figure 8-5 presents some additional dimensions that are useful for laying out parking facilities for the minimum module dimensions shown in Figure 8-6. It is important to note that the interlock dimension and stall width projection (parallel to the aisle) are calculated for an 8-foot, 6-inch stall.

The recommended minimum dimensions assume parking lot conditions without physical restrictions. When a curb stop is not provided, such as in a shopping center parking lot, vehicles occasionally pull into the parking space too far, thereby reducing the aisle width of the adjacent module. This can be a particular problem in the Snow Belt, where space markings are sometimes obscured. Therefore, when a curb, wall, or other physical restraint is provided at each parking space, the aisle width (and therefore the resulting module) can be reduced by one foot.

It is common in parking structures for columns to extend beyond the face of the bumper wall or vehicle restraint and therefore into the module. Encroachments also occur in parking lots at light poles. It is recommended that columns, light poles, or other appurtenances be allowed to encroach into the module and affect up to 30 percent of parking spaces. The encroachment should be limited to

- a maximum combined reduction of two feet (i.e., six inches into parking spaces on one side of the aisle and 1 foot, 6 inches on the other side) below the module widths recommended in Figure 8-2; or
- one foot below the module if the one-foot credit is taken for vehicle restraints at every parking space.

Column encroachments into the width of a parking space are occasionally used in short-span designs on the theory that if the column is clear of the door swing zone, the parking space width is maintained. However, the turning movement into the parking space is constrained by the column; the clear space for turning into a typical parking space between two design vehicles in the two adjacent parking spaces is the parking space width plus at least 20 inches. To maintain the same clear space for turning movement into each parking space, the parking spaces adjacent to walls, columns, or other obstructions must be widened by at least ten inches.

Why Small-Vehicle-Only Parking Spaces Do Not Work

At the time the small-vehicle-only parking space was introduced, the mix of automobiles consisted of very large and very small vehicles; therefore, the small-vehicle space was largely self-enforcing. One common layout placed angled large-vehicle spaces on one side of the aisle and 90-degree small-vehicle spaces on the other side of the aisle. The difficulty of the turning movement into the 90-degree parking spaces and the restriction on door opening discouraged larger vehicles from using the small-vehicle-only parking spaces.

The practicality of small-vehicle-only parking spaces was, however, short lived. Since manufacturers started downsizing larger passenger cars, much debate has raged over what is and is not a small vehicle. Confusion has increased as the dimensions of smaller-sized large vehicles and larger-sized small vehicles began to blur and, more recently, as certain models were upsized. Light trucks, vans, and the popular sport utility vehicles now account for half of total personal vehicle sales.

If a small-vehicle space is available in a convenient location in a parking facility, many drivers of intermediate or even larger vehicles park in the small-vehicle spaces, thus impeding traffic flow and compromising safety within the facility. In addition, when large vehicles park in small-vehicle parking spaces, they frequently encroach into the adjacent parking space such that a domino effect occurs down the row and eventually renders a parking space unusable. As a result, the effective capacity and improved efficiency provided by small-vehicle parking spaces is negated. If, on the other hand, small-vehicle spaces are placed at inconvenient locations, small-vehicle drivers may park their vehicles in standard-sized spaces, forcing later-arriving large vehicles into an inadequate and inconvenient small-vehicle parking space. It has thus become apparent that specially located small-vehicle spaces are not effective unless a facility is policed to prevent the use of large-vehicle spaces by small vehicles or vice versa.

Newspapers ranging from the *Wall Street Journal* to *USA Today* have run "exposés" on the inability of small-car-only stalls to accommodate today's vehicles. A number of cities, such as Honolulu, have dropped provisions allowing small spaces, and others (including Palo Alto, California) are increasing the fines imposed on large vehicles parked in small stalls. Therefore, small-car-only stalls should be used only in remnants of space and should not exceed 15 percent of total capacity.

Conclusion

Due to the convergence of vehicle sizes, small-vehicle-only parking spaces are no longer a rational parking design alternative. In addition, LTVUs are an increasingly important factor in parking design geometrics. Sales of small vehicles dropped significantly in the 1990s as the American passenger vehicle underwent a general, slow upsizing. Therefore, a rational approach to parking space and module sizing can and does support moderate module dimensions for one-size-fits-all designs

It is time for municipalities to review and revise their parking ordinances. Requiring excessively generous parking geometrics wastes resources, land, and money and conflicts with other community interests such as increased green space and reduced stormwater runoff. Where small-vehicle-only parking spaces are permitted, overly generous standard parking space dimensions virtually force facility owners to specify small-vehicle-only parking spaces to achieve a cost-effective design.

Moreover, excessive dimensions for standard parking spaces make it difficult for facility owners or operators whose properties include only small-vehicle-only parking spaces to restripe to a one-size-fits-all design without an unacceptable loss of parking spaces.

Notes

1 Parking Standards Design Associates, *A Parking Standards Report,* Los Angeles, March 10, 1971. Originally, square footage was used to describe class size, and compact vehicles were in what is now Class 8. By the time the PCC adopted this approach in 1989, the typical compact vehicle was in Class 7.
2 Mary Smith, "Parking Standards," *Parking,* July/August 1985.
3 Parking Standards Design Associates, *A Parking Standards Report*.
4 Mary Smith, "Parking Standards."

CHAPTER 9
SURFACE LOT FUNCTIONAL DESIGN

Abraham Gutman

BOB DUNPHY–ULI

Surface parking lots satisfy 80 percent of all parking demand in the United States. They vary in size from ten- to 15-space visitor and employee parking lots to several-acre lots serving major industrial complexes, large hospitals, shopping centers, apartment building developments, hotels, entertainment centers, convention and meeting complexes, sports venues, airports, universities, park-and-ride facilities, and large office developments.

Most surface parking is provided without direct charge to the user. Many employers provide free parking for their employees, shopping centers generally provide free parking for their patrons, and many suburban office buildings and hotel developments provide free parking for both employees and patrons. Therefore, a discussion on the design of surface parking facilities cannot be limited to parking lots that charge patrons to park.

Surface parking lots can be divided into four major service categories based on location or type of clientele: urban parking lots, suburban parking lots, parking lots that satisfy employee parking demand, and lots for special-use generators such as hospitals, airports, colleges and universities, sports complexes, entertainment centers such as theme parks, and convention and meeting facilities. An examination of each category illustrates the versatility of surface parking lots in satisfying a wide range of needs generated by the parking public.

Urban Lots

In general, the urban parking lot is comparatively small and may charge patrons for the use of its parking spaces. Such lots may meet the needs of the short-term (hourly) parker or the long-term parker—either on an all-day

An infill parking lot in Lexington, Virginia, preserved existing trees.

basis or under the terms of a monthly contract. Short- or long-term parking can be encouraged by varying a facility's rate structure. Facilities situated near retail and business establishments cater primarily to short-term parkers who generally are willing to pay a higher rate for the convenience of parking close to their destination; thus, short-term lots produce more revenue per parking space than do lots catering to long-term parkers. In the case of parking lots located progressively farther from the core of a community, the facilities' function shifts increasingly from short-term high-turnover hourly parking to long-term and monthly contract parking.

A facility can be operated as a valet-park system, self-park system, or honor-park system. With the increasing cost of labor, self-park and honor-park systems continue to predominate. Valet parking operations are somewhat restricted to smaller facilities that can be staffed by a few employees. Honor-park systems are generally used in facilities that are on the fringe of the central business district (CBD) and cater primarily to all-day and monthly parkers at a relatively low charge. They do not produce sufficient revenue to warrant employment of full-time personnel. All honor systems require periodic enforcement to ensure their effectiveness.

Suburban Lots

The past several decades have witnessed an explosion in business and commercial development in the suburbs of most major metropolitan areas. The shift in office building and shopping center development from urban to suburban locations is the result of lower land costs, development of the federal interstate highway system, the desire to conduct business near major single-family residential areas, and the convenience afforded by the automobile. Public transportation satisfies little of the demand currently generated by suburban commercial and business developments, thereby placing the onus on developers to provide parking for their tenants and tenant visitors.

The parking lot at a suburban shopping center functions in accordance with a completely different set of principles than those guiding an urban parking facility. For example, shopping center lots tend to be large; they vary from hundreds to thousands of spaces depending on the size of the shopping center. Moreover, the more generous parking space geometrics commonly found in suburban lots have now become the norm expected by the public.

Suburban office building parking lots also tend to be considerably larger than their urban counterparts. Suburban zoning regulations, lack of public transportation, and inadequate on-street parking create the need for a greater number of parking spaces per 1,000 square feet of net rentable office area. In addition, the ratio of visitor to employee spaces varies with the function of the office building. A medical office building, for instance, might require 50 percent of total spaces to be reserved for visitor and patient parking while a general office building might require only 10 to 15 percent of total spaces to be reserved for visitors.

Most suburban shopping center parking lots do not charge a direct fee for use of their facilities. Likewise, suburban office building complexes usually do not charge a fee for use of their facilities. However, the cost of developing, maintaining, and controlling suburban shopping center parking areas is factored into rents and ultimately into the costs of merchandise, services, and public use areas.

Employee Facilities

The largest individual segment of parking in the United States is provided by employers responding to the needs of their employees. In most instances, such parking is provided at no cost to employees. Free parking for employees has even been written into major labor agreements as an employee fringe benefit.

The design of long-term employee parking can differ somewhat from the design of short-term customer parking. Employees, who are familiar with the work facility and may enter and exit from the facility only once or twice a day, do not necessarily require the same degree of user convenience as medical center patients or retail/service customers. Employees can be expected to walk farther and use facilities with narrower aisles and reduced parking space widths.

Special-Use Facilities

Special-use parking facilities are distinguished from other parking facility types by their design requirements. That is, they must be designed to meet the brief peak parking demand generated by sports complexes, convention and meeting facilities, theaters, coliseums, and similar activity centers. However, other special uses such as hospitals, airports, and hotels generate parking demand 24 hours a day 365 days a year and thus exhibit still different peak parking needs. While certain design considerations are common to most special-use parking lots, proper evaluation of these facilities requires subdivision of the special-use category into special-use generators that operate 24 hours a day and special-use generators that operate only periodically.

Hospitals, airports, and hotels are excellent examples of special-use generators that create parking demand over a 24-hour day. They must accommodate parking demand associated with large numbers of employees and visitors as well as demand occasioned by daily periods of peak public parking. If an economical and efficient parking facility is to be developed for special-use generators, facility design must permit the operation of parking services with minimum manpower during periods of low demand while still providing sufficient entry/exit lanes to handle periods of peak in/out activity. Airports, in particular, offer public parking lots that are divided into long- and short-term parking areas. Furthermore, optimum revenue control can be achieved by segregating employee parking from paid parking, including separate entry/exit control points.

Uses that generate periodic parking demand, such as sports facilities, present a completely different set of parking problems that require different design considerations. Generally, the major design consideration is maximum entrance and exit capabilities to handle peak parking demand during a relatively short period of time. In addition, for special-event parking, fees are usually collected upon entry to rather than exit from the parking facility, with selection of a parking space rigidly controlled.

Parking Space Design Efficiency

The development of surface parking lots in lieu of multilevel parking structures is largely a function of economics. The cost of structured parking is much greater than the cost of surface parking. Thus, structured parking is usually developed when land is extremely costly or in short supply. Structured parking is also developed when optimal parking convenience is an issue.

In addition to meeting parking demand, urban parking lots can act as land banks. Urban property owners often convert downtown parcels into surface parking lots until the parcels are needed for development of office or commercial space. In the meantime, the property produces revenue for the owner and provides additional parking.

The cost of building a surface parking lot varies with its size, geographic location, and the quality and quantity of associated improvements. Installation of adequate paving, lighting, and drainage and of parking access and revenue control (PARC) equipment can be budgeted at a cost of $5 to $10 (1999 dollars) per square foot. The addition of landscaping, which is required by many communities, can further increase costs.

Within the parameters of acceptable design standards, the primary requirement for acceptable parking lot design is

Employee parking lot in Newport Beach, California, uses 90-degree parking for irregular parcel.

maximization of the number of parking spaces. Maximum capacity generally requires the development of parking modules that run parallel to the long dimension of the site. A repetitive modular increment for either angle or 90-degree parking can then be developed for the width of the site under consideration. A typical double-loaded parking module is a drive aisle with parking on both sides; 90-degree parking requires the largest modular width. As the angle of parking decreases from 90 to 45 degrees, the width of the module becomes progressively narrower. However, layout efficiency is reduced as the module angle decreases. Layout, or design efficiency, refers to the number of square feet per parking space.

Parking on the perimeter of a surface facility normally affords maximum capacity. However, where snow removal and storage is an issue, perimeter parking may not be feasible. Snow removal and storage should be considered at the outset of the design phase.

The width of parking stalls varies considerably depending on type of clientele, whether a location is urban or suburban, whether development is private or public, and whether parking is to be free or paid. Narrow parking stalls are generally developed in urban areas for employee use and thus achieve maximum revenue return while providing the most economical space possible for private development. In suburban areas with relatively low land costs, wider parking stalls are typically provided in high-turnover facilities as a matter of convenience and service. Current stall sizes in parking facilities vary from a width of about 8 feet, 3 inches to over nine feet. Chapter 8 provides recommended parking geometrics developed by the Parking Consultants Council. It is also essential to note the specific requirements of the Americans with Disabilities Act (ADA) with respect to the location, number, and size of signage for accessible parking spaces (see chapter 17 for more information).

Access controls facilitate managing employee parking.

Ingress and Egress

Usually, the larger a parking area, the more latitude there is in planning for street entrances and exits. One driveway opening per entrance or exit is often adequate for a small parking facility. In fact, local ordinances and codes frequently restrict the number of entrances and exits. Generally, though, the number of required driveway openings is related to lot size, turnover rate, the method of lot control, the lot's relationship with adjoining streets, and the type of clientele served. Ingress and egress are treated in more detail in recommendations as noted in chapter 4. In any event, adequate reservoir space should be provided at lot entrances to avoid hazardous queues on public roadways. To prevent friction with street traffic, driveway openings should not be located near street intersections.

Typically, the most efficient entrance and exit design can be achieved by favoring the traffic entering a facility, even at the expense of complicating the exit. Favoring entering traffic expedites the rapid movement of traffic from the street to the facility and avoids vehicle queues on public roadways. Moreover, given that traffic exiting from a parking facility tends to move slowly, drivers can comfortably negotiate the turns required to reach the exits. Driveways should minimize interruptions to the traffic flow within the facility itself.

Construction Details

Several critical construction details pertain to the proper design of surface parking lots, including pavement design, drainage considerations, location and design of curbs and sidewalks, lighting, striping, fencing, and landscaping. The remainder of the chapter describes recommended best practices to address each of these important components of surface lot design.

Pavement

The durability and serviceability of a surface parking lot largely depend on the quality and type of the lot's surface material. The most important consideration in the structural design of pavement is proper preparation of the subgrade material and selection of the appropriate pavement type and thickness. Excessive thickness results in unjustifiable construction costs; insufficient thickness results in unsatisfactory performance and expense, premature failure, and/or excessive maintenance. Proper subgrade preparation is mandatory and in many cases must be accomplished under the supervision of a geotechnical engineer. Concurrent with the subgrade work, the site must be sloped to ensure positive drainage, which often requires installation of surface drains and drain lines. Surface lots are typically paved with bituminous, concrete, gravel, or porous surface materials.

After the site is properly sloped, drains installed, and the soil compacted to the proper density, well-graded aggregate should be rolled onto the surface and compacted. For a bituminous pavement, asphaltic concrete is added over the prepared base. In some cases, an asphaltic binder course is applied before installation of the top course, the final level of paving that creates a smooth driving surface. Sealer coats are often applied to the top course to prevent deterioration of the asphalt from oil and gasoline.

Thickness designs for parking lot pavements are based on studies, road tests, and surveys of pavement performance. The most commonly used method is the American Association of State Highway and Transportation Officials (AASHTO) Design Equation, which was developed from data obtained from the American Association of State Highway Officials (AASHO) Road Test.

Many parking lot projects are not large enough to justify lengthy and detailed design analysis. Therefore, parking lot designers should be aware of and consider the design features used in similar local installations. For small parking lots, an engineer can often rely on personal experience and professional judgment to select conservative values for the design criteria associated with subgrade, soil reaction, imposed load, and traffic. Reference manuals recommended to assist designers in interpreting design needs and procedures for proper pavement thickness include the following:

- American Concrete Institute Committee 330, *Guide for Design and Construction of Concrete Parking Lots*;
- American Concrete Pavement Association, *Thickness Design for Concrete Highway and Street Pavements—Publication EB109P*; and
- Asphalt Institute, *Thickness Design—Asphalt Pavements for Highways and Streets*.

Drainage

Proper drainage is vital to ensure that rainwater will be carried away from the site. A surface parking lot should be sloped a minimum of 2 percent toward drain inlets, catch basins, or curb inlets. Designers should consult local ordinances and control standards to ensure compliance.

Curbs and Sidewalks

The parking lot perimeter should incorporate curbs and gutters of cast-in-place concrete or extruded concrete curbs or similar materials. Concrete is strong enough to withstand wheel impact and outlasts other types of curbs such as asphalt. Sidewalks should be provided for pedestrian circulation. To prevent the soils from washing out from under the sidewalk, edges should be more than four inches thick and turned down into the ground approximately six inches. An aggregate base course should be provided under all sidewalks. The sidewalk surface should be sloped for drainage and should have a light broom finish for safety. Control joints should be placed at a maximum of five feet.

Lighting

Large lots are usually illuminated with light standards located between parking stalls in the interior of the lot. The standards should be positioned along the centerline of a double row of vehicle stalls as well as along the stall line between vehicles.

Common fixture types include high-pressure sodium and metal halide. Fixture type, the number and height of fixtures per standard, and the desired illumination level all determine the spacing of standards. The type of fixture covering should be consistent with neighboring uses; for example, cut-off fixtures should shield residential areas from direct lighting. When security is a concern, lighting levels should be increased to a level that reasonably satisfies economic, security, and community concerns.

All wiring should be placed in buried conduits before completion of the paving operation. Photoelectric lighting controls can be located in a central area on poles or a nearby building and connected to a timing device. Parking facility lighting design is discussed further in chapter 14.

Striping

Parking lots should be striped in white or yellow paint. Many designers prefer to specify four-inch double-box, or hairpin, stripes approximately 18 to 24 inches apart to separate one parking stall from another. Double box-stripes help the driver center the vehicle within the area between the stripes. They also maximize the space between vehicles and minimize conflicts between door openings of adjacent vehicles. Most paint manufacturers offer a striping paint that meets federal specifications. Special acrylic paints should be applied over a newly constructed parking area to prevent paint discoloration.

Fencing

Fencing may be used to address security concerns, to screen the headlights of circulating vehicles, or to control access (for example, limiting cut-through pedestrian traffic). A six-foot-high chain link fence is usually most effective, although zoning codes may restrict heights and material types. Manufacturers offer a wide range of fencing materials, including plastic-coated fencing in various wire gauges and colors, chain link, wrought iron, treated wood, and composites.

Landscaped parking lot with stores closer to street.

Fencing should be located at an adequate distance from circulating drives or parking stalls to prevent damage from vehicles. The height of a fence, material type, and number of access points (ingress and egress) determine the degree of security provided by fencing. Access points in the fence should be minimized.

Landscaping

Properly designed plantings can help soften the visual impact of surface parking lots by screening circulating and parked vehicles. Many communities have enacted ordinances and requirements that govern landscaping for surface parking facilities.

Ideally, landscaping should be located in unusable parking or circulation areas, with the proper clearance from parked vehicles carefully maintained. To allow for vehicle overhangs, plantings should not be located within three feet of the curb unless low-lying groundcover is used. All planting areas should be mounded to promote drainage and salt runoff but should not be used for snow storage. Planter areas and tree wells should be installed in accordance with the planned lot dimensions and the needs of specific plant materials, thus avoiding any adverse impacts on parking functions due to improper location and/or design of landscaping features. A five-foot or greater turning radius is recommended for islands to accommodate sufficient vehicle maneuvering during circulation and to avoid breakdown of curbed areas and damage to plant materials.

If the parking layout is designed to accommodate future expansion, the landscaping plan should consider such expansion in order to maximize the efficiency of the initial landscaping.

The distance between interior parking lot islands and parked automobiles should never be less than the distance between two adjacent parked vehicles. Landscaping materials located within large parking areas should be sufficiently scaled so that the heat reflected from the pavement does not damage the vegetation. Underground sprinkler systems should be considered to ensure the long-term viability of plantings.

Other landscape design considerations are vehicle sight lines, particularly at points of ingress and egress and pedestrian routes that prevent cut-through traffic in planted areas. Bushy growth and leaves between three and eight feet above grade will severely reduce the sight line of drivers at critical ingress and egress locations. Low ground cover and tall trees without low branches are preferred. Final landscaping plans should be reviewed in conjunction with the Americans with Disabilities Act to ensure barrier-free design.

CHAPTER 10

FUNCTIONAL DESIGN OF PARKING STRUCTURES

H. Carl Walker and James E. Staif

A parking structure is part of the roadway system where vehicle occupants change from the vehicular mode to the pedestrian mode and back again. Every vehicle requires at least two parking spaces—the first at its trip origination point and the second at its destination. The need for parking structures is created by people driving to places of concentrated activity—a central business district, shopping center, airport, sports facility, college campus, medical center, or office building. The functional design of a parking facility varies with the type of user. A parking facility serving a retail shopping center or medical center experiences a high daily turnover of parking space use while a parking structure serving an office building may have a single turnover unless additional demand is created during evening and weekend hours.

Functional design involves the development of vehicular and pedestrian flows in a parking structure as well as the layout of parking spaces. Parking facility operation, including revenue control and security, is another functional design consideration.

Types of Parking Structure Operations

The two general types of parking operations are self-park and attendant-park facilities. In attendant-park facilities, the driver leaves the vehicle at the entrance and an attendant parks the vehicle. When the driver returns, the attendant retrieves the vehicle and transfers it to the driver at the exit. Attendant-park facilities maximize the number of vehicles that can be placed in a particular area, usually through stacked parking (see Figure 10-1). Such facilities are often associated with high-value properties in larger metropolitan areas.

FIGURE 10-1

ATTENDANT-PARK FACILITY

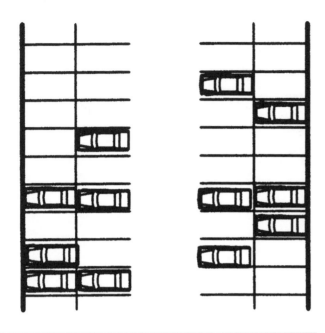

FIGURE 10-3

MORE THAN ONE ENTRANCE/EXIT

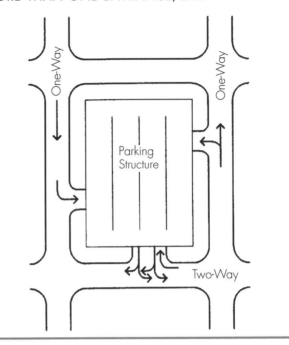

Today, the most common type of parking operation in North America is the self-park facility, in which drivers park and retrieve their own vehicle (see Figure 10-2). This chapter discusses the self-park approach to functional design.

The elements of functional design to be considered for self-park structures include the following:

- adjacent street traffic analysis;
- location and number of entrances and exits;

FIGURE 10-2

SELF-PARK FACILITY

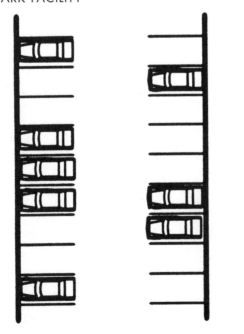

- transient versus monthly parking;
- large-vehicle/small-vehicle ratios;
- vehicle and pedestrian circulation;
- parking space geometrics;
- parking space resizing provisions;
- allowances for future expansion;
- stair and elevator locations;
- lighting intensity and control;
- drainage;
- security systems;
- access and revenue control and operating systems;
- graphics and signage; and
- maintenance and durability factors.

Street Traffic

Street traffic configuration—the pattern of adjacent one- and/or two-way streets—has a major impact on the use of a parking structure. It is always best to locate entrances on major streets inbound to the destination area, with exits located on outbound streets. The greatest fear of a parking facility owner is a change in the one-way street pattern after a garage is completed. Such a change requires the immediate reversal of all access directions to and from the facility's entrances and exits. The location of parking structure exits on low-volume streets is recommended as a means of minimizing street traffic conflicts with vehicles exiting from the parking facility.

Entrances

Generally, entrances to a parking facility are located on the high-volume streets that provide direct access from users'

FIGURE 10-4

DECELERATION LANE

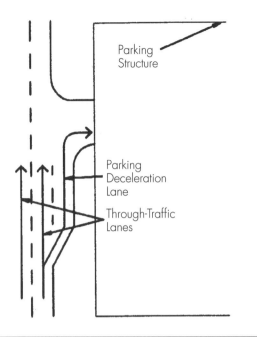

FIGURE 10-5

TICKET DISPENSER

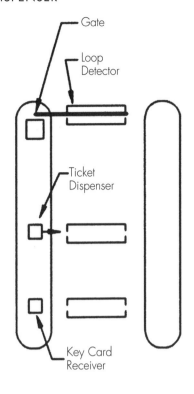

FIGURE 10-6

MONTHLY/HOURLY PARKING

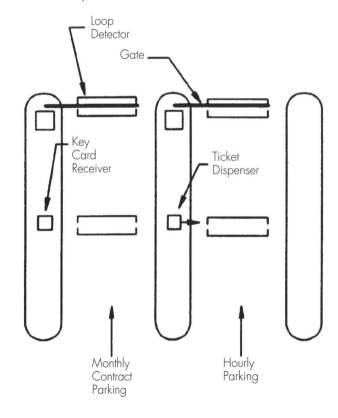

points of origin. Larger parking facilities generally incorporate more than one entrance and exit to provide access from various adjacent streets in the event of street repairs or emergencies (see Figure 10-3). Moreover, should entrance operating equipment fail, the additional entrance lane provides alternative access. As one solution to the problem of potential equipment failure, some operators place two ticket dispensers in tandem at a single entry lane and cover one with a removable canvas hood.

It is generally more convenient to enter a facility from a one-way street or by turning right from a two-way street. Left turns into a garage from a major two-way street during peak traffic periods can be difficult, if not impossible, because of the high volume of traffic approaching from the opposite direction.

The architectural design of entrances is a major element of successful facility operation. Entrances must be designed to be obvious and should be differentiated from facility exits. Special architectural features such as arches, canopies, marquees, or other distinguishing design elements help users identify a facility's entrance(s).

Where a parking facility is adjacent to a high-volume or high-velocity street, a deceleration lane leading to the entrance helps eliminate rear-end accidents and reduces street traffic slowdowns (see Figure 10-4). An entrance lane is usually equipped with a ticket dispenser, access card reader, control gate, and loop detectors (see Figure 10-5). An access card reader can be added to a typical entry lane but should be placed upstream of the ticket dispenser so it is not mistaken for a ticket dispenser. When installed in combination with an access card receiver, a ticket dispenser should be a push-

FIGURE 10-7

DIMENSIONAL CLEARANCES

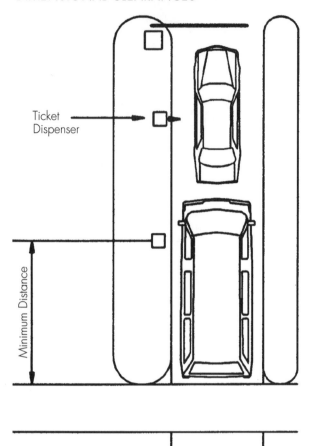

FIGURE 10-8

CASHIER BOOTH

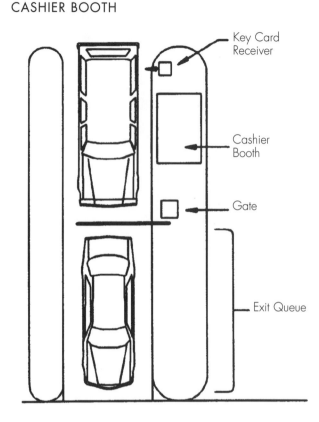

button unit so that entrance operations and activity reporting remain separate functions. Separate lanes can be designated for monthly and hourly parking (see Figure 10-6).

Entrance ticket dispensers and gates should be located far enough in from the street so that a vehicle entering behind a vehicle already at the ticket dispenser or access card reader can clear the sidewalk. When a deceleration lane cannot be accommodated on high-traffic streets, ticket-dispensing and card-reading equipment should be located at least three or four vehicle lengths into the building to provide queuing space. A large, van-type vehicle should be used as the design vehicle to test dimensional clearances (see Figure 10-7).

One inbound lane is adequate for a garage with an average turnover of 300 to 500 vehicles. For larger garages (500 or more vehicles) or smaller garages with high turnover, additional entrances or entrances on different streets help accommodate the higher entering volumes. A traffic operations assessment of the adjacent streets can determine the best possible access points. Entrances should be located at least 75 to 100 feet from any corner intersection to prevent conflicts between parking facility traffic and street intersec-

tion traffic. Traffic engineering principles can be applied to determine the appropriate vehicle queueing storage length.

Single entrance lanes from the street should be approximately 13 to 16 feet wide, tapering down to ten feet at the approach to the control equipment. Double entrance lanes should be a minimum 24 feet wide. Ramps leading directly from the entrances should have a short, level segment beyond the controlled exit/entrance area before beginning the slope upward or downward to the parking spaces.

Operators often use television cameras to monitor entrances that are remote from the cashier booth or manager's office. The cameras, coupled with an audio communication system built into the ticket dispenser, aid in communication if an equipment malfunction occurs or a patron has a question before entering the facility.

Exits

If possible, exits should be located on low-volume streets to reduce any exiting delay caused by street traffic in the vicinity of the exit. In addition, a turn in the drive aisle leading to an exit lane or plaza can slow exit speeds and help control vehicle release rates into the street. It is preferable to group together all cashier booths so that one cashier can operate the parking structure during low-volume periods, thus minimizing operating costs. The number of cashier-staffed and access-card exit lanes varies with the ratio of monthly contract (access card) patrons to transient parkers.

For a typical municipal garage with a combination of transient and monthly parkers, one cashier-staffed lane for each 400 exiting vehicles is usually adequate, with a minimum of two lanes for a structure accommodating at least 200 vehicles. One lane is the primary cashier-staffed exit; the other lane is a secondary or peak-load cashier-staffed lane. In addition, the second lane is available for monthly parker access-card exiting and therefore allows the monthly parker to bypass any backup that may occur at the adjacent cashier booth.

To keep cashiering delays to a minimum, the cashier booth should be located far enough from the sidewalk or street to provide space for at least one vehicle that has already completed the parking payment transaction (see Figure 10-8).

A cashier can handle approximately 90 to 180 vehicles per hour depending on the simplicity of the parking rates and the type of revenue control equipment. For example, parking rates charged in dollar increments permit vehicles to move through the cashier plaza faster than rates requiring coin change. Sometimes the primary cashier booth is an extension of the manager's office. In off-peak periods, the same staff person can serve the dual function of shift manager and cashier.

Operations Systems

Most self-park facilities use an exit cashiering system; however, some operate with parking meters located at each space or at centralized pedestrian exits. Sometimes a flat fee is collected upon entry. Operations systems can vary from simple metered systems to highly complex and sophisticated remote computerized systems. Other systems such as automatic pay-on-foot and central cashiering are common in Europe and gaining acceptance in North America.

Vehicle Circulation Patterns

The most common circulation pattern used in parking structures in North America is the continuous ramp, whereby sloping floors with aisles and parking spaces along both sides of the aisle provide access to the parking spaces themselves and the facility's circulation route. The basic continuous-ramp, sloping-floor configuration is called the single-helix or scissors ramp. It is used for 90-degree parking and two-way traffic (see Figure 10-9).

Architects generally like functional designs that provide horizontal and vertical façade lines. They often object to façades with sloping lines. Thus, functional designs that

keep the ramping on the interior bays, such as the three-bay double-helix ramp or the four-bay side-by-side ramp, are preferred.

Several systems use combinations of variations on the single-helix continuous ramp: the two-bay, end-to-end configuration (see Figure 10-10); the two-bay double-threaded helix configuration (see Figure 10-11); the three-bay, double-threaded configuration (see Figure 10-12); and the four-bay, side-by-side configuration (see Figure 10-13). All of these configurations lend themselves to one-way traffic and angle parking.

The two-bay split-level configuration (see Figure 10-14) was once a commonly used layout. Its geometry, however, requires special interfloor ramps that are not needed in continuous-ramp systems, thus leading to higher structural costs as well as to poor traffic circulation.

While 90-degree parking could be used with a one-way traffic system, it does not lend itself to the "automatic" one-way traffic flow pattern created by angle parking (see Figure 10-15). More specifically, 90-degree parking is frequently associated with the two-way traffic patterns that result in cross-traffic or conflict points within the structure, longer parking space search times for the driver, and larger overall building width. In contrast, the advantages of angle parking include ease of entry into a parking space and minimization of two-way traffic conflicts.

Nonetheless, 90-degree parking should not be dismissed outright. A 90-degree, two-way traffic pattern can sometimes operate much as a one-way traffic layout. In particular, a facility with high inbound traffic in the morning and high outbound traffic in the evening, as in the case of an employee parking facility, may effectively operate as a one-way traffic facility.

Access from floor to floor is typically provided by sloping one or more bays from one level to the next level. Multiple-bay sloped ramps can easily confuse the uninitiated parking patron. Where repeat parkers represent the largest share of facility patrons, however, users come to understand the ramp configuration. Under such circumstances, the efficiency and shorter travel distances afforded by intertwining ramps, such as with the double-threaded helix configuration, are particularly desirable.

For facilities that serve the infrequent parker at, for example, a convention center or hospital, the parking layout should be as simple as possible. In this case, the preferred practice is to replicate the shopping center type of parking lot by specifying level floors and, at the more remote bays, continuous-ramp parking that accommodates vehicle ingress/egress.

In a continuous-flow circulation system, drivers should not have to pass more than 600 to 750 spaces in a driving circuit to locate a parking space. The design should also permit a driver leaving a parking space to circulate directly to the exit as expeditiously as possible. A reentry point to the facility's internal flow pattern is desirable and usually located

FIGURE 10-9

SINGLE-HELIX RAMP (TWO-WAY TRAFFIC)

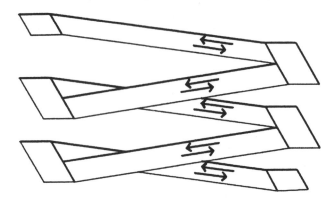

on the ground floor or first supported level before the entry to the cashier lanes.

Typically, grades in continuous-ramp facilities do not exceed 5 to 6 percent on the parking floors. For nonrepetitive short segments or in hilly areas where people are accustomed to steep grades, parking floor grades up to 7 percent are acceptable. In any event, the needs of persons with disabilities must be considered in establishing parking floor grades. Speed ramps (nonparking ramps) should be limited to a 12.5 percent grade unless signage specifically prohibits pedestrian use of the ramps. Ramps greater than 15 percent can be psychological barriers to some drivers, particularly in the case of a downbound ramp; however, again, in hilly areas, ramp grades up to 20 percent may be considered.

FIGURE 10-10

END-TO-END HELIX RAMP (ONE-WAY TRAFFIC)

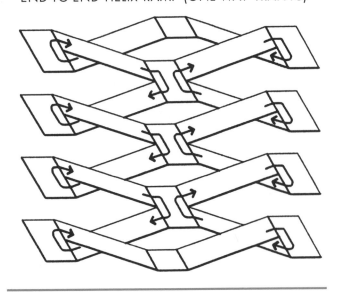

FIGURE 10-11

TWO-BAY, DOUBLE-THREADED HELIX RAMP (ONE-WAY TRAFFIC)

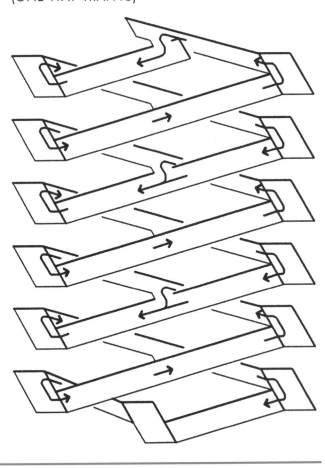

FIGURE 10-12

THREE-BAY, DOUBLE-THREADED HELIX RAMP (ONE-WAY TRAFFIC)

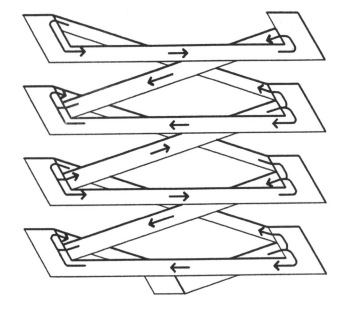

FIGURE 10-13

FOUR-BAY, SIDE-BY-SIDE RAMP (ONE-WAY TRAFFIC)

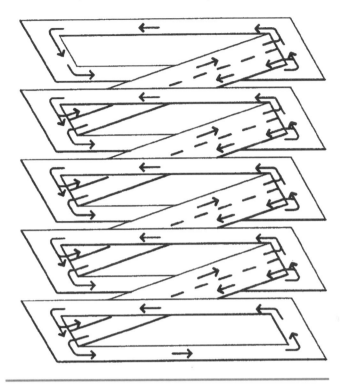

FIGURE 10-15

PERPENDICULAR AND ANGLE PARKING

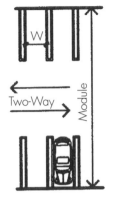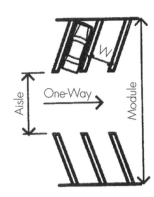

ply lowering the grade slab on the first or grade level. For passenger vehicles, a seven-foot minimum clear height is used, although a clearance of 7 feet, 4 inches to 7 feet, 8 inches conveys a sense of greater openness and accommodates higher vehicles. In the case of large, level multiple-bay parking areas, high floor-to-beam clearances can provide the user with more space and thus afford a greater degree of comfort. For vehicles used by the disabled, an 8-foot, 2-inch minimum clearance is used.

Circular or spiral express entrance and exit ramps are an efficient albeit expensive means of providing vertical access to a facility's parking levels. Airport parking facilities and other high-capacity (2,000 spaces or more) uses that generate long lengths of stay relative to the number of vehicle transactions often use flat-deck storage ramps with spiral express entrance and exit ramps. Spiral ramps range from 65 to 100 feet in outside diameter; drive aisles are approximate-

When the transition from floors to ramp grades exceeds 6 percent, a vertical curve transition (see Figure 10-16) should be used. Special attention should be given to height clearances on ramp breakovers, which should be checked from the wheel line, not from the floor surface (see Figure 10-17).

Some facilities are designed to accommodate overheight vans and recreational vehicles. In fact, accessibility design regulations may require special high-clearance areas. Often, the requirement for added clearance can be satisfied by sim-

FIGURE 10-14

TWO-BAY, SPLIT-LEVEL RAMP (ONE-WAY TRAFFIC)

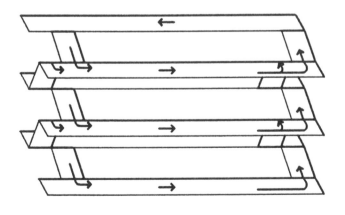

FIGURE 10-16

TRANSITION FROM FLOOR TO RAMP GRADES

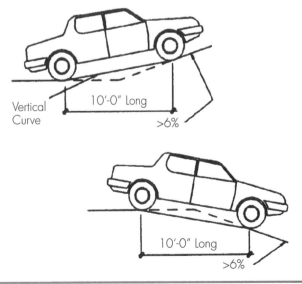

FIGURE 10-17

HEIGHT CLEARANCE

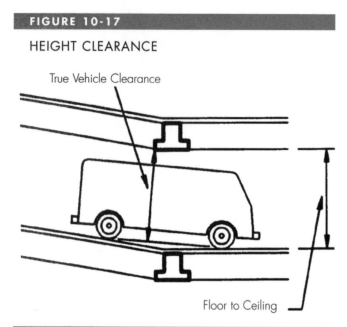

True Vehicle Clearance

Floor to Ceiling

ly 15 feet wide with an outer-curb width of 18 inches and an inner-curb width of 12 inches. Sometimes, circular ramps are designed in a double-threaded configuration in which each complete turn marks a descent of two parking levels.

The grade on a circular ramp varies with floor-to-floor height, the width of the driving path, the number of floors per revolution, and the overall diameter of the ramp. The grade also varies from the outer circumference to the inner circumference. All turns on the ramp should be a continuous ramp slope and superelevated between six inches and one foot with no reverse superelevation. Circular ramps should be as open as possible. Solid walls on the inner and outer circumferences of the ramp create a sense of confinement and thus should be discouraged. A circular express ramp should be limited to six complete turns, which in the case of a double-threaded ramp would allow the ramp to serve a 12-story structure.

Parking Space and Module Design

The most efficient parking structure in terms of square feet per space is not necessarily developed with 90-degree parking stalls. Properly designed angle-parking layouts with one-way end crossovers can sometimes be more efficient than 90-degree layouts. In fact, the ease of parking in a one-way traffic/angle layout often offsets any decrease in efficiency. Moreover, parking space width and parking module length (the dimension from bumper wall to bumper wall) can be varied in accordance with the desired level of comfort. As described in chapter 8, some parking structure designers provide separate spaces for large and small vehicles; however, today's recommended parking space calls for one size fits all. One-size-fits-all parking spaces now tend to be 8 feet, 6 inches wide compared with large-vehicle spaces of nine feet wide and small-vehicle spaces of 7 feet, 6 inches wide.

The ratio of large vehicles to small vehicles varies with different locations in North America as well as with different uses. For example, average vehicle size in the West is generally smaller than that in the Midwest. In addition, the average vehicle size at universities, particularly among student-driven vehicles, is smaller than average vehicle sizes at other locations. Often, a simple vehicle-size study at a given location can provide the parking facility designer with an accurate picture of the vehicle-size mix in that area. Current developments in designing for different vehicle sizes are discussed in chapter 8.

Local zoning codes and the Americans with Disabilities Act require accessible parking spaces for vehicles driven by persons with disabilities (see chapters 4, 8, and 17 for a more detailed discussion of zoning, geometrics, and the Americans with Disabilities Act). The incorporation of special design features for the disabled is mandatory in newly designed facilities. In some cases, designated spaces may have to comply with requirements for increased clearance and a prescribed location(s) within the parking structure.

Some parking consultants use a level-of-service concept to specify the size of parking spaces. Level of Service (LOS) as used in highway design ranges from LOS A for free, unimpeded flow of traffic to Levels B, C, D, E, and, finally, LOS F for gridlock. In fact, these considerations have little application to parking structure functional design. Other parking consultants, recognizing that parking functional design requires evaluation factors that differ from those used in roadway/highway design, prefer the User Comfort Factor approach to design. The User Comfort Factor approach takes into account variables such as one- or two-way traffic, 90-degree versus angle parking, parking space width, drive aisle width, queuing space available at entrances and exits, cashier systems, driver choices while circulating, and potential vehicle/vehicle and vehicle/pedestrian conflicts. It should also be noted that level of service and user comfort are improved by increasing module or space width.

Another consideration in sizing parking spaces is climatic factors. Given the inclement winter months in northern states, it may be desirable to specify a slightly wider space that permits drivers to exit from and enter their vehicles without their heavy outerwear making contact with adjacent vehicles that might be splattered with road chemicals and mud.

Clear-Span Design

The design of parking structures to span the parking module and thus eliminate columns between parked vehicles offers several advantages. First, clear spans promote easy entry into parking spaces without the "fender-bender" stigma. Second, columns between parking spaces consume space that could otherwise be used for parking. Most important, however, the clear span allows for the future restriping of parking spaces as vehicle sizes change.

Given that column locations seldom interfere with parking operations in clear-span structures, the structural bay size does not need to be identical to a specified increment of parking space width. In other words, if 90-degree parking spaces are laid out at 8 feet, 6 inches on center, the columns do not have to be placed at 25 feet, 6 inches on center or at some other increment of 8 feet, 6 inches. Columns can project into the parking module by up to two feet. While today's passenger vehicles vary considerably in length, some large vehicles may—but rarely do—park adjacent to the projecting column and extend into the parking aisle. Even then, they may not seriously disrupt a facility's operations.

Pedestrian Circulation

Pedestrian travel paths are typically located behind parked vehicles along the sides of drive aisles; the exception to this rule is special pedestrian routes that may be required for the disabled. In either case, pedestrians require a protected path of access to and from the parking structure and a safe, visible route to their parking space. Vertical transportation facilities for pedestrians such as elevators and stairs intended for patrons' use are usually located at the perimeter of the parking structure in the direction of major destinations. Fire escape exit stairs must be located in accordance with the applicable building code. Facilities with a high rate of vehicle turnover, which means high pedestrian volume, might incorporate wider drive aisles. Elevator lobbies and stair towers may be the most visible element of a parking structure and may provide interior architectural design opportunities for incorporating glass, special lighting, brick, and ornamental features.

Stairs and Elevators

Building code requirements dictate the exit travel distance to stair fire exits. If stairs are the only means of vertical pedestrian conveyance, as in a building of one or two supported levels, at least one stair should be oriented to major destinations. In parking facilities with four or more parking floors, stair locations may not be critical except in meeting building code requirements. In multilevel facilities, most patrons use the elevators, although one stairway should be located adjacent to the elevator tower. If the elevator is out of order, patrons use the nearby stairs. Even when an elevator is operating, some patrons prefer to walk to lower floors.

The general design standard is one elevator for up to 250 spaces, two elevators for up to 500 spaces, and three to four elevators for up to 1,000 spaces, although the number of levels, rate of vehicle turnover, and type of land use supported by the parking facility can be factored into the standard.

Common elevator size in a parking facility is a 2,500-pound-capacity unit with a five-foot-by-seven-foot cab that can accommodate a gurney for medical evacuation. Except in the case of low-rise hydraulic elevators, the vertical speed should be no less than 200 feet per minute. Hydraulic elevators can be used in structures up to six levels.

Where high peak-load pedestrian traffic is projected, extrawide stairs are recommended to encourage patrons' use of the stairs during periods of high activity.

Other Considerations

If a parking structure is enclosed or located underground and thus does not meet the open-structure wall area requirements for natural ventilation, mechanical ventilation and sprinklers may be required. Building codes usually prescribe the rate of ventilation. Generally, a rate of one cubic foot per minute per square foot of area is adequate for a parking structure except where extensive interior queuing is expected. Carbon monoxide sensors are recommended for underground facilities.

When required, sprinkler systems are installed in a conventional manner. In freezing climates, a dry system is preferable. A dry standpipe with hose cabinet is sometimes used instead of a sprinkler system.

Overall experience shows that the likelihood of fire in a parking structure is extremely low. Nonetheless, it should be noted that fire extinguishers located in a parking facility pose some risk of theft. Fire extinguishers stored in the cashier booth and manager's office usually should suffice for fire protection purposes in most cases.

Curbs in the vicinity of stair and elevator towers are trip hazards and thus should be discouraged. Often, curbs are used as wheelstops when facility design calls for cable rails instead of concrete bumper walls. Curbs between parking modules on a flat parking deck are also discouraged. Patrons may trip over them as they move from bay to bay between vehicles.

Precast concrete wheelstops are not recommended. They provide an area where trash and debris collect. If, however, wheelstops are required with angle parking, they should be placed in a straight line rather than perpendicular to the parking space. When wheelstops are placed perpendicular to the parking space, the wheelstop in the adjacent space poses a trip hazard for the driver exiting from a vehicle in that space. The hazard is particularly problematic with vans because the driver sits unusually close to the front of the vehicle.

The efficient functional design of a parking facility is a critical component in the success of a facility. Interaction between pedestrians and vehicles and between vehicles should be provided in a safe and efficient manner. Vehicular and pedestrian circulation within the facility and to and from the facility needs to be accommodated with appropriately designed entrances, exits, parking bays, elevators, and safety features. This will help ensure higher use levels, lower liability, and an efficient and cost-effective facility for the user and owner.

CHAPTER 11
BUILDING CODES

Donald R. Monahan and H. Carl Walker

The regulation of building construction in the United States is accomplished through a document known as a building code. The document is adopted by a state or local government legislative body and then enacted to regulate building construction within a particular jurisdiction. The design and construction of a parking structure is governed by the applicable building code of the jurisdiction in which the facility is built (see Figure 11-1).

Three model codes have gained widespread acceptance throughout the United States. They are

- the Uniform Building Code (1997), promulgated by the International Conference of Building Officials (ICBO)—used mainly in the upper Midwest and the western half of the United States;
- the BOCA/National Building Code (1999), promulgated by the Building Officials and Code Administrators International, Inc. (BOCA)—used predominantly in the central and northeastern part of the United States; and
- the Standard Building Code (1999), promulgated by the Southern Building Code Congress International, Inc. (SBCCI)—used primarily in the southeastern part of the United States.

On December 9, 1994, the three model code organizations joined together to form the International Code Council (ICC). Their joint goal was to develop a single set of comprehensive and coordinated national codes by 2000. The process culminated in the approval of the International Building Code 2000 (IBC) in fall 1999 along with publication of the final document in

FIGURE 11-1

WHICH STATES USE WHAT CODES

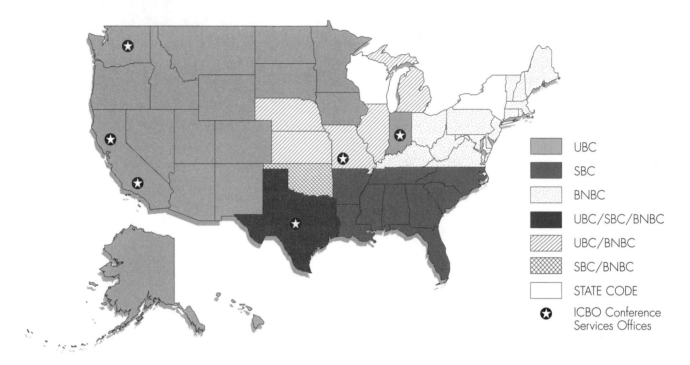

Legend:
- UBC
- SBC
- BNBC
- UBC/SBC/BNBC
- UBC/BNBC
- SBC/BNBC
- STATE CODE
- ⭐ ICBO Conference Services Offices

UBC–ICBO's *Uniform Building Code*; SBC–SBCCI's *Standard Building Code*; BNBC–BOCA's *National Building Code*.
Source: The International Conference of Building Officials (ICBO) Web site http://www.icbo.org/Code_Talk/code-map.html.

April 2000. It is now up to the different states or cities to enact enabling legislation to adopt the new national code.

In addition, since 1972, the Council of American Building Officials (CABO) has served as the umbrella organization for BOCA, ICBO, and SBCCI. In November 1997, CABO agreed to incorporate itself into the ICC and to become the secretariat for the committee that maintains the standard for Accessible and Usable Buildings and Facilities (CABO/ANSI A117.1), which is referenced by the three model codes.

Finally, the National Parking Association's Parking Consultants Council (NPA/PCC) revised and published its *Recommended Building Code Provisions for Open Parking Structures*. The NPA/PCC recommendations do not represent a legal document unless adopted by a local governing authority by reference. They do, however, represent the collective opinion of many of the top experts in the parking industry. In the absence of specific code requirements, the NPA document represents recommended parking industry standards.

The purpose of a building code is to establish the minimum acceptable requirements necessary for protecting the public health, safety, and welfare in the built environment. Building codes establish structural design requirements for live loads, dead loads, wind loads, and earthquake loads. They also establish life safety requirements related to the number of fire exits (stairs), travel distances to fire exits, fire suppression systems, railing protection at changes in elevation, and so forth. Dispersion of vehicle emissions is a partic-

ular concern in parking facilities because a parking facility is a warehouse for a tankful of potentially hazardous material in every vehicle. Ventilation and fire protection requirements therefore differ markedly for a parking structure versus other building types. Accordingly, the development team must identify a parking facility's type of use or occupancy classification in order to determine the specific building code provisions that apply to the given facility.

This discussion of building code requirements for parking structures is intentionally general in nature and should not be construed as explaining any specific code.

Occupancy Classification

The three model codes classify parking structures as low-hazard storage facilities or Group S occupancy under the codes. Parking garages are further subdivided into open parking garages and enclosed parking garages.

Open parking garages are those with sufficient openings around the exterior to provide for natural ventilation. For a parking facility to be classified as an open parking garage, Section 411.3.2 of the 1999 Standard Building Code states,

> The exterior and interior walls of the garage shall be designed in accordance with one of the following: 1) At least 50 percent of the clear height between floors shall be open to the atmosphere for the full length of at least two exterior walls, excluding required stair

FIGURE 11-2

OPENING BELOW GRADE FOR
NATURAL VENTILATION

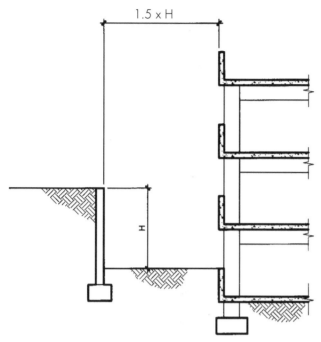

Source: *The Dimensions of Parking,* Third Edition (Washington, D.C.: ULI, 1993), p. 115.

and elevator walls and structural columns. Interior wall lines and column lines shall be at least 20 percent open and uniformly distributed or, 2) the exterior walls of the structure shall have uniformly distributed openings on two or more sides totaling no less than 40 percent of the building perimeter. The area of such openings in the exterior walls on each level shall have at least 20 percent of the total perimeter wall area of each level. Interior wall lines and interior column lines shall be at least 20 percent open and uniformly distributed."

The other codes specify similar provisions.

The building codes do not require mechanical ventilation, sprinkler systems, or enclosed stairways when a structure is classified as an open parking garage.

Portions of parking structures that are partially or entirely below grade may be classified as enclosed even though upper portions are classified as open. Designers can provide natural ventilation to basement levels by constructing area walls or light walls around the perimeter of the basement (see Figure 11-2). Generally, a basement is that portion of the building that is eight feet or more below the exterior grade; the codes do not specify requirements for natural ventilation associated with exterior openings.

The 1999 BOCA Code (Section 1208) states that "openings below grade shall be acceptable for natural ventilation provided that the outside clear space measured perpendicular to

the opening is one and one-half times the depth below the average adjoining grade."

For a parking structure to be classified as open, it must meet other special provisions under the various codes. The Standard Building Code requires that the *distance* from any point on any floor level to an open exterior wall facing on a street or to other permanently maintained open space at least 20 feet wide and extending full-space width to a street shall not exceed 200 feet. The NPA recommends a respective width and length of ten and 250 feet. The UBC also requires a maximum distance of 200 feet from any point on the floor to a perimeter wall opening. If a structure fails to meet this provision, its occupancy classification defaults to an enclosed garage.

The 1999 UBC requires an open parking garage to be used *exclusively* for the parking of private motor vehicles. Mixed occupancies are not allowed in an open parking garage. Therefore, if a mixed use is included under or over the parking garage, the occupancy classification defaults to an enclosed garage.

Parking structures that do not meet the above criteria for an open parking garage are classified as enclosed parking garages and thus require mechanical ventilation, fire sprinklers, enclosed stairs, and shorter travel distances to fire exits (stairs).

Specific Use Provisions

The remainder of the chapter discusses the following specific provisions:

- location on property;
- height and area allowances;
- mechanical ventilation;
- guardrails;
- design live loads;
- means of egress; and
- fire protection.

Location on Property
Open parking garages must have a ten-foot setback from a common property line or from an imaginary line midway between buildings. Protected openings (i.e., fire sprinklers at an opening) or a one-hour–rated firewall is required within five to ten feet of a property line. Openings are not allowed at less than five feet from the property line.

Height and Area Allowances
Open parking structures are required to be constructed of noncombustible material (Type I or Type II construction per chapter 6 of UBC-1999). The allowable heights and areas of parking structures are governed by construction type and vary with the codes as shown in Figure 11-3.

The codes allow increases in the limits if more than two sides are open or an automatic fire sprinkler system is installed.

FIGURE 11-3

OPEN PARKING GARAGES AREA AND HEIGHT

Construction Type[1]	Fire Rating of Structural Frame	Area per Tier (square feet)	Allowable Height
Type I	Three-hour	Unlimited	Unlimited
Type II—FR.(1)[1]	Two-hour	125,000	12 tiers
Type II—One Hour[1]	One-hour	50,000	10 tiers
Type II—N[1]		30,000	8 tiers

[1]May be unlimited in area when the height does not exceed 75 feet.
Source: 1999 UBC Table 3-H and Table 6-A.

The minimum clearance to overhead pipes, beams, and other obstructions is seven feet. A minimum clearance of 8 feet, 2 inches is required for handicap vans.

Mechanical Ventilation

When a parking garage does not meet the definition of an open parking garage, mechanical ventilation is usually required. The 1999 Standard Building Code (Section 411.4.2) requires a mechanical ventilation system capable of providing at least six air changes per hour on each level, with continuous ventilation providing a positive means for both inlet and exhaust of 0.75 cubic feet per minute (cfm) per square foot of floor area.

The 1997 Uniform Building Code (Section 1202.2.7) requires a ventilation system capable of exhausting a minimum of 1.5 cfm per square foot of gross total floor area unless an alternative ventilation system is designed to exhaust a minimum of 14,000 cfm for each operating vehicle. Such alternative systems must be based on the maximum number of vehicles circulating through the parking structure at any instant but not less than 2.5 percent (or one vehicle) of the garage capacity. Automatic CO (carbon monoxide) sensing devices may be employed to activate a modulated ventilation system to maintain a maximum average

CO concentration of 50 parts per million (ppm) during any eight-hour period, with a maximum concentration not greater than 200 ppm for a period not exceeding one hour. Connecting offices, waiting rooms, ticket booths, and so on must be supplied with conditioned (uncontaminated) air under positive pressure. Fresh air intakes to the cashier booths are generally recommended.

Guardrails

The 1999 UBC requires guardrails to be provided at all exterior and interior vertical openings in all floor and roof areas where cars are parked and where the vertical distance to the ground or surface directly below exceeds 30 inches. The 1999 Standard Building Code specifies guardrails where the elevation difference is three feet. The codes require such handrails to extend 42 inches above the floor line. Intermediate rails must be spaced such that a four-inch-diameter sphere cannot pass through the opening. The BOCA Code does not allow the intermediate rails to be horizontal as the "ladder effect" potentially allows children to climb the rail, fall, and injure themselves.

Vehicle restraint is also required at changes in elevation of adjacent surfaces. The Standard Building Code and NPA code require that impact guardrails, spandrels, and walls that act as impact guardrails in parking structures must be designed for a minimum horizontal ultimate vehicle load of 10,000 pounds applied 18 inches above the floor at any point along the guardrail. Impact guardrails not less than two feet in height shall be placed at the ends of drive aisles, at the ends of parking spaces at the perimeter of the structure, and at the ends of parking spaces where the difference in the adjacent floor elevation is greater than one foot. The 1999 UBC specifies a 6,000-pound service load acting at 18 inches above the pavement. The minimum vertical dimension of the vehicle barrier is 12 inches. A vehicle barrier is required where any parking area is located more than five feet above the adjacent grade.

Design Live Loads

Design uniform live loads for parking structures are 50 pounds per square foot. Often, an additional requirement

CHOATE PARKING CONSULTANTS

Guardrails placed at perimeter of parking structure.

applies to passenger vehicles accommodating not more than nine passengers: a 2,000-pound concentrated load on an area of 20 square inches. Building codes allow a reduction in live load for the design of beams, girders, columns, tiers, walls, large precast floor members, and foundations. One exception is the BOCA code, which allows no live load reduction for parking structures except for walls and columns.

All codes require parking facilities to be designed to withstand earthquake-induced loads for the seismic zone in which they are located. The design of structures for seismic resistance is highly specialized. In parking structures, rigid frames, shear walls, or shear frames normally resist seismic loads.

Assuming a fully enclosed building, wind loads are applied to the exterior of the parking structure, with the code-specified load applied to the gross area of the façade. No additions or reductions are made to the wind load for the openness of the structure's façade or the impact of the wind on interior elements.

Means of Egress

Where no persons other than parking attendants are permitted, at least two, three-foot-wide stairs are required. Where persons other than parking attendants are permitted, the travel distance to a stair in an open parking garage shall not exceed 300 feet. If automatic fire sprinklers are provided, the travel distance may be increased to 400 feet. The travel distance to a stair in an enclosed garage is 200 feet without fire sprinklers and 250 feet with fire sprinklers. A minimum two stairs are required per tier. At least two stairs must be placed a distance apart equal to not less than one-half the length of the maximum overall diagonal dimension of a tier. The travel distance must include the path around permanent construction features and building elements.

Stair enclosures are not required in open parking garages; however, stair enclosures are required for enclosed parking garages. Wireglass stair enclosures are sometimes allowed in enclosed parking garages.

The 1997 UBC requires that ramped surfaces along the exit travel path not exceed a slope of 1:20 (5 percent). Ramps that exceed a 5 percent slope must have a five-foot-long landing for every five feet of rise. The 1999 BOCA and SBC codes require landings for every 2.5 feet (30 inches) of rise if the ramp slope exceeds 1:20. Before 1997, the maximum slope requirement was 1:15 (6.67 percent). The IBC 2000 also specifies a landing for every 30 inches of rise if the ramp slope exceeds 1:20. This new requirement is controversial as many designers do not believe it was intended to apply to parking structure floors. Finally, speed ramps must have landings if they are part of the exit travel path; however, if pedestrians are prohibited from using the ramps, then the speed ramp may be at a 1:8 slope (12.5 percent). It may be necessary to provide a separate walkway and steps around interior speed ramps to accommodate fire exit requirements.

Fire Protection

Fire protection for open parking structures in freezing climates usually consists of a dry standpipe system located in each stairway and/or at a spacing that provides adequate coverage for a 75-foot hose with a 30-foot spout of water. When more than one standpipe riser is provided, they must be interconnected at ground level. Exterior Siamese connections must be provided at ground level to connect to a tanker truck or fire hydrant. In addition, local fire marshals often require fire extinguishers spaced at regular intervals (75 feet) throughout the parking floor area. Unless they are enclosed in a glass-door case, however, fire extinguishers on parking floors are often stolen.

For enclosed parking structures, the codes generally require automatic fire sprinkler systems throughout the parking areas. These systems are dry when used in freezing climates but are connected to a water supply that is activated by heat or smoke detectors placed throughout the structure. Sprinkler systems are often ineffective at extinguishing vehicle fires as the fire is usually contained inside the steel shell of the automobile in either the passenger or engine compartment. According to the Parking Market Research Company in *Parking Garage Fires in 1992*, only 13.6 percent of fires in garages with fire sprinklers were controlled or extinguished by the sprinkler system. Sprinkler systems in a parking structure can actually create more problems than they solve. In particular, sprinkler water can disperse the fuel from a ruptured gas tank and thus spread a fire.

Code Changes

Building codes are periodically amended, typically on a three-year cycle. In April 2000, the International Building Code 2000 was issued. The intent of the new code is to combine all three model codes into one uniform document.

CHAPTER 12
STRUCTURAL SYSTEMS FOR PARKING FACILITIES

Thomas J. D'Arcy and James E. Staif

PARKING MAGAZINE

Over time, parking facilities have been constructed of a wide variety of building materials, including cast-in-place concrete, precast concrete, and steel. This chapter provides a history of structural systems, describes the most commonly used systems, explains how designers choose structural systems, and examines issues for consideration by planners and designers as a project develops.

History of Structural Systems

Most early parking structures, many of which are still in operation, used short-span construction typified by large columns with massive capitals and flat slabs. Other early structures were constructed with steel frames and concrete decks. Eventually, the relationship between clear-span construction and improved parking efficiency became apparent so that structures spanning 50 to 65 feet are now the norm. The impetus for the construction of clear-span facilities emerged in the mid-1950s and early 1960s with the advent of precast pretensioned concrete and cast-in-place, post-tensioned systems with tendons of high-tensile steel. The new technologies allowed for the possibility and economy of long, shallow-depth spans. Today, precast concrete; long-span cast-in-place, post-tensioned concrete; and steel systems are commonly used in most new parking structures.

Precast Concrete Systems

Most precast concrete structures consist of precast concrete columns bearing on and connected to a foundation. The columns support precast beams and spandrels that in turn support a precast deck member (see Figure 12-1). The

71

Long-span precast concrete structural systems.

type of precast deck member generally lends its name to a given structural system, as in the double-tee structure, single-tee structure, hollow-core system, pretopped system, or precast joist system. The double-tee is by far the most common structural system used today.

A double-tee slab system consists of units eight, ten, 12, or 15 feet wide that span between supports (see Figure 12-1). The double-tees may employ either a thicker flange (typically four inches thick) called a pretopped unit or a hardrock (normal-weight) or light-weight concrete topping cast on top of the double-tee units. The depth of the double tees is governed by the span, member width, design loads, and local availability.

The typical double-tee floor system is supported at the perimeter by either L-beam spandrels or pocketed spandrels. A typical precast interior framing system consists of columns plus inverted tee-beams and load-bearing walls (called lite-walls), with large openings for increased security. In parking facilities, lite-walls are employed at ramp bays to support the sloping floor tees at their different elevations.

Supported double-tee precast member.

FIGURE 12-1

PRECAST CONCRETE DECK

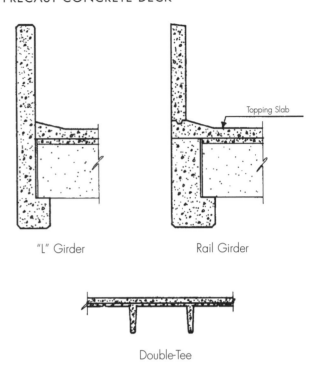

"L" Girder   Rail Girder

Double-Tee

Single-tee systems are seldom used today because of economic considerations. The single-tee unit varies in width from six to ten feet and in depth from 24 to 48 inches depending on span and loading conditions.

A hollow-core slab is a shorter-span system with less depth than the double-tee unit. The hollow-core unit is manufactured in sections four to eight feet wide and six to 12 inches deep. Deeper hollow-core units have been used for 60-foot clear spans. Special care must be taken in places where temperatures fall below the freezing point. Holes must be drilled or cast in the low ends of the hollow-core units to prevent the accumulation of water. In addition, all joints must be sealed and the application of a traffic-bearing membrane is recommended.

Pretopped systems employ double-tees with a thickened flange (typically four inches) that eliminates the need for a field-cast topping. The system can incorporate small pour strips at the ends to accommodate tolerances or can function as a dry system with no field-placed concrete. The top surface is roughened for traction, and the joints between members are sealed. The minimization or elimination of field-placed concrete has earned pretopped systems wide acceptance for speed of construction.

A precast joist system typically includes deep joists that clear-span a bay supported by precast concrete columns. The joists support cast-in-place floor slabs and provide some of the shoring required during construction. Joists can be spaced from ten to 25 feet on center and can range from

Cast-in-place, post-tensioned system.

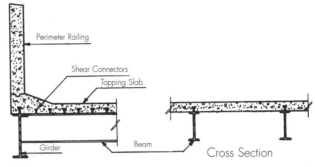

FIGURE 12-2

STRUCTURAL STEEL SYSTEM

Perimeter Railing

Shear Connectors

Topping Slab

Girder

Beam

Cross Section

eight to 24 inches deep. The cast-in-place floor slab is typically post-tensioned.

Cast-in-Place Systems

Cast-in-place concrete systems were developed before precast concrete became an economically competitive option. The several types of cast-in-place structural systems include two-way flat slabs, pan-joist systems, slab-beam-girder systems, flat-soffit construction, and dropped-beam construction. These systems rely on conventional or post-tensioned reinforcement (see photo). The use of cast-in-place, post-tensioned construction in parking structures offers considerable flexibility, with almost no limit to the variety of shapes that can be formed.

A two-way flat-slab structure accommodates less structural depth than a precast structural system and thereby minimizes floor-to-floor heights. However, the structure requires a large number of columns that typically fall between parking spaces, consume valuable space, and constrain future restriping efforts. A flat slab can be conventionally reinforced or post-tensioned.

A pan-joist system is sometimes referred to as flat-soffit construction. When a design requires beams to be deeper than joists, the system is often called a dropped-beam system. The pan-joist system uses steel or fiberglass pans approximately 30 inches wide. Placement of the pans on designated centers produces a joist of a certain width. If pan depths are increased, joists can span 60 feet or more. The system may also use shallow pans ten to 12 inches deep to extend between long-span girders. The slab cast on top of the pans varies from two to five inches depending on local fire codes and structural requirements. It should be noted that the system's thin slab is particularly susceptible to corrosion and deterioration in salt-use regions and therefore is seldom used today.

Thin-slab systems such as waffle slabs are susceptible to corrosion because of the small concrete cover over the reinforcing steel. In addition, the slabs' penchant for cracking demands careful analysis. The two-way, post-tensioned, cast-in-place slab has been used to make concrete slabs more watertight. Because prestressed concrete induces compression, it reduces the tendency toward cracking and produces structures that are relatively watertight.

Structural Steel Systems

A structural steel system uses columns, beams, and girders with a concrete slab installed between the beams (see Figure 12-2). The slab may be precast or cast-in-place. The steel structure can be adapted to short or long spans depending on design requirements.

The use of long-span steel beams with composite concrete floor slabs has made inroads into the parking structure market. In composite construction, steel beams are fixed to the concrete slab above so that the slab and beam act as a single unit to resist bending and deflection from parking loads. The benefits of composite construction are possible not only with cast-in-place slabs but also with various types of precast construction. High-strength steels have reduced the required tonnage for long-span steel structures. Another system, termed hybrid, employs steel beams and columns with precast double tees providing the deck member. In any event, the fire safety and corrosion protection of unprotected steel should be investigated.

Comparison and Selection of Structural Systems

The selection of a structural system usually follows from an analysis of available options that considers the following:

- owner preference;
- first cost;
- life-cycle cost;

- availability of materials;
- safety and security; and
- construction schedule.

A brief description follows.

Owner Preference

Owners are often familiar with structural system options and usually favor a particular system. If an owner has analyzed systems in the past and specifies a preference, further analysis is unnecessary.

First Cost

The first or construction cost of various systems can vary significantly. While first cost is not the best tool for comparing systems, owners are sometimes willing to accept lower first costs with the understanding that a lower-cost system may mean higher operations and maintenance costs.

Life-Cycle Cost

A widely accepted measure of total system cost is life-cycle cost. Life-cycle costs include all costs expected to be incurred over the life of a structure, including first cost and operations and maintenance costs. The assumed life of a structure varies, but designers often use an expected life of 50 years. All costs are projected over the same time period and brought back as present value (PV) costs and compared with one another.

Availability of Materials

Materials are not always available at all project locations. For example, a project site may be hundreds of miles from a precast concrete fabrication plant. Designers need to research material options as they begin their analysis of potential structural systems.

Safety and Security

Owners and designers must consider users' safety and sense of security as related to structural systems. For example, precast designs often incorporate shear walls that limit lines of sight and create corners. Designers can overcome perceived design deficiencies in all structural systems by providing openings in precast shear walls or employing shear frames.

Construction Schedule

Selection of a structural system is influenced by the time of year that construction is slated to begin, weather conditions, and the availability of materials. Another consideration is the capacity and schedule of the factories that produce precast concrete. In addition, local preferences, construction customs, and the workload and skill level of available contracting companies may influence both the construction schedule and choice of structural system.

The analysis of structural systems often concludes with the development of an evaluation matrix. The project team then weights and scores individual factors; the highest-scoring system moves into final design.

Other Considerations

Column Location and Spacing

The development of long-span structural systems has greatly improved the efficiency and cost-effectiveness of parking facilities. Whenever possible, designers should maximize a facility's usable area by keeping drive aisles and stalls free of columns. Chapter 8 provides additional information on geometrics.

Loading

Loading requirements for parking facilities vary from code to code and often from city to city; national codes frequently are modified to satisfy local conditions or the desires of local officials. Local conditions can require particular design loads. Where applicable, it is generally recommended that the actual service live loads range from 25 to 30 pounds per square foot. In some cases, parking decks must be designed to support the weight of emergency equipment, such as fire trucks. If deliveries are to be made on the parking deck, designs must include provisions for appropriate truck loading and other types of heavy vehicular traffic. The available clear head room also will affect the type of vehicles that can enter a parking structure.

Designing for full snow loads plus full vehicle loads would be excessive. A higher snow load should result in a lower vehicle load because fewer vehicles can be parked in the snow.

Lateral Loads

Parking structures present special consideration in regions with high seismic activity. However, properly designed parking structures have performed well during seismic events. Typical lateral load-resisting systems in cast-in-place post-tensioned parking structures employ moment frame while those of precast concrete employ shear walls. To maximize personal safety, large openings in the precast shear walls frequently are provided. The design of the diaphragm must consider potential long spans between the lateral load-resisting elements, such as shear walls, and the impact of internal sloping ramps, which can break up a floor diaphragm. Diaphragm reinforcing must be continuous and must properly transfer the lateral load to the lateral load-resisting system.

Framing members not a part of the lateral load system must be connected together and designed to support their loads under expected drift.

Lateral load systems similar to seismic load systems also withstand wind loads. Moment frames are typical for cast-in-place structures and shear walls for precast systems although recent development in connection design has produced acceptable precast concrete moment frames.

Underground parking structures present the problem of lateral earth loads, which usually are supported either by cast-in-place retaining walls or through the diaphragm by shear walls.

Expansion Joints

The expansion and contraction of structural materials should be considered in the design of any structure, whether used for parking or for commercial purposes.

Because the coefficient of linear expansion is an absolute value, if the temperature-related contraction exceeds the capacity of the structure or its connections, severe stresses can cause cracking and in some cases structural failure, unless appropriate mechanisms allowing for these differential strains are provided. In a parking structure with two or more levels, it is not unusual for the top level to reach a temperature of 140 degrees Fahrenheit on a hot summer day, then to cool down to 75 or 80 degrees at night. In winter, the temperature at this same level may drop to 10 degrees or lower in cold climates.

In most cases, changes in length are calculated, based on published temperature range charts, and an expansion joint is designed to allow for maximum changes. The same joint is then used at each level—a repetition that normally provides greater construction economy. Upon exposure to solar radiation, the exterior walls or columns normally expand or contract slightly more than inside columns.

Once the amount of expansion or contraction has been estimated, allowance in the design must be made for the change in length. Care should be taken not to design physical restraints inside the structure and/or around the perimeter of the structure. The type of structural system also should be considered when spacing expansion joints. A cast-in-place, post-tensioned structure requires closer spacing of expansion joints than a precast or mild steel-reinforced, cast-in-place structure. This is because a mild steel-reinforced parking structure will relieve temperature strain through shrinkage cracks, and a precast parking structure can relieve temperature-related strains through properly designed connections. However, without such means, a post-tensioned structure must be able to accommodate elastic shortening, and in addition, creep and shrinkage are more important for post-tensioned structures than a precast concrete structure.

When the joint width has been calculated, design and detailing of the expansion joint follow. The material to allow the joint to expand must be highly durable and capable of surviving the weather conditions to which it will be subjected. The joint itself must be kept free of all extraneous materials and/or restrictions. If an electrical conduit penetrates an expansion joint, it must have an expanding coupling, and no materials should be left in the joint. An expansion joint should be sealed to prevent water leakage.

Snow and Ice

Snow customarily is removed from surface lots by plowing and stacking. Stacking a large amount of snow on a parking structure can create excessive loads and damage to the structure and should not be allowed. In areas of heavy annual snowfall and few winter thaw periods, snow must often be hauled away to maintain the maximum capacity of a lot. When piled snow thaws on warm days and the runoff water freezes at night, it creates unsafe conditions.

Snow removal from the roof of a parking garage is more difficult. Heavy accumulations of snow are not permissible, and large trucks cannot go to the roof because of the danger of exceeding the maximum floor load. Only lightweight, rubber-tired equipment should be used if snow must be hauled from a roof.

A number of methods have been devised to remove snow from garages. For instance, after snow has been plowed to an edge, it can be dumped over the side of the building. Both the plowing and dumping can be done by a front-end loader, whose weight cannot exceed the permissible floor load. Removable rail sections might be required depending on the height of the rail. This method should only be used when garages have adequate setbacks from the sidewalks or alleys so that pedestrian and vehicle movements at grade will not be impeded by the dumped snow. Any dumped snow should be removed from the site as soon as possible. If the top parking level has wheel stops, however, snow removal is difficult.

A melting pit is a boxlike container five feet deep, about six feet wide, and ten feet long. It is two-thirds filled with water heated by steam or by hot-water coils. The snow is dumped or pushed into the pit and then drawn off through an overflow pipe. A drain with a shutoff valve should be located at the bottom of the pit. Because mud, dirt, and trash accumulate in the pit, it should be cleaned regularly. The pit can be built on the roof as part of the garage structure, or it can be portable. Some lot operators use a portable one so that they can move it to different locations. Portable pits are four feet wide, six feet long, and three feet deep. After a heavy snow, the roof should be blocked off, with no parking allowed until most of the snow has been removed.

Durability

Durability of structural systems is a major consideration in any design. Many books, articles, and other publications provide detailed information on durable designs. The high cost of repairing structures built without adequate durability measures attests to the importance of durability. Readers are strongly encouraged to retain durability experts at the outset of the design process.

Ground-Level Retail Space

The inclusion of ground-level retail space is now common in downtown areas and, in the case of garages located in areas of high pedestrian activity, is desirable for two reasons. First, commercial frontages are more pedestrian-friendly than plain concrete garage facades and add a measure of attractiveness to CBDs. Second, the income potential (dollars per square foot) is generally far greater for commercial uses than for parking facilities.

Many multilevel garage sites are located in areas of high retail and commercial activity or serve hospital and medical center complexes. Therefore, it may be appropriate to incorporate or provide for ground-level commercial space designed to complement adjacent land uses.

Conclusion

The selection of a structural system for a parking facility is a complex process that must address several factors. Many systems or combinations of systems are available. Careful thought must be given to events that occur during construction as well as throughout the lifetime of a facility. Precast and cast-in-place concrete structural systems both have advantages and disadvantages depending on the owner's needs. First cost, maintenance costs, desired ceiling height and column spacing, labor and precast concrete availability, and aesthetics all affect the choice of systems to be selected. An owner needs to evaluate available options to make an informed decision.

CHAPTER 13
MECHANICAL VENTILATION AND DRAINAGE SYSTEMS

Abraham Gutman and I. Paul Lew

Whether natural or mechanical, ventilation in a parking facility prevents the accumulation of carbon monoxide, which is the deadliest of the gases constituting automobile exhaust. When carbon monoxide is successfully controlled, other gases are eliminated at the same time. The most cost-effective way of preventing carbon monoxide accumulation is natural ventilation. A mechanical ventilation system must be used if natural ventilation is not an option. Surface water, which often contains corrosive material, must be removed by a drainage system.

Natural Ventilation

Natural ventilation requires openings of sufficient size in exterior walls distributed in such a way that fresh air will disperse and displace contaminated air. For a building to be classified as an open-air parking facility, the building codes require a specified minimum standard in terms of the area and distribution of the openings in the facade of the parking structure.

It is useful to compare the specific ventilation requirements of the three major building codes in terms of how they address the practical considerations faced by parking facility designers. The Uniform Building Code, promulgated by the International Conference of Building Officials, is used in the upper Midwest and in western states; the BOCA/National Building Code, issued by the Building Officials and Code Administrators International, Inc., is used in the central and northeastern states; and the Standard Building Code, published by the Southern Building Code Congress International, Inc., is used in the southeastern states. Over the years, the codes' criteria for open parking

An open parking structure does not require mechanical ventilation.

garages have grown more alike than dissimilar. The three organizations developed a simple code in 2000, as described in chapter 11.

Uniform Building Code (UBC) (1997)

The UBC describes an open parking garage as a structure with uniformly distributed openings on two or more sides. The area of such openings in exterior walls on a tier must be at least 20 percent of the total perimeter wall area of each tier. The aggregate length of the openings considered to be providing natural ventilation shall constitute a minimum of 40 percent of the perimeter of the tier. Interior wall lines and column lines shall be at least 20 percent open with uniformly distributed openings.

BOCA/National Building Code (1999)

BOCA describes an open parking structure as a structure with uniformly distributed openings on not less than two sides totaling not less than 40 percent of the building perimeter. The aggregate area of such openings in exterior walls in each level shall not be less than 20 percent of the total perimeter wall area of each level. Interior wall lines and column lines shall be at least 20 percent open with openings distributed to provide ventilation. Openings are not required to be distributed over 40 percent of the building perimeter if the required openings are uniformly distributed over two opposing sides of the building.

Standard Building Code (SBC) (1999)

The SBC describes an open parking structure as a structure with uniformly distributed openings on two or more sides totaling no less than 40 percent of the building perimeter. The area of such openings in the exterior walls on each level shall be at least 20 percent of the total perimeter wall area of each level. Interior wall lines and column lines shall be at least 20 percent open and uniformly distributed.

Mechanical Ventilation

When a parking facility lacks sufficient openings to provide natural ventilation, a mechanical system is required for the removal of carbon monoxide. Among the several methods used to establish criteria for the quantity of ventilation, most specify a number of cubic feet per minute (cfm) for satisfactory ventilation of a facility.

Code Requirements

The 1997 Uniform Building Code provides three alternative criteria for evaluating the required mechanical ventilation.

- "In parking garages used for storing or handling automobiles operating under their own power and for loading platforms in bus terminals, ventilation shall be provided capable of exhausting a minimum of 1.5 cubic feet per minute (cfm) per square foot (0.71 liter/square meter) of gross floor area."
- "The building official has the latitude to approve an alternative ventilation system designed to exhaust a minimum of 14,000 cfm (6,608 liters/second) for each operating vehicle. Such system shall be based on the anticipated instantaneous movement rate of vehicles but not less than 2.5 percent (or one vehicle) of the garage capacity."
- "Automatic carbon monoxide-sensors may be employed to modulate the ventilation system to maintain a maximum average concentration of carbon monoxide of 50 parts per million during any eight-hour period, with a maximum concentration not greater than 200 parts per million for a period not exceeding one hour."

Connecting offices, waiting rooms, ticket booths, and similar uses shall be supplied with conditioned air under positive pressure.

The 1999 BOCA/National Building Code requires mechanical ventilation at a rate of 1.5 cfm per square foot. The 1999 Standard Building Code states that a mechanical ventilation system shall be capable of providing at least six air changes per hour for each level.

Mechanical exhaust.

To determine the total ventilation requirement for a parking facility based on cfm-per-square-foot criteria, a simple calculation can be performed. For example, if a parking level to be ventilated has an area of 30,000 square feet and the code requires 1.5 cfm per square foot, the required ventilation is 1.5 x 30,000 = 45,000 cfm.

Cars-in-Motion Criterion

To use the number of cars in motion, the designer must estimate the expected peak rates of traffic flow along with the average driving time of a vehicle in motion within the facility. For example, if a 1,000-stall facility is expected to achieve a peak of 60 percent of vehicles exiting over a one-hour period, the flow rate equals ten vehicles per minute. If the average driving distance to an exit in the facility is 880 feet and the estimated driving speed is six mph (8.8 feet per second), the average driving time to an exit is 100 seconds. If three exit lanes are available with a flow capacity of 400 vehicles per hour, a queue equal to the length of two vehicles will develop (on average). An additional 20 seconds of waiting time per vehicle is added to the 100 seconds of driving time to the exit. Therefore, with a flow rate of ten vehicles per minute and an average exit time of two minutes per vehicle, the number of vehicles operating at one time is 20. The total ventilation requirement would be 20 x 14,000 = 280,000 cfm.

Dilution Criteria. To determine the ventilation requirement when carbon monoxide sensors are employed per the UBC or to satisfy the BOCA code requirement, the designer must perform a dilution method analysis in accordance with the following formula:

$$C = \left(\frac{G - Ge}{Q'}\right)^{-\left(\frac{Q't}{V}\right)}$$

where,

C = concentration of carbon monoxide
G = rate of generation of contaminant or 0.352 cfm of carbon monoxide per car times the number of cars in motion during the specified period
e = 2.71828
Q = actual rate of ventilation
Q´ = effective rate of ventilation or actual rate (Q) divided by a safety factor of 3
t = time in minutes
V = volume of ventilated space

American Society of Heating, Refrigerating, and Air Conditioning Engineers recommends a ventilation rate that maintains a carbon monoxide level of 25 ppm with peak levels not to exceed 120 ppm.

Methods Used to Achieve Ventilation

The three types of mechanical means for ventilating a parking facility involve supply air only, exhaust air only, and a

Mechanical exhaust room.

combination of supply and exhaust air. The effectiveness of any one system depends on the distribution of supply and/or exhaust points relative to the geometry of the facility. Openings between floors, openings to the outside, or the proximity of supply and exhaust points can cause short circuits in the air flow, leaving portions of the facility unventilated. It is therefore important to consider probable air flow throughout the entire facility. Generally, exhaust points should be located near the floor because exhaust air tends to be heavier than clean air. Outside air supply outlets should be located to effect a cross flow of air in the travel aisle of each floor. Occupied areas such as stairways require a supply of outside air to ensure positive pressure in the garage, especially at major pedestrian locations such as stairways and elevator cores.

Areas of a parking facility where employees work for long periods, namely, the parking office and cashier booths, should be ventilated with an air supply that is separate from the air supply to the rest of the facility. All air supplies should be located where they are least likely to be contaminated from the ventilation system's exhaust or other outside sources.

The parking area of the garage should be maintained at a negative pressure and should not be connected to adjacent buildings or occupied spaces except through pressurized vestibules.

Each area of the facility should be provided with air flow to eliminate pockets of contaminated air. Several small fan units are often preferable to a few large units, although the number of fans should provide sufficient flexibility with respect to variations in maintenance demands and fluctuations in efficiency and traffic. Smaller units permit greater flexibility in the fan control system and, in the event that a single unit is out of service for repair or maintenance, help ensure that only a small area of the facility is affected.

The designer of enclosed parking facilities must consider the impact of duct locations and duct size. Ducts must be located such that overhead space and other aspects of facility operation are not compromised. Air distribution should be vertical wherever possible and long horizontal runs of duct-work avoided. Duct material should be selected for its long-term maintenance properties as well as for its appearance. Concrete or noncorroding metals are preferable.

As with other parts of the parking facility, a regular program of inspection and maintenance is essential for the proper operation of the ventilation system. Each fan should be checked daily; needed repairs should be performed immediately. Fans and motors, carbon monoxide monitors, and control equipment should be maintained regularly as recommended by the manufacturer.

Although the safest method of controlling fans is through continuous operation, the associated energy consumption may not be justified given that alternative means of control may satisfy required safety margins. While various codes may specify and approve a variety of control systems or redundancies, all systems must operate on a fail-safe basis. The failure of any link in the control system may trigger continuous operation of the ventilation system.

Ventilation systems can be controlled by timing devices. If a system is programmed to turn on its fans during periods of expected automobile movements, the control method is considered safe, provided that no peaks of activity occur at other times. To warn of emergencies, however, carbon monoxide detectors can indicate the need for ventilation during off-peak hours associated with special events or unexpected conditions. Complete manual operation of a ventilation system is not recommended. Even when a carbon monoxide detection system advises the garage staff of the facility's ventilation needs, human control is unsatisfactory.

The most satisfactory ventilation control system, and probably the least expensive in terms of power consumption, is a system of carbon monoxide detectors. The detectors measure the concentration of carbon monoxide in the garage air at various sampling stations and adjust fan motor speeds or set volume controls accordingly.

No matter how sophisticated a ventilation system design or the type of carbon monoxide detection equipment installed, every facility needs emergency procedures. Operating personnel must be trained in how to recognize a ventilation problem and how to institute the necessary emergency procedures. Certain provisions are appropriate for any such emergency procedure. They include the following:

- signs that warn motorists to turn off their engines until they receive further instructions;
- portable loudspeakers that can be used by operating personnel to direct motorists to turn off their engines;
- emergency oxygen equipment; and
- authorization for operating personnel to permit cars to exit without payment to speed the movement of large numbers of cars, thus reducing the number of engines operating simultaneously.

CHOATE PARKING CONSULTANTS

Results of inadequate drainage.

Drainage Systems

Whether liquid or frozen, standing water represents a major threat to parking structures. Often, wastewater from vehicles contains corrosive elements, particularly salts, which, if not removed rapidly from the floor surfaces of the structure, can compromise a parking facility's structural elements. Each level of a parking structure requires a drainage system for the removal of surface water.

To prevent the ponding of water on the floor surface, a parking structure must be appropriately sloped and incorporate a properly designed drainage system. The pitch of floors to drains, the location and size of drains, the slope of drainage lines, and the careful selection of piping materials must work together to remove standing water from all parking levels. Generally, the parking surface should slope away from the exterior façade so that any standing water does not saturate the façade. Furthermore, cambering of floor members must be considered. If the slope to the interior is not steep enough or there is too much beam camber, a reverse slope to the exterior of the slab edge may result, permitting the accumulation of standing water.

The recommended slope of a parking floor to the drain is a minimum 1 percent, with a 1.5 to 2 percent recommended minimum in all directions. While the recommended slope is achievable in cast-in-place concrete slabs, it is more difficult to achieve in precast concrete double-tee construction. Normally, the main slope in precast parking structures is 2 percent (typically in the span direction) with a limited cross-slope (perpendicular to the direction of the main slope).

Sloping a facility's slabs requires attention to detail at the edges of interior slabs and ramps in order to prevent water from flowing over the edge of one bay onto another. Typically, swales (thickening of edges) or curbs provide the necessary containment. At the roof level, large quantities of water drain down the ramps and can easily overrun standard-sized roof drains. Consequently, larger-than-calculated drain heads should be provided. Full-width trench drains are not

Drain pipe.

rainwater washdowns. Sometimes, however, a washdown system is incorporated into facility design (hose bibbs on each level); if so, the local jurisdiction might require under-cover floors to drain into a separate wastewater system. To prevent oil, sand, debris, leaves, and the like from entering the system, municipalities sometimes mandate interceptors (oil/water separators) on the final connection from the inter-mediate parking levels before discharge to the sewer. Others require a sand filtration system before rainwater is discharged to the sewer because of the pollutants that accumulate during drainage.

Some ordinances call for the use of detention tanks or basins, generally located under the lowest ramp, to control the discharge of runoff water. Other methods of water retention include large-diameter concrete, plastic, or corrugated metal pipes located below the pavement of the lowest level. To avoid the construction of detention tanks, designers often must convince local authorities that a proposed parking facility will not produce increased runoff.

Because most parking structures are open, unheated, and subject to freezing temperatures, long horizontal runs of drainage piping should be avoided. Vertical leaders and/or sanitary stacks should be placed at each drain location and extend through the lowest level. They should run horizontally when buried below the slab. Likewise, horizontal runs in the supported levels should be avoided because they tend to restrict headroom or require openings in beams. If horizontal drainage piping cannot be avoided, an electric heat tracing system with insulation, especially at "elbow" joints, might be considered in localities where temperatures dip below freezing.

Piping materials can vary from cast iron to galvanized steel to copper to plastic (PVC). The selection of piping material depends on acceptance by local authorities and cost considerations. PVC has the advantage of long-term corrosion resistance. Bumper guards or pipe bollards can protect vertical piping against damage from vehicles.

Regularly scheduled floor washdowns by maintenance personnel can help alleviate clogging and backup within the drainage system. Care should be taken in the draindown of the drainage system during winter months if freezing is a possibility.

feasible because they cut off the continuity of structural slabs and present an ongoing maintenance problem. Partial trench drains or multiple drains are usually placed at the bottom of ramps.

The first step in designing a drainage system for a parking facility is to obtain the local rainfall intensities so that the roof level can be designed with an adequate number of drains and properly connected to adequately sized leaders. Generally, tributary roof drainage areas per drain on a horizontal projection vary, but they should ideally not exceed 10,000 square feet; the preferred area per drain is 5,000 to 6,000 square feet. Many communities require the roof to drain directly into the stormwater management system. Some codes, however, require separate stormwater and sanitary systems; thus, runoff from intermediate and lower levels must be directed to a sanitary sewer. Other codes do not distinguish between waste systems and thus permit the entire structure to drain into a storm sewer.

A covered parking level accumulates latents and oil drippings from automobiles without the benefit of routine

CHAPTER 14
LIGHTING

Donald R. Monahan

The primary purpose of adequate lighting in parking structures and parking lots is to permit the safe movement of vehicles and pedestrians. Lighting enhancements in excess of minimum illumination levels may be necessary for guidance, space definition, and crime deterrence. The lighting design must consider the illumination necessary to achieve these objectives balanced against the need to control costs—both initial costs as well as long-term operational and maintenance costs.

This chapter discusses visibility issues, lighting industry standards, lighting system design issues, and related economic considerations so that designers, owners, and operators can make informed decisions about lighting for their parking facilities.

Visibility Issues

A parking facility's lighting system should provide drivers with adequate visibility of signage, physical obstructions, and pedestrian movements as well as provide pedestrians with adequate visibility of signage and trip hazards.

The visibility of an object is a function of the following factors:
- luminance (brightness) of an object;
- luminance of the background (adapting luminance);
- contrast between object and background;
- size of the object;
- duration of the emission of light by the object;
- location of the object relative to the line of sight; and
- movement in a person's field of view (30 to 150 degrees).

FIGURE 14-1

FIGURE 14-2

REFLECTANCE OF VARIOUS COLORS

Color	Reflectance	Glidden Color
White	90%	AC-98
Yellow	74%	AC-630
Pink	53%	AC-296
Gray	41%	AC-516
Orange	29%	AC-592
Green	20%	AC-677
Brown	19%	AC-595
Red	18%	AC-528
Blue	11%	AC-722
Purple	11%	AC-749
Black	4%	AC-780

REQUIRED CONTRAST VERSUS ILLUMINANCE

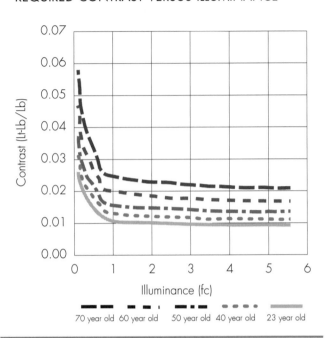

In addition, factors such as attention, expectation, and habituation generally affect the ability to detect and recognize objects.

Two quantifiable factors have been investigated to determine the minimum and maximum amount of beneficial illuminance in a parking structure. They are the amount of illuminance required for adequate visibility of curbs or wheelstops in parking stalls and the amount of illuminance required for confident facial recognition of potential intruders.

Object Detection

Slip or trip and fall injuries represent 50 to 75 percent of the liability claims in a parking facility. The first means of preventing trips and falls is to eliminate all wheelstops and to minimize the use of curbs or islands. Other means are available for channeling vehicles or providing bumper protection, including pipe bollards or guardrails. For existing facilities with curbs that cannot be removed, the visibility of the hazard should be improved to minimize personal injury.

Visibility of trip hazards (steps, wheelstops, curbs, and islands) is a function of illuminance on the hazard and the reflectance contrast of the hazard against its background. The light reflected from a surface or object is called luminance. Luminance is calculated as follows:

$$\text{Luminance} = \text{Illuminance} \times \frac{\text{Reflectance}}{\pi}$$

Illuminance is the amount of direct light falling on a surface; it can be measured with a light meter. Reflectance varies for different colors and is available from paint manufacturers as illustrated in Figure 14-1.

Painting objects to sharpen their contrast against their background enhances their visibility. A concrete wheelstop against a concrete floor has minimal contrast because the object and its background have similar reflectance. Painting the wheelstop yellow greatly enhances its visibility.

The Roadway Lighting Committee of the Illuminating Engineering Society has undertaken extensive research into the amount of contrast required for adequate visibility of an object. As illustrated in Figure 14-2, the required contrast varies with the light level and age of the observer.

Figure 14-2 indicates the contrast required at a 99.9 percent probability of observing a six-inch-high concrete curb viewed at a distance of 20 feet. The required contrast increases significantly at light levels less than 0.6 footcandle. At the same time, it should be noted that little additional benefit with respect to object detection is derived at minimum light levels above 0.6 footcandle. The average illuminance is three to four times higher than the minimum illuminance depending on the configuration of the luminaires and uniformity of the lighting system. Therefore, an average illuminance of approximately three footcandles on the pavement could provide adequate visibility of curbs and wheelstops in a concrete parking structure with a uniform lighting configuration.

Crime Deterrence

How much lighting is necessary to deter criminal activity? Unfortunately, no hard data exist to correlate light levels with criminal activity. In general, many facilities that have increased their light levels have found a reduction in some types of accidents and criminal activity, but there is no conclusive evidence that improved lighting reduces crime. However, attitude surveys before and after lighting improvements indicate that patrons feel safer after the introduction of light-

FIGURE 14-3

VERTICAL ILLUMINANCE VERSUS DISTANCE FOR CONFIDENT FACIAL RECOGNITION

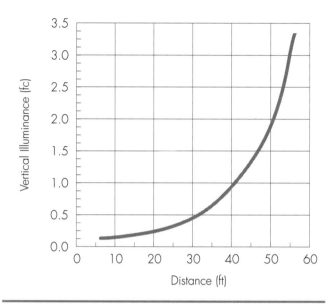

than that required for correct detection (approximately 15:1 at a 90 percent probability).

Rombauts et al. have investigated facial recognition under street lighting conditions. Figure 14-3 depicts the relationship between vertical illuminance and confident facial recognition at various distances. Approximately 0.1 footcandle of vertical illuminance is required for confident facial recognition at a distance of two meters (6.6 feet). Approximately 0.5 footcandle of vertical illuminance is required for confident facial recognition at a distance of ten meters (33 feet). Approximately three footcandles are required for confident facial recognition at a distance of 17 meters (56 feet). Rombauts concluded that confident facial recognition is not possible beyond 56 feet.

Therefore, these studies suggest that a minimum vertical illuminance in the range of 0.5 footcandle to one footcandle at five feet above the floor should be provided to allow for confident facial recognition at a distance of 30 to 40 feet. A patron sensing a threat to security would then have adequate reaction time to take evasive action. Further, it follows that if a parking facility's lighting is adequate for confident facial recognition, then a potential criminal may avoid the facility because of increased likelihood of apprehension.

Other Visibility Issues

Ambient lighting of overhead signage is an important consideration. Overhead signs are typically mounted at approximately seven to eight feet (minimum vehicle clearance) above the floor. As shown in Figure 14-4, a combination of illuminance and corresponding contrast between the message and its background is required for readability. To ensure relatively little contrast, the vertical illuminance at the sign face should be a minimum of one footcandle for adequate visibility. However, one footcandle of minimum ambient illuminance is difficult to achieve at seven to eight feet above the floor. Therefore, signage designers often require a minimum reflectance difference of 75 percent for adequate visibility at low light levels. If ambient lighting for overhead signage is insufficient, then internally illuminated signs should be used. Ambient lighting of signage is an important consideration in the selection of the fixture type.

ing improvements owing to greater distance visibility and an enhanced ability to identify potential assailants and take evasive action.

Boyce and Rea performed studies on the effects of perimeter security lighting on people's ability, first, to detect someone walking toward them along a lighted path and, second, to identify the person from a set of four photographs. The results indicated that a vertical illuminance of about 0.1 footcandle (1 lux) is sufficient to obtain about a 90 percent probability of correct detection (able to recognize someone's presence but unable to distinguish the person's facial features). At about two footcandles (20 lux), the probability of detection approaches 100 percent. A vertical illuminance of about 1.5 footcandles is sufficient to obtain a 90 percent probability of correct recognition (able to identify a person's features and expression). The vertical illuminance required for correct facial recognition is considerably greater

FIGURE 14-4

RECOMMENDED MAINTAINED ILLUMINANCE VALUES FOR PARKING LOTS

	Unit	Basic	Enhanced Security
Minimum horizontal illuminance on floor	Lux	2	5
	FC	0.2	0.5
Uniformity ratio, maximum to minimum		20:1	15:1
Minimum vertical illuminance at five feet above floor	Lux	1	2.5
	FC	0.1	0.25

Source: Illuminating Engineering Society of North America, *RP-20-98, Lighting for Parking Facilities* (New York: IES, 1998).

FIGURE 14-5

RECOMMENDED MAINTAINED ILLUMINANCE VALUES FOR PARKING GARAGES

	Minimal Horizontal Illuminance on Floor		Maximum/Minimum Horizontal Uniformity	Minimum Vertical Illuminance at Five Feet	
	Lux	Footcandles	Ratio	Lux	Footcandles
Basic	10	1	10:1	5	0.5
Ramps					
Day	20	2	10:1	10	1
Night	10	1	10:1	5	0.5
Entrance areas					
Day	500	50		250	25
Night	10	1	10:1	5	0.5
Stairways	20	2		10	1

Source: Illuminating Engineering Society of North America, *RP-20-98, Lighting for Parking Facilities* (New York: IES, 1998).

For closed circuit television surveillance, a minimum illuminance of 0.5 footcandle is required for today's state-of-the-art color cameras without paying an equipment premium for increased light sensitivity. Care should be taken in positioning the camera. If a camera is aimed directly at or scans across a light fixture, it will adjust to the brightness of the light source and cause the background detail to be lost.

Lighting Industry Standards

Except for emergency lighting requirements (typically one footcandle along the path of egress), most cities and states do not legislate lighting levels in parking lots or parking structures. Nonetheless, to minimize the owner's risk of liability for personal injury in a parking facility because of allegedly poor lighting, light levels should meet minimum industry standards as described below.

The Illuminating Engineering Society of North America (IESNA or IES) publishes illuminance guidelines for a variety of building types and activities. The guidelines are generally

considered the industry standard. IES document *RP-20-98, Lighting for Parking Facilities*, specifies the design guidelines for lighting surface parking lots and parking structures. Figures 14-4 and 14-5 outline the latest (1998) design standards.

Lighting System Design

The lighting system design should consider the following items:

- luminaire design;
- glare;
- color rendition of light source;
- maintenance; and
- economics.

Luminaire Design

Luminaires are generally classified as cutoff or noncutoff. Figures 14-6 and 14-7 illustrate fixture types.

A cutoff luminaire is defined by the IES as a fixture that controls emitted light to less than 2 percent above horizontal

FIGURE 14-6

NONCUTOFF LUMINAIRE

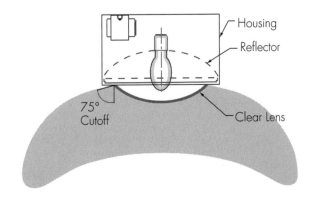

FIGURE 14-7

CUTOFF LUMINAIRE

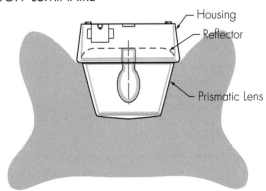

Lighting in cast-in-place concrete parking structure.

Lighting in precast concrete parking structure.

and less than 10 percent above an 80-degree angle from a vertical line through the light source. The advantage of cutoff fixtures is reduced glare through minimization of high-angle light. However, the spacing of the fixtures must be close enough to provide overlap of the light distribution at the driver's eye level.

In addition, the fixture spacing must be close enough to provide for adequate light distribution over and between parked vehicles. For an 8.5-foot mounting height and a 75-degree cutoff angle, fixture spacing must be approximately 15 feet to provide adequate illumination at five feet above the pavement. At lower mounting heights, even closer fixture spacings are required. If adequate overlap is not provided, the user feels uncomfortable passing through the light and dark areas along the critical visual plane.

The advantage of a noncutoff luminaire is better distribution and uniformity of light at high elevations above the floor, which is important for the visibility of pedestrians between cars and for adequate ambient lighting of signage suspended from the ceilings or overhead beams. The disadvantage is the potential for glare produced by high-angle light.

To obtain adequate vertical illumination at five feet above the pavement, cutoff luminaires can often be used at mounting heights above 12 feet while noncutoff luminaires are generally recommended at mounting heights at or below ten feet. Specific lighting calculations must determine which type of light fixture is appropriate at mounting heights from ten to 12 feet. Because the floor-to-floor height in most parking structures is on the order of ten feet, noncutoff luminaires should be used on covered levels.

On the roof level of parking structures and in surface parking lots, cutoff luminaires are recommended to minimize light trespass and to hide the light source from the view of adjacent properties. For roof-mounted pole lights on interior column lines, the mounting height should equal approximately half the horizontal distance to be illuminated (for instance, a 30-foot mounting height for a 60-foot horizontal

throw). A mounting height less than 25 feet will likely require light fixtures at the perimeter of the roof or surface lot.

Glare

As stated in the *IES Lighting for Parking Facilities*, 8th Edition, "Discomfort glare is a sensation of annoyance or pain caused by a high or nonuniform distribution of brightness in the field of view." Discomfort glare can be reduced by

- offsetting the fixture from the direct line of sight;
- decreasing the luminance of the light source;
- diminishing the area of the light source; or
- increasing the background luminance around the source.

Fixture Location. Proper integration of the lighting system with a facility's structural components is important. Light fixtures should be centered between structural beams or joints to minimize light blockage, although the beams or joints also shield the fixtures and minimize glare. Beams or precast concrete tee stems shield the light fixture at distances of more than 60 feet. The overhang of the vehicle roof shields the driver from fixtures at distances less than approximately 15 to 20 feet. Therefore, the fixture can be seen only in a range of 20 to 60 feet.

Locating the light fixtures away from the driver's direct line of sight can minimize the potential for discomfort glare. Research has shown that a lateral offset of 10 degrees or more from the direct line of sight greatly reduces the potential for glare. If fixtures are located over the parking stalls on each side of the drive aisle, the lateral offset will be approximately 12 feet from the driver's direct line of sight. At a distance of 60 feet, the lateral distance represents an angular offset of 11 degrees.

According to the foregoing dimensions, the driver's potential glare zone occurs from nine to 15 degrees above the horizontal line of sight (75 to 81 degrees with respect to a vertical line through the fixture). The designer should therefore select a luminaire that is designed to reduce the light output in the glare zone. For pedestrians, the potential glare zone is reduced even less as the pedestrian's line of

Lighting at roof level can reduce unwanted glare in surrounding neighborhoods.

sight is at approximately 60 inches above the floor compared with 45 inches for the driver. Additional shielding may be required at the crossover aisles that are perpendicular to the parking access aisles.

Light Source Intensity and Background Contrast. Discomfort glare is a function of the contrast between the light source and its background. For instance, vehicle headlights can be discomforting at night but are almost unnoticeable in bright sunlight. Reducing lamp intensity and/or increasing the brightness of the surfaces that form the background around the light fixture can minimize glare.

Background brightness can be increased by a factor of two to 2.5 times by painting the interior parking structure surfaces (including ceilings) off-white or white. Painted ceilings and beams also reduce the potential for discomfort glare by 50 to 60 percent. In addition, painted ceilings increase illuminance by approximately 10 to 20 percent for noncutoff luminaires owing to increased reflectance and thus greatly enhance the psychological perception of the space's brightness. Increased reflectance has a greater impact on the illuminance of darker areas and thereby enhances lighting uniformity. There is little or no uplight with cutoff luminaires such that painted ceilings and beams provide little benefit with that fixture type. Painting precast double-tee soffits that do not contain a light fixture offers little advantage as a direct source of uplight.

Optical Control of Light Source. Many fixture manufacturers control glare through the use of reflectors and lenses that redirect the light output of the lamp and minimize the lighting intensity between 75 and 85 degrees from a vertical line through the fixture. Limiting the light output in the glare zone to less than 2,500 candela (a unit of measure of lighting intensity) generally minimizes the potential for glare.

For roof fixtures, recommendations call for cutoff-type light fixtures that limit the light output above a 75-degree angle from a vertical line through the fixture. The pole height and/or shielding of the roof fixtures should be designed to prevent the light source from being viewed from less than a 75-degree angle from a vertical line through the fixture or greater than 15 degrees above horizontal. Based on obtrusive light research performed in Australia and Germany, a maximum luminous intensity of 2,500 candela is recommended at the angle of view to the light fixture by an observer standing at the property line. This requirement generally limits the light source to a 400-watt lamp. Further, the vertical illuminance should not exceed 0.5 footcandles at a height of five feet at the property line.

Color Rendition. "White" light from fluorescent or metal halide lamps provides the most accurate color rendition. High-pressure sodium (HPS) lamps produce a yellowish light that slightly distorts the hues of many colors, making it difficult to distinguish some shades of blue from green. However, the color distortion is not so severe for most people as to prevent recognition of their vehicle.

Recent research indicates that the color-naming accuracy of metal halide lighting was 86 percent, and the accuracy of high-pressure sodium lighting was 65 percent at an adapted luminance of one candela per square meter (equivalent to approximately one footcandle of illuminance in a concrete parking structure). Color-naming accuracy generally decreases at lower light levels and increases at higher light levels. Color-improved, high-pressure sodium lamps are available, but their significantly reduced life and output offer no advantage over metal halide lamps.

Given that the color of metal halide lamps (MH) varies significantly from lamp to lamp and that color deteriorates with age, fluorescent lamps provide better color rendition than metal halide lamps.

Many designers have exaggerated the importance of color rendition in parking structures. In fact, color discrimination is not a high-priority requirement in parking structures. Color-related tasks consist of owners' identification of their vehicle or perhaps recognition of floor color coding. Both tasks can be performed if the hue is slightly distorted; "true" color rendition is not necessary. Moreover, the eye adapts to the lighted environment as well as to the recognition of different colors for that environment. Further, 5 percent of the population is color-blind and 30 percent color-impaired. Therefore, the design of the wayfinding and orientation system should not rely exclusively on color schemes. In addition, patrons occupy the parking facility for a short period of time. Color rendition may be most significant in the elevator lobbies or other waiting areas where messages conveyed by colored graphics and signage are important. Finally, some designers believe that white light adds to the starkness of a concrete parking structure and that the yellowish-white light of high-pressure sodium adds some "warmth" to the environment. Therefore, high-pressure sodium lamps are acceptable light sources for general parking areas; however, white light sources such as metal halide or fluorescent may be more desirable in pedestrian lobbies.

FIGURE 14-8

LAMP LIFE

Type	Life
150W HPS	28,500 hours
150W–175W/PS MH	15,000 hours
4-foot, T8 Fluorescent	30,000 hours
4-foot, T5 Fluorescent	24,000 hours

FIGURE 14-9

LAMP LUMEN DEPRECIATION FACTOR

Type	Depreciation Factor
4-foot, T5 Fluorescent	1.0
4-foot, T8 Fluorescent	0.9
175W/PS MH	0.7
100W and 150W HPS	0.73

Maintenance

Fixture Design

Luminaires should have an IP (International Protection) rating established by publication IEC 529 of the International Electrotechnical Commission to protect against dust and moisture infiltration. The rating is indicated by the letters "IP" followed by two characteristic numerals. The first numeral indicates protection against dust deposits and the second protection against water. A minimum rating of IP51 is recommended, although a rating of IP55 is required if power washing of luminaires is performed. These requirements may be more comprehensive than a UL damp or wet location listing.

Fixture design must be vandal-resistant. Lenses should be impact resistant. Tamper-proof hardware should be used to prevent unauthorized dismantling of fixtures. Polycarbonate lenses are not recommended as they become progressively brittle with age until they are no stronger than high-impact acrylic. Further, polycarbonate lenses are more prone to yellowing and degradation, particularly when exposed to ultraviolet radiation. Polycarbonate lenses also have lower light transmission characteristics than acrylic or glass. Given that metal halide lamps produce ultraviolet radiation, they should be outfitted with UV (ultraviolet) stabilizers in plastic lenses or a tempered-glass lens. Alternatively, a coated lamp that reduces the UV output can be used.

Lighting calculations should include a minimum reduction in light output of 10 percent due to accumulation of dirt and bugs in or on the lenses and some lens discoloration. Annual cleaning is recommended to ensure that the reduction in light output does not exceed 10 percent.

Lamp Life

Maintenance of light fixtures consists primarily of relamping expired fixtures. The lamp life for light sources typically used in parking facilities is based on a 24-hour-per-day burn time as noted in Figure 14-8.

The "T" designation for fluorescent lamps indicates the diameter of the tube in eighths of an inch. Therefore, a T8 fluorescent lamp is one inch in diameter. T5 lamps represent the technology of the future; they produce higher light output at the same energy as T8 lamps.

Pulse-start metal halide (MH) lamps with specialized ballasts and igniters are now available. They offer increased lamp life from 10,000 hours to 15,000 hours and provide higher maintained lumen output than standard MH lamps. All subsequent references herein are to pulse-start metal halide lamps. Metal halide lamps that burn continuously must be turned off for 15 minutes a week to prevent violent, premature termination.

Lumen Depreciation

In a phenomenon known as lamp lumen depreciation (LLD), the light output of a lamp decreases with the amount of time that the lamp operates. Therefore, lighting calculations should be based on the fraction of light output available at the end of the rated life of the lamp (see Figure 14-9).

Note that the rated life is determined in the laboratory as the number of operating hours at which 50 percent of the lamps have expired. Fifty percent are then still functioning. The light output of the lamps will continue to depreciate below the design values after they have exceeded their rated life. Therefore, attention to relamping is important to maintain the minimum illuminance in any discrete area for safety and security. The lamps should be replaced when the horizontal illuminance directly under the fixture is below a predetermined value based upon the lighting calculations. Annual surveys with a light meter should be performed to maintain the fixtures with adequate functioning lamps.

The ambient temperature may affect the light output of some lamps. The light output of metal halide and high pressure sodium (HPS) lamps is not affected by temperature; however, the light output of fluorescent lamps is significantly affected by temperature (see Figure 14-10).

Typically, fluorescent lamps are not recommended where the ambient temperature falls below freezing during normal operating hours. A protective tube around the lamp or a wrap-around, prismatic lens could capture the heat from the lamp and increase the bulb-wall temperature of the fluorescent lamp by approximately 15 to 20 degrees. This approach allows the use of fluorescent fixtures in colder weather; however, the lens adversely affects the light loss at

FIGURE 14-10

FLUORESCENT LIGHT OUTPUT VERSUS TEMPERATURE

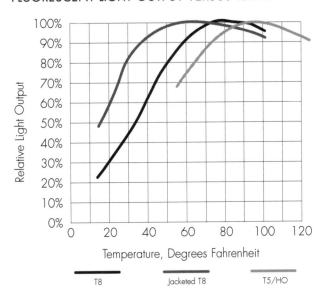

waveform) for starting and operating. Both fluorescent lamps and high-intensity discharge (HID) lamps (i.e., metal halide, high-pressure sodium, mercury vapor, and low-pressure sodium lamps) require a ballast. The ballast supplied with the fixture may result in lower light output than the reference ballast used to determine the photometric characteristics of the luminaire in the testing laboratory. The ratio of light output of a ballast versus the reference ballast is called the ballast factor.

The ballast factor for HID lamps is typically in the range of 0.9 to 1. The ballast factor for fluorescent lamps varies significantly and can range from 0.7 to 1.2. The ballast factor is published in manufacturers' catalogs.

The advent of electronic ballasts for fluorescent lamps has made fluorescent lighting systems much more energy-efficient. The lamp plus ballast watts for a luminaire with four, 32-watt T8 lamps and one high-frequency electronic ballast is on the order of 110 watts with a ballast factor of 0.88. A luminaire with T5 high-output (54-watt) lamps and one full light output electronic ballast (i.e., ballast factor equals 1) uses approximately 117 watts. These fixtures produce almost the same light output as 150-watt metal halide fixtures at approximately 60 percent of the energy consumed.

high temperatures as illustrated in Figure 14-10. However, the ambient temperature correction at night generally is much lower than the temperature correction for the daily maximum. A light loss factor of approximately 0.8 is recommended for a protected fluorescent lamp where historical climatological data indicate that the mean number of days below freezing on an annual basis is less than 36 days (less than 10 percent of the days below freezing on an annual basis). Therefore, a closer fixture spacing resulting in additional fluorescent fixtures is required to make up for occasionally reduced light output during the winter.

Lighting System Economics

The costs associated with the lighting configuration include the construction or first cost, the operating cost (energy cost), and the maintenance cost for fixture cleaning and lamp replacement.

Construction Cost

Construction cost largely depends the number of fixtures and individual fixture cost. The number of light fixtures is a function of type of light source, mounting height, fixture design, and the fixture spacing required to achieve the desired illumination and lighting uniformity. The higher the lumen out-

Ballast Factors

A ballast is a device used with an electrodischarge lamp to obtain the necessary circuit conditions (voltage, current, and

FIGURE 14-11

DESIGN LUMEN COMPARISONS

Light Source	Initial Lumens	Design Lumens	Ratio to HPS
150W HPS	16,000	11,680[1]	1.0
175W Standard MH	14,000	8,540[2]	0.73
175W/PS MH	17,500	12,250[2]	1.05
150W/PS MH	15,000	9,300[2]	0.80
4-foot, T8 Fluorescent	11,600	9,200[3]	0.79
2-foot, T5/HO Fluorescent	10,000	8,550[2]	0.81

[1] At rated life.
[2] Includes ballast factor of 1.
[3] Includes ballast factor of 0.88.

FIGURE 14-12

FIXTURE ENERGY CONSUMPTION

Type	Watts
150W HPS	188
150W/PS metal halide	190
175W/PS metal halide	208
4-foot, T8 fluorescent	110±
2-foot, T5/HO fluorescent	117

FIGURE 14-13

ANNUAL OPERATING COST PER FIXTURE

Type	Cost
150W HPS	$132
150W/PS metal halide	$133
175W/PS metal halide	$146
4-foot, T8 fluorescent	$ 77
2-foot, T5/HO fluorescent	$ 82

put of the light source, the smaller is the number of required fixtures. Figure 14-11 compares lumen outputs for equivalent light sources typically used in parking structures.

The illuminance of 150W/PS metal halide fixtures or fluorescent fixtures with either four, four-foot T8 lamps or two, four-foot T5/HO lamps is approximately 20 percent less than for HPS on a one-for-one replacement basis. In other words, approximately 25 percent more fixtures will be required to produce the equivalent illuminance of 150W HPS. Given that brightness perception and visual acuity are better under white light than the yellowish light of HPS, a somewhat lower illuminance for the white light sources is likely justifiable; however, the lighting system must still meet minimum industry standards for illuminance. For equivalent illuminance to 150W HPS, a 175W/PS MH lamp should be used.

The material cost for a 150W HPS or 175W MH fixture typically ranges from $140 to $250 per unit, including the lamp (all costs herein represent 1999 dollars). An eight-foot-long fluorescent fixture with four T8 lamps and a wrap-around, high-impact acrylic lens costs approximately $125 to $175 per unit. The most common luminaire configuration in a parking structure for the above fixtures is 30-foot-by-30-foot spacing. With the installed cost approximately double the fixture cost, the installed fixture cost is approximately $0.30 to $0.50 per square foot. Beyond the installed cost is the cost of wiring, conduit, transformer, generator, switch gear, lighting panels, and lighting controls, which yields a total lighting cost of approximately $1 to $1.50 per square foot for the general parking area. Another $0.50 to $1 per square foot should be included for lighting stairs, elevator lobbies, storage rooms, and the office and for exterior lighting. The total lighting cost is then on the order of $1.50 to $2.50 per square foot. However, the initial construction cost is typically less than 10 percent of the 25-year life-cycle cost of the lighting system.

Operating Cost

Operating cost is determined by multiplying the lamp plus ballast wattage for each fixture times the number of fixtures, times annual operating hours, times the utility cost for electricity in the project area. If the number of fixtures is the same for each lighting option, then the lamp plus ballast wattage of each different fixture type determines the most economical choice in terms of operating cost. Figure 14-12 depicts the lamp plus ballast watts for the five typical light sources used in a parking structure.

The fluorescent fixtures with electronic ballasts will save approximately 40 percent in operating cost versus the 150W HPS or 150W/PS MH fixtures at 20 percent lower illuminance. Even if the number of fluorescent fixtures is increased by 25 percent to produce equivalent illuminance, fluorescent fixtures still represent a 25 percent savings in operating costs.

Based on a national average utility cost of $0.08 per Kwh and a 24-hour-per-day operation, Figure 14-13 presents the annual operating cost per fixture. When evaluated over the life of the luminaire (approximately 25 years), the operating cost typically represents approximately five times the initial cost or approximately 85 percent of the total life-cycle cost.

Maintenance Cost

A lighting system's maintenance cost is typically less than 10 percent of the system's 25-year life-cycle cost. Metal halide fixtures incur the highest maintenance cost because their lamp life is approximately one-half that of either HPS or fluorescent lamps. Stated another way, twice as many MH lamps expire on an annual basis compared with either HPS or fluorescent lamps. However, the equivalent fluorescent system uses four, T8 lamps per fixture. Therefore, four times as many fluorescent lamps will be replaced on an annual basis compared with the HPS fixtures while twice as many fluorescent lamps will be replaced compared with MH fixtures. Since the cost per fluorescent lamp is 10 to 20 percent of the cost of a metal halide lamp, the relamping material cost for the fluorescent lamp replacement is still much less than the cost of MH lamp replacement, but the labor cost for relamping is much higher for fluorescent fixtures. Therefore, the annual maintenance cost for a fluorescent lighting system is equivalent to that for a metal halide lighting system, but the maintenance cost for the HPS lighting system is less than that either for a fluorescent or metal halide system.

Conclusion

For all areas of a covered parking facility, IES guidelines recommend a minimum maintained (i.e., immediately before lamp burnout) horizontal illuminance of one footcandle and a minimum maintained vertical illuminance of 0.5 footcandle at five feet above the floor. Because of lower background luminance in asphalt surface parking lots at night, minimum horizontal and vertical illuminance should be 0.5 and 0.25 footcandle, respectively.

To meet the IES vertical illuminance criteria, noncutoff light fixtures should be used where mounting heights are less than ten feet. Cutoff luminaires are recommended where mounting heights typically exceed 12 feet, as in the case of surface parking lots and the roofs of parking structures. The spacing-to-mounting-height ratio should be approximately 4:1 (half that distance to an unlighted perimeter).

High-pressure sodium lamps are the most cost-effective light source in northern climates while fluorescent fixtures are the most cost-effective light source where winter temperatures generally remain above freezing.

Metal halide or fluorescent lamps are recommended for illumination of pedestrian destination areas. The average horizontal illumination on the pavement and average vertical illumination at five feet above the pavement should meet or exceed an average of ten footcandles in these areas.

References

Adrian, Werner. "The Physiological Basis of the Visibility Concept." 2nd Annual Symposium on Visibility and Illuminance in Roadway Lighting, Orlando, Florida, October 26–27, 1993.

Boyce, P.R., and J.M. Gutkowski. *Street Lighting and Street Crime*. Troy, N.Y: Rensselaer Polytechnic Institute, 1990.

Boyce, P.R., and J.M. Gutkowski. "The If, Why, and What of Street Lighting and Street Crime." CIBSE National Lighting Conference, Cambridge, England, 1995.

Boyce, P.R., and M.S. Rea. "Security Lighting: Effects of Illuminance and Light Source on the Capabilities of Guards and Intruders." *Lighting Research and Technology*, Vol. 22, 1990, p. 57.

Box, Paul C. "Avoiding Tort Claims in Parking Lots." *Public Works Magazine*, January 1994.

Box, Paul C. "Parking Lot Accident Characteristics." *ITE Journal*, December 1981.

Cunnen, J.M.L. *Crime and Lighting, Lighting Design and Application*. New York: Illuminating Engineering Society of North America, 1990.

English, William. *Safety Engineering Guidelines for the Prevention of Slips, Trips, and Falls*. Del Mar, California: Hanrow Press, 1989.

Monahan, Donald R. "Safety Considerations in Parking Facilities." *The Parking Professional,* September 1995.

Nam, Sheela H., and Joseph B. Murdoch. "Lighting for Bus Stops." Proceedings of the IESNA Annual Conference, New York, July 30–August 2, 1995.

Painter, K. *Lighting and Crime Prevention: The Edmonton Project*. London: Middlesex Polytechnic Institute, 1988.

Painter, K. "An Evaluation of Public Lighting as a Crime Prevention Strategy: The West Park Estate Surveys." *The Lighting Journal*, December 1991, p. 228.

Rombauts P., H. Vandewyngaerde, and G. Maggeto. "Minimum Semi-cylindrical Illuminance and Modeling in Residential Area Lighting." *Lighting Research and Technology*, Vol. 21, 1989, p. 7.

Illuminating Engineering Society of North America. *RP-20-98, Lighting For Parking Facilities*. New York: IES, 1998.

Illuminating Engineering Society of North America. *Lighting Handbook, Reference and Application*, 9th Edition. New York: IES, 1999.

CHAPTER 15
WAYFINDING, SIGNAGE, AND GRAPHICS

Stephen J. Rebora and Donald R. Monahan

Most of today's forward-thinking businesses, industries, and municipalities recognize the importance of image, efficiency, convenience, and automation in delivering promised goods and services. This is as true with parking facilities as with any other business pursuit. A properly designed wayfinding system in a parking facility leaves parking patrons with a positive image of both the facility and their primary destination.

Parking facilities are notorious as labyrinthine structures that defy logic. For patrons, searching for the facility entrance, finding a parking space, identifying pedestrian access, and locating their vehicle upon return to the facility all contribute to a less-than-favorable image of parking facilities.

If designers paid greater attention to the environmental design concepts of spatial orientation, cognitive mapping, and wayfinding, they would recognize that it takes more than signage to direct patrons into, through, and out of a parking facility. In fact, a facility that relies almost entirely on signage for wayfinding is likely to frustrate its users.

This chapter provides background on the principles of wayfinding and discusses how those principles relate to parking structure design. In addition, it offers guidelines for the design of signage and graphic systems that assist in wayfinding and user orientation.

The benefits of good wayfinding design should be obvious. Satisfied tenants will renew their leases, and patrons who find a facility easy to negotiate will become repeat customers. And staff will have more time to spend maintaining and operating the parking facility rather than escorting

93

or consoling lost or emotionally distraught customers. Most important, increased patronage will increase revenues.

Wayfinding Design

Overview

The primary purpose of a wayfinding system is to guide patrons safely along a pleasant and efficient route that takes them from the roadway system to a parking place near their destination and then back to the roadway system.

Parking facilities and signage systems must be designed with the overall objective of providing a concise and informative series of verbal and nonverbal messages that are understandable by the full range of facility patrons. To be effective, the signage system must function as an integral part of its environment; therefore, designers must understand the principles of wayfinding and incorporate wayfinding design steps into the overall facility design process at the outset of that process.

Principles of Wayfinding

Introduced in the late 1970s, wayfinding is a relatively new term. People's representation of their surrounding environment, also called an image or cognitive map, is the psychological concept that underlies the notion of spatial orientation. Spatial orientation, in turn, involves the ability to situate oneself within a space. Thus, wayfinding describes the process of reaching a destination that is located in either a familiar or unfamiliar environment.

Wayfinding is spatial problem solving that involves
- decision making and the development of a plan of action;
- decision execution that transforms the plan into appropriate behavior at all decision points; and
- information processing, which comprises environmental perception and understanding and permits the above decision-related processes to occur.

Cognitive mapping is the process of creating an overall mental representation of a setting that cannot be obtained from a single viewpoint. The cognitive map is a source of information used in making and executing decisions. Perception is the process of obtaining information through the senses. Cognition is understanding and being able to manipulate that information.

Most settings are laid out in a plan or shape that people can relate to and that allows them to determine their location within the setting, recognize that their destination is within that setting, and formulate a plan of action that will take them from their location to their destination.

People tend to feel disoriented when, first, they cannot situate themselves within a parking garage, and, second, they do not have or cannot develop a plan to reach their destination.

Environmental Design

Successful wayfinding design starts with a facility's architectural systems and functional design and the surrounding environment. The design must help patrons make correct intuitive decisions that are then reinforced by verbal and nonverbal information.

As patrons approach a parking structure, they form a mental image of the shape of the space (circular or rectangular, number of levels, and so forth). While they circulate through the structure, they develop a mental image of the facility's interior layout. Circulation past elevator cores provides landmarks that organize the mental image of the space. Repetitive ramping systems located in the same position on each level assist in cognitive mapping and reinforce the mental image of the space. Therefore, the functional design or environmental design of the space has as much to do with wayfinding as directional signage.

Some of the characteristics of parking structures that make wayfinding difficult are noted below.
- *Poor visibility.* Low ceilings, poor lighting, disruption of sight lines by internal ramps, and views obstructed by columns, shear walls, and pipes challenge the user to locate destination points and may even prevent the parking patron from forming a cognitive map.
- *Size of the space.* Large floor areas with more than four parking modules (bays made up of a drive aisle and parked vehicles on either side) make it difficult to comprehend or recall the layout of the space.
- *Number of floors.* When structures exceed six levels, they can compromise the user's vertical orientation.
- *Multiple ramping and/or circulation systems.* More than one circulation system through a parking facility complicates the user's understanding of the space and leads to confusion.

The spatial characteristics of a parking facility—that is, its size, its organization, and the nature of its circulation systems—all contribute to or work against a patron's wayfinding.

Spatial Planning

Spatial planning is the first major component in wayfinding design. It provides the context for wayfinding and sets the stage for problem-solving performance. It also determines the location of a setting's entrances and exits as well as the location of major destinations, the organization of its spaces, and the visual accessibility of its architecture.

Wayfinding begins with a definition of the trip segments that users must take to find a parking place, walk to their destination, retrieve their vehicle, and then return to the roadway system. By identifying paths of travel and decision points within each facility, the designer can provide patrons with visual cues and needed information at the right time at the right location.

Environmental Communication

Once the circulation system is determined, the designer can study each trip segment and develop instructions for navigating within each segment and from one segment to the next. The instructions make up the wayfinding system, whereby visual, tactile, and audible cues between and along trip segments help users identify decision points and find their way through the facility. The cues can be architectural as well as take the form of signage.

The architectural features that identify the route to the users' destination should be designed to provide an intuitive path of travel. In other words, the designer should create a layout that is in keeping with users' most direct route to their parking space as well as their final destination. Signage should coincide with architectural features by providing users with additional directions as they move into, through, and out of the parking facility.

Content and Location

Signage should convey a message to the user in a quick and easy-to-read format. A sign's content and location are critical for smooth vehicle and pedestrian flow throughout a facility. Signage is usually located at decision points within the facility such as at an intersection. Information must be provided at or shortly before a decision point otherwise it may go unnoticed or become ineffective. To identify an acceptable location for a sign, the designer must take note of the physical characteristics of the setting such as light levels, ceiling heights, and aisle widths. Use of the trip segment approach (imagining the driver's route through the facility) facilitates the design of sign content and location. It indicates patrons' most common behavior or path of travel from each of the facility's primary destinations for identification and mapping. The designer can then focus on each decision point to determine the size, message, and placement of specific signs.

Legibility and Readability

In wayfinding design, legibility and readability are not interchangeable terms. Legibility is the ease with which information can be seen and perceived by the senses. Readability is the ease with which information can be understood. Typically, when information cannot be understood, it is subject to shortcomings. First, the information is not legible because it is obstructed, poorly located, too small, garbled, or too busy to be perceived. Second, the information is not helpful because it cannot be understood. To avoid these flaws, the designer must understand and apply accepted graphic standards and be aware of the importance of placement, sight lines, sight distances, lighting levels, and message content.

Wayfinding in Parking Structures

The following discussion tracks the progression of a typical user through a parking facility. First, the driver must find and recognize the structure as a parking facility. While it is

Signs that tell when parking areas are full help drivers avoid unnecessary searching.

appropriate for a parking facility's architecture to complement the architecture of the surrounding area, the structure should not be camouflaged or otherwise hidden. The most important consideration is that the vehicle entrance is clearly identifiable to drivers who may be dealing with many visual distractions. Canopies or portals placed perpendicular to approaching patrons' path of travel are useful.

The facility's entrance area must be welcoming and well lighted. Parking control equipment, if any, should be placed to allow patrons to recognize its presence. Where exit or restricted lanes are provided in the same area as the entrance lanes, the driver must have adequate sight distance to determine which lane to enter. It is often desirable not to give the driver any choices immediately after passing through the entry lane. Driving into the structure for some distance before any further decisions are required often helps the driver become acclimated to the facility.

A primary element of wayfinding design is visual cues. A simple, easily understood traffic pattern that is repeated on every floor greatly eases decision making. Drivers should be routed past visual anchors such as the main stair/elevator tower shortly after reaching each floor. Anchors orient the parking patron for the shift to the pedestrian mode. In large facilities, light wells and other architectural features may also serve as visual anchors.

Visibility across the parking floor to the patron's destination is another component of wayfinding. Why are shoppers willing to walk relatively long distances at suburban shopping centers but complain about parking around the corner downtown? The answer is that shoppers can see the shopping center entrance from the moment they leave their car.

Both security and wayfinding concerns have caused the parking industry to reduce the use of complicated, sloping parking floor designs in favor of more simply understood layouts that maximize the number of spaces on flat floors. In addition, the industry is seeing a trend toward maximizing

Signs in cast-in-place structure.

Express ramps provide direct access to floors with available space.

the slope of parking ramps (up to 6 percent). Where a site is long, the tendency is to keep the sloping aisles to a minimum length, leaving the remaining aisles flat.

Other issues affecting visibility are the facility's floor-to-floor height and its structural system. It is generally recognized that a cast-in-place, post-tensioned parking facility has a higher perceived ceiling height than facilities constructed with other structural systems. Such a structure may enhance other aspects of wayfinding: that is, signage may be more visible because sight lines can be more direct, and lighting may be more uniform because of fewer obstructions. Cast-in-place, post-tensioned construction also results in more openness along bumper walls at both interior sloping ramps and exterior walls. When precast concrete is the preferred structural system for parking structures, sight lines can be improved by increasing the floor-to-floor height.

Minimizing the number of turns (in terms of 360-degree revolutions) along the path of travel has long been a priority of parking designers. Drivers have a tendency to become disoriented when the path of travel requires several turns. It

---

FIGURE 15-1

RECOMMENDED DESIGN STANDARDS FOR WAYFINDING

Design Standard for	Level of Service D	Level of Service C	Level of Service B	Level of Service A
Maximum walking distance within parking facilities (feet)				
Surface lot	1,400	1,050	700	350
Structure	1,200	900	600	300
Front parking to destination (feet)				
Climate controlled	5,200	3,800	2,400	1,000
Outdoors, covered	2,000	1,500	1,000	500
Outdoors, uncovered	1,600	1,200	800	400
Floor-to-floor height[1]				
Long span, post-tensioned[2]	9.5 feet	10.5 feet	11.5 feet	12.5 feet
Long span, precast	10.5 feet	11.5 feet	12.5 feet	13.5 feet
Percent spaces on flat floors	0%	30%	60%	90%
Parking ramp slope	6.5%	6.0%	5.5%	5.0%
360-degree turns to top	7	5.5	4	2.5
Short circuit in long run[3]	400 feet	350 feet	300 feet	250 feet
Travel distance to crossover[4]	750 feet	600 feet	450 feet	300 feet
Spaces searched or compartment size[5]				
Angled	1,600	1,200	800	400
Perpendicular	1,000	750	500	250

[1]Minimum vertical clearance for van accessibility is 8 feet, 2 inches, which requires minimum floor-to-floor heights per LOS C.
[2]LOS D clearance for post-tensioned design set by minimum 6-foot, 8-inch overhead clearance; most codes require seven feet.
[3]To shorten exit path of travel.
[4]In one-way designs, it is necessary to continue on the inbound path of travel before connecting to the outbound path.
[5]Spaces passed on primary search path or spaces per floor in express ramp design.

Wayfinding is improved when parking aisles are oriented toward the pedestrian destination.

Exit from airport parking facility at Reagan National Airport.

is also important to minimize the number of decision and/or conflict points. While placing parking spaces away from the main path of travel expedites flow capacity, it is desirable to select a parking circulation system that allows parkers to see all spaces as they progress through a facility. Conversely, when drivers are in the exit mode, they prefer short driving circuits that minimize cross traffic and limit travel distance.

At some point, patrons might find themselves searching an excessive number of parking spaces to locate an available space. In a larger facility, it is desirable to break the facility into smaller "compartments" with express ramp systems that speed users to a floor with available space where drivers search a limited area of stalls for a vacant parking space. Depending on facility size, another option is to break the structure into two (or more) structures with independent circulation systems.

Once the driver has found a space and parked the car, pedestrian considerations come into play. The first issue is to help patrons remember where they left their car. Markers, easy-to-remember images, and location signs provide necessary landmarks, which are enhanced when a facility enjoys a high level of visibility across the parking floor.

Figure 15-1 presents guidelines for acceptable walking distances for different levels of service (for further information on the development and application of these guidelines, see Smith and Butcher, 1994). Similar to the highway level of service described in chapter 4, decreasing Levels of Service represent less convenience to the user.

Wayfinding is greatly improved when the patron's instinctual behavior can be reinforced. Thus, it is generally desirable to orient parking aisles toward the pedestrian destination. In a freestanding parking facility, that destination is usually the main stair/elevator tower. When bays are oriented transverse to the destination, pedestrians typically cut between parked vehicles, potentially causing security and safety problems. If necessary or appropriate, cross aisles

should be aligned with the stair/elevator tower or the building entrance(s).

The proper location of stair/elevator towers in the overall path of travel relative to the user's ultimate destination is important. Just as the pedestrian wants to see the tower from within the structure, he or she uses the tower as a beacon when returning to the parking facility. Accordingly, circuitous routes to and from towers should be avoided. Once patrons have retraced their route to the parking stall, they return to a vehicular wayfinding mode. The exit route should be equally simple and understandable and follow the shortest path of travel between the facility's parking spaces and the public roadway system.

Conclusion

It is clear that proper wayfinding design starts during the early stages of facility planning. Its goal is to ease facility operations and performance. A well-designed wayfinding, signage, and graphics program enhances a patron's parking experience. It also creates a positive image for the facility owner and operator and therefore can increase patronage and customer satisfaction and perhaps even help create new opportunities for both owner and operator.

References

Boldon, Charles. "Signing and Graphics for Parking," 1983. Presented at the 32nd annual convention of the National Parking Association, New York Hilton, New York City, May 18, 1983.

Monahan, Donald R. "Parking Structure Signing and Graphics." *The Parking Professional*, April 1990.

Sawka, Richard, and Ted R. Seeburg. "Signage and Graphics." *The Dimensions of Parking,* Third Edition. Washington, D.C: ULI–Urban Land Institute, 1993.

Smith, Mary S. "Signage and Graphics." *Parking Structures*, 2nd Edition. Indianapolis, Ind.: Walker Parking Consultants, 1996.

Transportation Research Board. *Guidelines for Transit Facility Signing and Graphics*. TCRP Report 12. Washington, D.C.: National Academy Press, 1996.

CHAPTER 16
SECURITY

I. Paul Lew, Abraham Gutman, and Richard C. Rich

When a parking patron is the victim of theft or personal attack in a parking facility, the owner of that facility often faces a lawsuit alleging inadequate security. In such a situation, the owner's position is often evaluated in accordance with the reasonable man test. Simply stated, would another reasonable person under similar circumstances deploy similar security measures? If the reasonable man would use more security measures, then the responsible party's position is tenuous. If, however, the actions of the responsible party are equal to or exceed those of the reasonable man, then the responsible party's actions are defensible.

While this chapter offers insights into means of improving security, it should not be perceived as a checklist of items to be included in a specific facility. Owners need to retain experts to evaluate their properties.

Security Options

Security measures are usually classified as active or passive. Active security measures are normally defined as any technique that involves a human response, such as security guards or persons monitoring a closed-circuit television. Passive security measures are normally defined as any measure not requiring a human response and that is a physical part of the facility, such as lights, fences, or screening devices. This article primarily addresses passive security measures but examines how physical design can facilitate active security measures such as alarms and cameras.

Physical Design of a Parking Facility

The underlying goal of security measures is to create an atmosphere that makes potential perpetrators feel that they can be seen, sense that they will

PARKING MAGAZINE

Camera monitors.

be caught, and realize that criminal activities are not worth the effort.

Perimeter Control

Perimeter control thwarts unwanted pedestrian access to a facility. It typically requires the perimeter to be fenced and is more common in a parking structure than in a parking lot. Landscaping is also a critical element in perimeter control. It should discourage persons from hiding along the facility perimeter. Low bushes that do not provide cover are preferable so long as they are not planted near points of access to the facility.

Vehicle Access Locations

Vehicular access can be an effective security tool. Potential perpetrators can be deterred by the prospect of being seen by staff or other patrons and perhaps even recorded. Given that vehicular access control is primarily a function of opera-

Perimeter control limits unauthorized access.

tions related to types of users and hours of operation, security measures at vehicular access points must be complementary to operations.

An important issue in vehicular access as a security measure is the number of ingress and egress points. Although increasing the number of ingress and egress points is operationally advantageous for circulation, it is not desirable from a security perspective, particularly during periods of low vehicular volume. One technique commonly used in parking structures is to design pedestrian and vehicular access paths to pass by an attendant and security monitoring point even if the monitoring point does not function as a primary checkpoint that otherwise stops each vehicle or pedestrian. Closing certain points of vehicular ingress and egress is advisable during periods of low activity. Once again, it is important to send the message that potential perpetrators will be seen.

Pedestrian Access Control

The key to controlling pedestrian access is to direct patrons to areas of high pedestrian activity and away from areas of low pedestrian activity. Controlling pedestrian access concentrates activity along preferred routes. Tools available for controlling pedestrian access are the closing and alarming of stairwells intended for emergency egress only.

In some cases, the potential perpetrator walks in and drives out. The posting of guards at pedestrian entries is by far the exception to the rule. Where possible, though, patrons entering the facility on foot should have no option but to pass by attendant booths and security offices. Once again, the visibility associated with a controlled entry should help deter would-be perpetrators.

Clear Line of Sight

The more a parking structure's design approaches an open lot, the easier the facility surveillance because clear sight lines do not conflict with the facility's other functional requirements. To that end, interior walls should be minimized unless economic considerations dictate multilevel parking structures or seismic considerations require interior shear walls capable of resisting earthquake-induced lateral loads. In lieu of eliminating interior walls, holes or windows can create a perforated wall.

Interior ramps located near the center of the facility may be functionally preferable for circulation, but they limit sight lines. Therefore, where security conditions warrant, supplemental security measures may be in order. One security option that provides nearly ideal sight lines is exterior vehicle-only express ramps (either straight or helical). The exterior placement of the ramps affords a relatively unobstructed view of level, open floors. The added cost of the ramps, however, typically limits the exterior express-ramp layout to large parking structures (over 2,000 cars) that serve airports or shopping centers.

A major parking structure security issue occurs when the parking structure is below another use such as a residential

Stairway open from the interior.

or office building. In this case, columns from the building above typically land not only at the front bumper of the cars but also at the sides of cars, thus greatly reducing sight lines across parking levels. Furthermore, pedestrians must typically negotiate a column obstruction when opening the door to their vehicle. These conditions can be partially mitigated with express ramps between levels; the ramps permit level floors and thereby increase sight lines. Once again, where security conditions dictate, more active security measures should be instituted.

Stairways

Parking structures are often required by code to incorporate several emergency staircases that may be underused because of their distance to ground-level uses. It therefore becomes important to direct pedestrians to the stairways closest to their intended destination and away from stairways with limited activity. Appropriate signage or, where warranted, alarms may be used. One major consideration in stairway security is openness. Stairways should be visible from grade, particularly from at-grade areas with high levels of pedestrian activity.

Whether or not the interior of the stairway is open to the floor is the prerogative of the local code. Indeed, debate continues to rage over whether or not stairways should be open from the interior. Where stairways are enclosed from the interior, they are a target for perpetrators. In lieu of opaque interior-wall stairwells, a three-quarter-hour–rated wireglass firewall is sometimes acceptable when firewalls are required. Where stairwells cannot be open, doors to the stairwells should have a glass panel that complies with the fire code. Corner mirrors should also be used if security conditions dictate.

The underside of the lowest run and first landing of a stairway should be enclosed to prevent persons from hiding under the stairway or landing. Similarly, if the stair continues above the last parking level to an elevator penthouse, the stair to the level above should be fenced off with a locked gate.

Noise-activated alarms are of limited value in the vehicular areas of parking facilities because of competing vehicle noises. This is not the case in enclosed stairwells, which are insulated from vehicle noises. Screech alarms are therefore effective in enclosed stairways.

Elevators

Elevators are the main means of vertical pedestrian circulation in parking structures. Probably the most accepted method of elevator surveillance is the glass-backed or -walled ele-

Glass-walled elevator.

ATM machine located near security office.

Conclusion

Security in a parking structure is not a simple matter. The primary purpose of a parking structure is to park automobiles so that users can go about their business. Security should not unnecessarily impede patrons' activities, although additional security measures should be instituted as needed. Seeking the advice of a security specialist is always advisable, particularly as new security systems are constantly entering the marketplace. Security will always be a major issue in the design and operation of any parking facility, and knowledge of available measures is essential for ensuring proper use.

vator, which is a stock item for most elevator manufacturers. Glass-walled elevators should face an area of high pedestrian activity.

Most elevators are equipped with an alarm that should be audible to a potential perpetrator. Two-way communication between the elevator and the attendant or security station is also important.

Lighting

Lighting is a major factor in security. Readers should refer to chapter 14 for additional information.

Cash Security

The exterior location of the cashier booth coupled with periods of low activity and the possible use of an automobile as an escape vehicle places the booth at risk of a hold-up. To minimize the possibility of an incident, the first and most effective tool is the drop safe, to which the attendant has no access. Signage near the cashier booth must state that cash is safe-deposited and that the attendant has no access to the safe. Signage might also indicate that only exact change is accepted, particularly during off-peak hours. If an exact-change policy is in effect, that policy must be posted at the facility entry for patrons' information. The second tool is the silent hold-up alarm in the attendant's booth. A concealed button, typically foot-operated, sounds an alarm in a remote location, usually at a central security or police station. Assistance can be en route while the robbery is still underway.

Alarms and Emergency Communications

Alarms and emergency communications go hand in hand. A panic alarm can be located in elevators, elevator lobbies, stairwells, and prominent locations in parking areas. Typically, the alarm is connected to an intercom. When the panic button is pushed, it activates a pulsing blue light to indicate where assistance is sought.

CHAPTER 17
ACCESSIBILITY AND THE ADA

Richard S. Beebe and I. Paul Lew

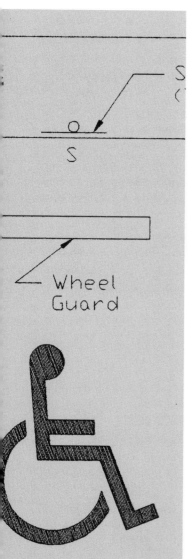

Wheel Guard

The Americans with Disabilities Act took effect on January 26, 1992. Six months later, the Architectural and Transportation Barriers Compliance Board (ATBCB) published the Americans with Disabilities Accessibility Guidelines (ADAAG) and, on April 13, 1992, issued a final rule in the *Federal Register.*[1] The rule contained no significant changes relative to the parking requirements outlined in the earlier guidelines. It should be noted that while the ATBCB prepares the guidelines, it is the Department of Justice that accepts and enforces them. This chapter highlights the guidelines as they affect parking and site access.

The Americans with Disabilities Act (ADA) establishes design priorities for providing persons with disabilities with access to existing sites and buildings and new construction. The basic criterion for implementation in existing facilities is whether accessibility is readily achievable (private sector) or not an undue burden (public sector). If not, then the required work must be performed. The ADA guidelines state, "First priority should be given to measures that will enable individuals with disabilities to get in the front door."[2] This chapter explores major features of the ADA design guidelines for new construction. Issues of whether the actual work to be performed involves a new facility, an addition, an alteration, or just barrier removal are legal matters beyond the scope of the discussion, as are requirements for public transportation.[3]

Number and Location of Accessible Parking Spaces

Figure 17-1 presents the required number of accessible parking spaces based on the total number of spaces to be provided in any given facility. How-

FIGURE 17-1

REQUIRED ACCESSIBLE SPACES

Total Parking Spaces in Lot	Required Minimum Number of Accessible Spaces*
1 to 25	1
26 to 50	2
51 to 75	3
76 to 100	4
101 to 150	5
151 to 200	6
201 to 300	7
301 to 400	8
401 to 500	9
501 to 1,000	2% of total
1,001 and over	20 plus 1 for each 100 over 1,000

*Medical facilities have higher requirements; see text.

FIGURE 17-2

ACCESSIBLE SPACE DIMENSIONS

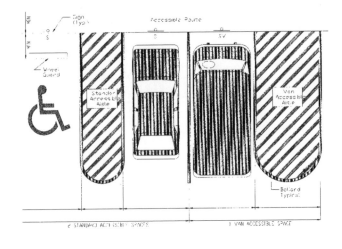

ever, the requirements are not applicable to medal centers where 10 percent of spaces should be accessible for outpatient facilities and 20 percent of spaces accessible if a facility specializes in treatment of persons with mobility impairments. For hospitals, rational analysis for the 10 and 20 percent requirements is suggested here. For example, if the local zoning code requires four parking spaces per 1,000 square feet of hospital space and the hospital encompasses 250,000 square feet, then 1,000 cars must be accommodated. In this example, if 20,000 square feet serves the outpatient facility and 5,000 square feet serves the facility for mobility-impaired treatment, then, of the 1,000 parking spaces, 20,000/250,000 or 8 percent (80 spaces) may serve outpatients and 5,000/250,000 or 2 percent (20 spaces) may serve patients treated for mobility impairments. The remaining 900 spaces are allocated to employees and the general public. Thus, the following minimum number of accessible spaces would be required:

General	2% of 900 spaces	= 18 spaces
Outpatient	10% of 80 spaces	= 8 spaces
Mobility treatment	20% of 20 spaces	= 4 spaces
Total spaces required		= 30 spaces

User surveys may also provide a basis for parking space allocations. In all cases, the opinion of local governing authorities should be sought.

If multiple lots or parking facilities are involved, each lot or facility must be considered individually to determine the required total number of accessible spaces. Once the vehicle space count is determined for each lot or facility, the spaces can be distributed to the most accessible locations. It is essential to note here that all accessible parking spaces must

be located and designed in strict conformance with the ADAAG requirements.

The ADA guidelines require accessible spaces to be the closest spaces to all accessible building entrances while still conforming to the general public's preferred pedestrian access route(s). Thus, clustering all accessible spaces near only one accessible entrance does not meet the intent of the guidelines. In addition, longer distances are preferable to steeper slopes on shorter pedestrian travel routes.

The process of determining the location of the accessible parking spaces within a parking facility serving a particular building or facility must consider the requirement that at least 50 percent of all public building entrances must be accessible and have an accessible route to them. Furthermore, at least one direct accessible route from any garage to a building must be provided if any such route is provided for pedestrians. Similar criteria apply to pedestrian tunnels or walkways.

Sizes of Accessible Parking Spaces

With the location of the accessible parking spaces determined, the next task is to define the size of the parking spaces. The three types of accessible parking spaces are

- standard-accessible parking spaces;
- van-accessible parking spaces (one of every eight accessible spaces must be a van-accessible space, and at least one space must be van-accessible wherever accessible spaces are provided); and
- passenger loading zones, which are mandatory with valet or attendant parking.

The standard-accessible parking space is eight feet wide and must have a five-foot-wide demarcated accessible aisle adjacent to it (see Figure 17-2). Two accessible spaces may share the same accessible aisle except in the case of angle

Accessible spaces and aisle.

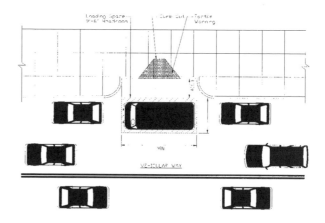

FIGURE 17-3

ACCESSIBLE PASSENGER LOADING ZONES

parking; in that instance, each space must have an adjacent accessible aisle. Only in the case of 90-degree parking can a vehicle back into a parking space and still have access to an oversized aisle. Vertical clearance for accessible spaces may be the same as in the rest of the parking structure (7-foot, 2-inch minimum or as per local code, whichever is higher) unless spaces are provided for vans. The standard van-accessible space is also eight feet wide but has an eight-foot accessible aisle (see Figure 17-2). Bollards or other barriers should be considered to stop vehicles from parking in the accessible aisle. Van-accessible spaces and the vehicle access route to the spaces must have a minimum vertical clearance of 8 feet, 2 inches. Van spaces may be grouped on one appropriate level in a parking structure. It is important to note that several states, such as Illinois, have enacted ADA-type legislation with more stringent requirements than those in the ADAAG.

Finally, accessible passenger loading zones must be at least 20 feet long (by eight feet or more in width) with a five-foot accessible aisle adjacent to the space (see Figure 17-3). A raised curb must not be located within the accessible aisle, and a curb ramp must lead from the parking space, via the accessible aisle, to any raised curb. Furthermore, the vertical clearance at loading zones must be 9 feet, 6 inches. All accessible parking spaces and loading zones, including the accessible aisle, must not have slopes exceeding 2 percent and must be connected to an accessible route.[4]

Accessible Route

Once the number and location of accessible spaces is determined, the next step is to focus on the ADA's accessible route guidelines. An accessible route is defined as "a continuous unobstructed path connecting all accessible elements and spaces of a building or facility."[5] Exterior accessible routes may include parking access aisles, curb ramps, crosswalks at vehicular ways, walks, ramps, and lifts.

An accessible route must meet the following minimum requirements as defined in Section 4 of the ADAAG—

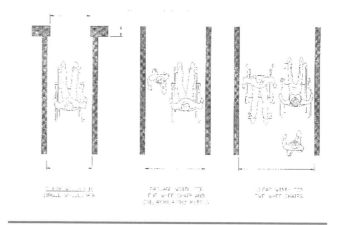

FIGURE 17-4

ACCESSIBLE ROUTE

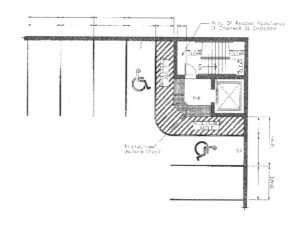

FIGURE 17-5

ACCESSIBLE SPACES AROUND ELEVATOR TOWER

FIGURE 17-6

ACCESSIBLE SPACES AROUND ELEVATOR TOWER AT ON-GRADE ENTRY

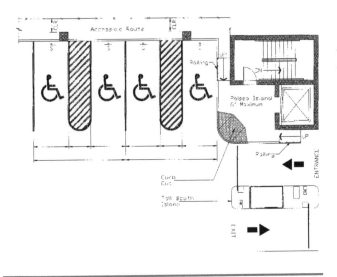

Accessible elements and spaces: scope and technical requirements:

- "At least one accessible route shall be provided within the boundary of the site from public transportation stops, accessible parking spaces, passenger loading zones, if provided, and public streets or sidewalks to an accessible building entrance."[6]

- "At least one accessible route shall connect accessible buildings, accessible facilities, accessible elements, and accessible spaces within the same site. The accessible route shall to the maximum extent feasible coincide with the route for the general public."[7]

Although a minimum accessible route is only 36 inches wide (see Figure 17-4), such width presents several limitations. First, two wheelchairs cannot pass each other; passing zones at least 60 inches wide and no greater than 200 feet apart are required to resolve wheelchair-wheelchair conflicts. Furthermore, at least a 48-inch width is needed to allow a pedestrian to pass a wheelchair (see Figure 17-4). Again, an accessible route at least 60 inches wide can resolve wheelchair-pedestrian conflicts. Limitations on turns along the accessible route can be met by T-intersections at corridors or by providing passing spaces along the route.

Slopes on an accessible route must be less than 1:20; if conditions do not permit such slope, the affected section is to be designed as a ramp that meets more stringent design requirements. All floor surfaces must be stable and slip-resistant. Equally important, no objects can protrude into the accessible route and otherwise reduce the route's clear width.

Many parking facilities provide accessible spaces adjacent to the corner stair and elevator towers (see Figure 17-5). Whenever possible, accessible spaces should be located on grade at the perimeter of a parking lot or structure with direct access to an accessible route that merges with the main pedestrian entry (see Figure 17-6). Parking directly across the

FIGURE 17-7

ACCESSIBLE SPACES ACROSS FROM VEHICULAR WAY—PARALLEL ORIENTATION

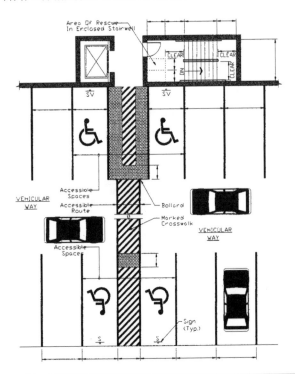

FIGURE 17-8

ACCESSIBLE SPACES ACROSS FROM VEHICULAR WAY—PERPENDICULAR ORIENTATION

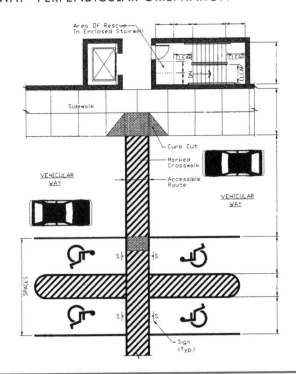

Ramp on accessible route from garage to destination.

Signage for accessible spaces in surface parking facility.

drive aisle from an elevator is considered acceptable (see Figures 17-7 and -8). In this case, though, the crosswalk must be clearly marked on the aisle floor. Nonetheless, parking across the drive aisle from an elevator is less desirable than parking along an accessible pedestrian route located in front of parking spaces.

Ramps, Signage, and Detectable Warnings

Ramps and curb ramps are two of the major design elements of an accessible route. The more prevalent of the two ramps is the curb ramp. The revised curb ramp criteria specified in the ADA guidelines now require a maximum slope of 1:12 (see Figure 17-9) while the adjoining accessible route must follow the 1:20 limit for accessible routes. The sides of a curb ramp must be flared 1:10 if pedestrians use the ramp. Curb ramps must have the same 36-inch-minimum width of the accessible route exclusive of sides, slopes, and accessible routes perpendicular to the direction of travel. Any built-up curb ramps must not project into the path of vehicular traffic.

Ramps in general must have a slope no greater than 1:12. The maximum rise for any run cannot exceed 30 inches without a landing. A landing must be at least 60 inches long; if a change of direction is involved, the landing must be at least 60 inches by 60 inches. Handrails are required on ramps with more than a six-inch rise or a length greater than 72 inches. The cross slopes of ramps may not exceed 2 percent.

For the ADA to be effective, persons with disabilities must know where accessible spaces and routes are located. Signage must be provided to direct a person to accessible entries, parking spaces, and loading zones. Elements and spaces of accessible facilities must be identified by the International Symbol of Accessibility (see Figure 17-10).

The ADA guidelines govern signage, including brailled and raised letters and symbols. Brailled or raised signs are required to designate permanent rooms and spaces such as stairs and elevator towers. Local standards for site and parking signage typically exceed the strict minimum ADA standards for directional signs. For example, the minimum ADA character height is three inches for overhead signs, but larger character sizes, up to eight or ten inches, are typical in parking facilities. In general, characters must be sized according to the viewing distance, with larger letters required for signs viewed from longer distances.

FIGURE 17-9

CURB RAMP SLOPES

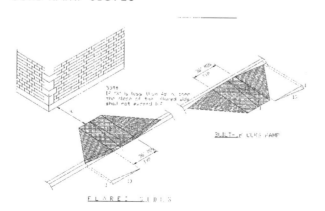

FIGURE 17-10

SIGN TYPES

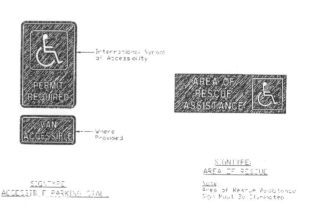

On November 15, 1999, the Architectural and Transportation Barriers Compliance Board (hereinafter referred to as the board) published a proposed comprehensive revision to the *Americans with Disabilities Act Accessibility Guidelines for Buildings and Facilities* (ADAAG). Among other things, the revision consolidates the requirements under the ADA and those under the Architectural Barriers Act of 1968 (ABA). Buildings leased or owned by the federal government or built with federal funds are required to comply with ABA, which in turn requires compliance with the Uniform Federal Accessibility Standards (UFAS). ADA was adopted in 1990 to require accessibility of buildings not covered under ABA, with ADAAG the standard for design; however, state and local governments have the option of complying with either UFAS or ADAAG. In sum, with the issuance of ADAAG as a final rule, UFAS will probably disappear before the end of 2000, and there will be one standard for all entities.

The revisions were principally developed by an advisory committee, which worked over a two-year period. The board, however, as the ultimate issuing authority, made all final decisions and declined to adopt some advisory committee recommendations.

Some of the changes in the proposed section that may be of interest and/or concern to those involved in parking design, ownership, or operation are noted here. The proposed section

- Dropped any distinction in requirements between exterior facilities and buildings.
- Clarified the requirements for accessible routes to indicate clearly that vehicular ways, such as parking aisles (if otherwise meeting requirements such as floor slope), can be used as the accessible route from a parking space to the destination.
- Clarified that the increased requirements for accessible spaces at "outpatient" (10 percent) and "rehabilitation" (20 percent) facilities apply only to visitor and patient parking and further clarified the definition of outpatient as treatment facilities not requiring an overnight stay in a hospital and not doctors' offices, independent clinics, and so forth, not located in a hospital.
- Clarified requirements for the number and location of accessible parking spaces at residential units. The requirements may be summarized as a minimum of one parking space per accessible dwelling unit; if additional spaces are provided for residents, 2 percent but not less than one of the additional spaces shall be provided; if additional spaces are provided for guest parking, they shall comply with the same ratios. Where accessible spaces are specifically located at or assigned to specific dwelling units, they do not have to be signed or dispersed; however, where they are not assigned, the accessible spaces shall be dispersed.

- Added a long-requested height for signage at parking spaces (60 inches from the ground to the bottom of the sign) and removed the requirement for designation of van-accessible spaces (interpreted as reserving spaces only for vans, which was never the intent).
- Clarified the requirement for certain design details. Access aisles for accessible parking spaces must be marked, and changes in level beyond the maximum 1:48 (2.08333 percent) slope are not permitted for either the space or the aisle. The access aisle must be at the same level as the parking space, i.e., it cannot be at curb height, which is a common mistake in parallel parking. The same provisions generally apply to accessible passenger loading zones.
- Changed the location requirements for accessible parking spaces; in fact, the omission of any change such as prohibitions on passing behind parked vehicles is considered significant. Access aisles may be shared; there is no new requirement that they be provided on a specific side and there is no new prohibition of shared-access aisles by angled parking. Adding bollards to van-access aisles is not required but is considered "helpful."
- Suspended the requirement for detectable warnings until further research about where and what detectable warnings actually work; however, detectable warnings are still required on transportation system station platforms in the interim.
- Changed the requirements for elevators so that an accessible route must be provided between floors; an elevator is the most common means of meeting it.
- Eliminated the linkage between the required number of accessible entrances and the required number of exits because the purpose of entries/exits may differ substantially. This is beneficial to parking facilities with major security concerns, where there is specifically a single entrance for daily pedestrian access, even though the building code requires several emergency exits.
- Adopted the model building code language for accessible means of egress, including exceptions not requiring areas of refuge at either stairs or elevators in open parking structures and in buildings "protected throughout" by a "supervised automatic" sprinkler system. Therefore, most parking structures will not require areas of refuge.
- Clarified other signage requirements to make it clear that tactile information is required only at exit doors (but apparently not at an open exit stair without a door) and at permanent rooms and spaces such as restrooms (but not on most other signs in parking facilities).

Mary S. Smith
Parking Consultants Council

One of the new features of the ADA guidelines is the requirement for detectable warnings on walking surfaces. Guidance should be sought from the ATBCB on this matter.

Elevators and Areas of Rescue

The pedestrian elements of a parking structure must also comply with the ADA. All full-size elevators must be accessible, and multistory buildings must have at least one elevator. Under some limited circumstances, two-story buildings do

not require an elevator[8] but must instead incorporate an accessible pedestrian route ramp.[9] The requirements for accessible elevators are extensive and should be addressed by an expert.

Another pedestrian element in parking structures, particularly in enclosed structures, is areas of rescue. Areas of rescue are normally not mandated unless a facility requires a fire-rated enclosed exit. Where required, an area of rescue must have a smoke-proof, fire-resistive enclosure. It must be located along the accessible route adjacent to or as a part of

FIGURE 17-11

ACCESSIBLE CASHIER BOOTH

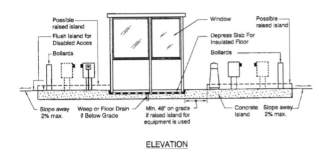

ELEVATION

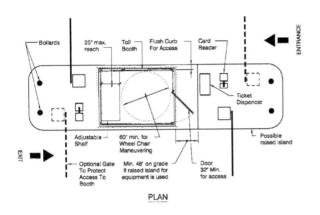

PLAN

the exitway. The area must be clearly identified with illumination and provide a means of two-way communication (both visible and audible). In addition, all fire and other emergency alarms must be both visible and audible. Areas of rescue must be able to accommodate at least two 30-inch-by-48-inch areas or one 30-inch-by-48-inch area per 200 occupants (whichever is greater) and cannot encroach on any required exitway. Stairways adjoining areas of rescue must be 48 inches wide from face of railing to face of railing to allow rescue workers to take wheelchair-bound persons down the staircase. If there is a supervised automatic sprinkler system in the building, an area of rescue is not required.

The provision of areas of rescue in an open parking structure is an issue requiring some further clarification. According to the ATBCB, open parking structures are not required to have areas of rescue under most circumstances unless the exit stairs must be enclosed.[10] Thus, areas of rescue would be required only when the local code requires enclosed stairways. Guidance from the local code authorities should be sought on this matter. It should be noted that in some cases local building codes may be in conflict with the requirements of the ADAAG and specific decisions sought from local officials

Cashier Booths

The ADA guidelines appendix, which addresses employment within a parking facility, requires at least 5 percent of all

work stations but not less than one station to be accessible. Work spaces must be at least five feet by five feet clear to allow for wheelchair turning space. All cashier booths must be accessible to and through the door. Two percent of all booths, or a minimum of one booth, must be fully accessible. In addition, if cashier booths are located on raised islands, curb ramps are required. Curb ramps can be eliminated at accessible booths if the booths are not placed on raised islands (see Figure 17-11). Beyond the required wheelchair maneuvering space, the height and depth of work surfaces must meet strict guidelines covered by the ADA. It is important to remember that the booth will be used by other than persons with disabilities and therefore must include adjustable shelves and other elements that ensure flexibility in use of the workplace. Employee toilets must be accessible as in any place of employment.

Conclusion

This chapter on the ADA provisions concerning parking site access is hardly exhaustive. Moreover, some state or local regulations may be more stringent than the ADA guidelines. For these reasons, only a complete review of the ADA guidelines by a knowledgeable designer can address the full range of accessibility issues. In any event, it must be stressed that one of the highest priorities of the ADA is parking and site accessibility. Further modification to the ADAAG guidelines is anticipated in 2000 and in future years as the ATBCB and Department of Justice continue to review the issues of mobility for the disabled.

Notes

1 *Federal Register*, July 26, 1991, Vol. 56, No. 144, Part III, U.S. Department of Justice, 28 CFR, Part 36.
2 U.S. Department of Justice, "Title III Highlights," p. 6.
3 *Federal Register*, September 6, 1991, Part II, ATBCB (Architectural and Transportation Barriers Compliance Board), Vol. 56, No. 173.
4 Appendix, *Federal Register*, Volume 56, No. 144, 28 CFR, Part 36, p. 35,676.
5 *Federal Register*, July 26, 1991, Vol. 56, No. 144, Part III, U.S. Department of Justice, 28 CFR, Part 36, p. 35,608.
6 *Federal Register*, July 26, 1991, Vol. 56, No. 144, Part III, U.S. Department of Justice, 28 CFR, Part 36, p. 35,611.
7 *Federal Register*, July 26, 1991, Vol. 56, No. 144, Part III, U.S. Department of Justice, 28 CFR, Part 36, p. 35,611.
8 *Federal Register*, July 26, 1991, Vol. 56, No. 144, U.S. Department of Justice, 28 CFR, Part 36, p. 35,613.
9 *Federal Register*, July 26, 1991, Vol. 56, No. 144, U.S. Department of Justice, 28 CFR 36, p. 35,613.
10 *Federal Register*, July 26, 1991, 36 CFR, Part 1191, p. 35,420.

CHAPTER 18
FINANCIAL FEASIBILITY

Larry Donoghue, Jean M. Keneipp, and William Surna

©COMSTOCK, INC.

The purpose of a financial feasibility study of a parking facility is to estimate a proposed facility's future financial performance. In many cases, a project cannot be developed unless its projected net income meets specified criteria. One frequently applied criterion is the debt coverage ratio or the ratio of projected net income divided by projected debt payment. The criteria may, however, vary with the proposed financing method. For example, a public agency that plans to finance a project with revenue bonds needs to show that net income will total 150 percent or more (a debt coverage ratio of 1.5 or more) than the debt service. A private developer planning to finance a parking project to support an office building may simply require that the estimated deficit is at an acceptable level.

Financial feasibility studies are prepared by experienced parking consulting firms. Experience in the preparation of feasibility studies is especially important for projects that will be financed with municipal bond sales. In fact, bond sales are often conditioned on the completion of a feasibility study prepared by a consultant with a proven record.

In particular, the need for feasibility studies is strongly associated with revenue bond financing. Typically, purchasers of revenue bonds do not have collateral rights; instead, they depend in part on assurances of impartial studies that their investment will be safe. The objective of a financial feasibility study is to determine whether the funds available for annual payment of principal and interest will be greater—after the deduction of expenses—than required.

Study Approach

It is useful to prepare a feasibility study in two phases. A preliminary financial analysis can be performed relatively rapidly and inexpensively. If the preliminary analysis indicates that the project as originally conceived or with some modification could succeed, a more detailed feasibility study is in order.

In many situations, the owner/developer of a proposed parking structure needs to know at the project's conceptual stage the degree of financial exposure associated with the proposal. The owner/developer might ask, "Should I pursue this project, modify the concept, or forget it?" An informal analysis can suggest what a project will cost to build, compare income and costs for future years, determine whether the project should go forward, and serve as a first step in a detailed feasibility study.

Often, the initial examination does not yield a favorable conclusion. In that case, the next step is to explore a number of alternatives through a series of sensitivity analyses. With the preliminary financial analysis and the results of the sensitivity analyses in hand, the owner/developer may then be able to modify the original assumptions to achieve a satisfactory approach. The number of scenarios that might be considered for a modified plan is almost endless.

- What is the impact of garage efficiency (square feet per space) on the cost of construction?
- What impact would front-end funds or a downpayment have on project financing?
- Would it be possible to reduce operations and maintenance costs? What is the effect on project feasibility?
- How can the method of financing be changed to reduce debt service costs?

If warranted by the preliminary analysis, the consultant prepares a detailed feasibility study well before the owner/developer makes final commitments for land, design and engineering services, and other components of the project. Should the conditions of feasibility prove unacceptable, the owner/developer may take appropriate actions. A completed feasibility study informs the development decision: whether to proceed with or abandon a project.

Study Components

At a minimum, a financial feasibility study includes three broad parts: demand estimation, projection of net revenues, and the pro forma until debt retirement. More specifically, a typical feasibility study comprises the following sections:

- description and cost estimate of the proposed project;
- existing parking supply and demand;
- projected parking supply and demand;
- proposed rate schedules and estimates of use and gross revenue;
- estimates of expenses for operations and maintenance;
- debt service; and
- recommended financial program.

Project Description

A written project description should be supplemented by a location map and schematic drawings that show the dimensions of the parking structure and the means of vehicular and pedestrian circulation. Stairs, elevators, stall sizes, and driving aisles should be depicted in sufficient detail to assure those who would put capital at risk that the project will result in a usable facility. Identification and description of the surrounding streets on the ground-floor plan help the potential lender or investor envision the capacity of the streets to carry traffic to and from the proposed facility.

Sometimes the project description includes outline specifications and standards of quality for material and equipment. An estimate of the project cost, including any applicable land cost, must be incorporated into the project description.

Parking Supply and Demand

Supply and demand factors are determined by first establishing the project's area of influence—that area containing the generators of demand for parking that the proposed facility is expected to satisfy. Second, an inventory of the existing supply of parking spaces and use of those spaces is required, along with descriptions and locations of all demand generators related to the area of influence. Use data for existing parking facilities include accumulation counts at selected hours during the day when significant activity occurs as well as information on turnover (the number of times a space is used during the day). Estimates of any new demand generators must also be prepared and factored into existing data.

Projected parking supply and demand are, respectively, the estimated number of parking spaces in the area of influence following project completion and, at the time of projection completion, the total number of spaces expected to be required by the demand generators in the area of influence. To formulate these estimates, it is necessary to account for spaces added or removed during the course of project development as well as for any other changes in the area of influence. An accounting of significant changes in demand because of development changes is needed to project future demand.

Studies are often prepared for parking structures that are part of completely new redevelopment projects expected to contain a mix of land uses. The demand for parking associated with each use must therefore be estimated in accordance with the development's projected tenancy.

Area of Influence

A parking facility serving a central business district generates its patronage from parking demand generators located close to the facility. Depending on the type of parking patronage, the extent of the area of influence area can vary. For example, a parking facility in a high-demand area may experience heavy use by short-term patrons who park for only one or two hours while conducting business at destinations within one or, at most, two blocks of the parking facility. On the other hand, a parking facility used predominantly by long-term patrons who park for eight to ten hours attracts most of its business from persons whose destinations are as much as three or four blocks from the parking facility.

The parking consultant usually determines the area of influence by surveying parking patrons in the vicinity of the proposed parking facility. Parking patrons using existing on- and off-street parking facilities are queried about the following:

- What is the purpose of your trip?
- Where did you park?
- What is your destination?
- How long will your vehicle be parked?

Trip purpose might include commute to work, attending an entertainment event, frequenting a restaurant, a visit to a professional office, a sales call, shopping, or some combination.

From the responses obtained from parking patrons, the consultant can estimate the proposed facility's area of influence. Generally, smaller cities mean smaller influence areas and larger cities mean larger influence areas. In larger cities, it is not uncommon for monthly contract parking patrons, especially eight- to ten-hour patrons, to walk as far as six or eight blocks (2,000 to 2,600 feet) to their place of employment.

Parking Rates

Even though a parking facility may be built to provide parking for a particular development, there is no assurance that potential patronage will not be lost to other facilities with more competitive rates. Therefore, the consultant must make a survey of the various parking rates charged by all parking facilities located in the proposed facility's area of influence. Professional judgment then informs the selection of a parking rate schedule that is competitive with the rates charged in facilities within the area of influence.

Parkers may be categorized by their length of stay, which has a significant influence on the rates they pay.

Short-Term or Transient Parkers. Short-term parkers are patrons who park for as short a period as one-half hour and as long as up to ten or even 24 hours. They pay for parking on an hourly or daily basis, with fees generally proportional to their length of stay. Patrons usually pay their parking fee when they exit from the facility.

Short-term or transient rates usually have a high first-half-hour or first-hour rate that may be as much as one-quarter or even one-third of the daily maximum rate, e.g., $3 for the first hour with a $10 daily maximum rate. The second and succeeding hours are usually less, say $1 to $2. There is a strong tendency to try to achieve the eight- to ten-hour rate within the first three or four hours by, for example,

charging $3 for the first hour, $5 for up to two hours, $7 for up to three hours, and $9 for up to four hours, with a $10 daily maximum rate.

Early Bird Parkers. Within the transient-parker category is the early bird parker who arrives at a facility between 8:30 a.m. and 9:00 a.m. and remains until 4:00 p.m. to 6:00 p.m. Early bird rates usually equal about 50 or 60 percent of the daily maximum rate. For example, if the daily maximum rate is $10, the early bird rate might be $6.

Special-Event Parkers. Special-event parkers are patrons attending a sporting event, concert, or similar activity. They usually pay a flat, fixed parking fee when they enter the parking facility. Special-event rates are the widest-ranging of all parking rates. If the parking facility caters primarily to the usual mix of downtown parking demands, the special-event rate might be as low as the first-hour rate, say, $3. If, however, parking demand is related almost exclusively to a professional sports activity, the rate may range from $5 to as high as $10.

Saturday, Sunday, and Holiday Parkers. For most urban parking facilities, demand declines on weekends and holidays. The rate for these periods is therefore often a flat, reduced fee that is typically equal to about what is charged for one hour of parking during weekdays. A rate of $4 per use would be reasonable.

Monthly Contract Parkers. Contract patrons are parkers whose place of employment is conveniently located to the parking facility. They are usually permitted to use the facility 24 hours per day, seven days a week. Some facilities, however, limit the parking privilege to day-time use and charge a reduced monthly rate for evening or night use.

Monthly contract rates usually range from ten to 15 times the daily maximum rate, e.g., if a facility has a $10 daily maximum rate, the monthly rate would range from $100 to $150. The reduction in monthly contract rates is based on the concept that the patron is a repeat user and thereby entitled to a discount.

In rare circumstances, the monthly contract rate is set at 20 to 22 times the daily rate to account for the 260 weekdays in a year. Parking facilities that use the higher contract rate stress that a monthly patron enjoys the convenience of key-card ingress and egress and forgoes any exit delay at the cashier booth. The repeat use concept is not a consideration.

Estimated Use

Once the proposed rate schedule is established, the consultant prepares an estimate of the expected number of users for each of the facility's many different types of demand. Users may include some or all of the groups previously identified.

Estimated Revenue

Revenue is estimated by multiplying the estimated number of patrons for each expected category of use by the rate proposed for that type of use. Frequently, the consultant takes a conservative position and assumes a smaller number of patrons during the early years of use compared with the likely level of use after two or three years of facility operation. In this way, the consultant recognizes that a new facility does not experience full demand from the outset. Usually a facility needs two to three years to reach stable demand before it achieves near-capacity operation on a fairly consistent basis.

Estimated Operations and Maintenance Expenses

The expenses involved in operating and maintaining a proposed facility typically include salaries, wages, and fringe benefits for operating and administrative staff; equipment maintenance; expendable supplies; taxes; insurance; utilities; and minor repairs. Ideally, a sinking fund for major repairs should be established. In fact, one common requirement of revenue bond financing is the creation of a replacement fund. Operations and maintenance expenses differ widely from location to location depending on factors such as climate, utility costs, and wage scales. Therefore, the consultant should try to obtain comparable figures from facilities in the proposed project's locale to help guide the formulation of reliable expense estimates.

The likely operational arrangement for the proposed parking facility also affects the project's feasibility. Operations expenses vary depending on whether the facility is self-operated or uses a management agreement or concession agreement. In some cities, the type of operating arrangement dictates whether union-scale wages must be paid. The requirement to pay union wages can have a significant impact on a parking facility's financial feasibility.

Effects of Inflation

The time frame embodied by feasibility studies varies. Some studies project revenues and expenses for only the first three to five years of facility operation and make no allowance for inflation that, at the time of project construction, might average only 3 to 4 percent per year. Under these circumstances, it could be assumed that current conditions will prevail, followed by an equal escalation of parking fees and expenses.

If a feasibility study involves a longer-range projection, say, 20 or more years, it should include the effects of estimated inflation. In particular, parking facilities that are constructed with the proceeds of a loan or bonds benefit from inflation because the revenues and expenses directly affected by inflation tend to offset one another. At the same time, debt service is not affected by inflation and usually remains constant from the time the facility opens until the debt is retired. Consequently, inflation can improve net income and cash flow such that the facility becomes more financially feasible with the passage of time.

Financing Program

When projected revenues, costs, and operations and maintenance expenses are in hand, the consultant might want to consider engaging the services of a financial adviser to develop the facility's financial program. The financial program should show expected or possible sources of financing; the basic terms of financing such as interest rates, length of borrowing, and amount borrowed; estimated net revenues based on cash flow; facility use at proposed rates adjusted by expenses for operations and maintenance; and a summary of debt retirement. The financial program need not be structured around only one funding source. Subsidies, special assessments, or other credit instruments such as tax-increment bonds or general obligation bonds retired by project revenues may be considered. The ability to realize the necessary funding for the proposed project thus becomes a major condition of feasibility.

Possible Adverse Conditions

Several factors can undermine the financial feasibility of parking facilities, especially garages. If construction costs increase and must be passed along to patrons in the form of higher parking rates, the owner/developer could likely meet with resistance, especially where demand is decreasing because of loss of business or regional unemployment. Other problems are high land costs and high interest rates. Feasibility studies must therefore delineate business and economic conditions and explain in some detail what must be done to achieve a program that will attract credit capital.

Financial Sweeteners

For the public sector, it is common for municipalities to finance parking facilities with revenue bonds. Revenue bonds usually do not affect local real estate ad valorem taxes because they are pledged against the net revenues generated by the project itself. In cases where projected net revenues may not be sufficient to retire the revenue bond debt fully, the public sector sometimes turns to "sweeteners," which are net revenues generated by other revenue sources that are not based on ad valorem taxes. Sources include the parking meter system, other off-street parking facilities, municipal sales taxes, and municipal utility taxes.

Finding of Feasibility

The final step in the feasibility study is to reach a conclusion about the analysis. There is no universally applicable definition of a feasible project. The traditional test of financial feasibility is an estimated future debt coverage ratio of 1:5 or higher, although the debt coverage ratio may not be the controlling factor for certain projects. For example, when an owner is prepared to subsidize a proposed parking facility, the project becomes financially feasible if future subsidies are projected to fall within an acceptable range. In other cases, "back-up" funds can be pledged to a project such that a debt coverage ratio of 1.1 or even 0.9 is acceptable.

It is the nature of most projects to generate higher net revenues in each successive year if fees increase to match increases in operating costs. Assuming that the debt payment remains constant, the debt coverage ratio thus increases each year.

Assumptions

Generally, any feasibility study that evaluates estimated or projected values is subject to error if any of the study's underlying assumptions changes. Specifically, a financial feasibility study is an evaluation of the estimated future financial performance of a proposed project under a given set of circumstances. One of the most significant assumptions is patronage of the facility. Indeed, because assumptions are so important to a feasibility study, they should be listed prominently in the report.

The following list illustrates the types of assumptions that should be addressed in a feasibility study's concluding section, although it is important to recognize that each project is based on certain unique assumptions.

- The proposed parking facility will be designed and constructed so that it will be acceptable to its projected patrons and so that there will be no impediments to its use.
- The proposed parking facility will contain the specified number of spaces plus, if applicable, the specified area of commercial/retail space.
- The proposed parking facility will be constructed and opened in accordance with the specified time frame and assumed construction and financing costs.
- Parking fees will be charged in accordance with projected fees.
- The operating costs of the parking facility will not exceed the levels reflected in the estimates.
- The parking facility will be properly maintained during its service life to ensure its continuing viability; maintenance costs will be as estimated.
- There will be no significant changes in the availability and cost of motor fuel and in transit competition during the period of the analysis.
- The assumed level of new development or redevelopment in the area of influence will take place according to the described time frame.
- The level of economic activity in the metropolitan area and the parking facility's trade area of influence will continue to be normal, and parking demand and the demand for commercial space will continue to be at normal levels during the period of the analysis.

The project assumptions identify some of the factors that affect the financial feasibility of a parking structure, including changes in the character of the area surrounding the proposed facility. If, following preparation of the feasibility study, changes occur that differ significantly from the assumptions spelled out in the study, the revenue generated by the parking structure may prove insufficient or even exceed expectations. The following changes could occur:

- A major employer in the area decides to move out of the area. Likewise, a new employer could decide to move into the area, thus increasing the demand for parking.
- A large evening demand generator moves out of the area or closes.
- Proposed mixed-use developments increase or decrease in size.
- New, competing parking facilities are constructed in the area.
- The direction of traffic flow near the proposed facility changes.

For these and other similar reasons, it is important to update financial feasibility studies, particularly if a planned project has been put on hold for an extended time.

Conclusion

Finally, the feasibility study should be summarized in an executive summary that includes conclusions and recommendations as well as important information about the project and the proposed financing plan. To expedite the lending decision, the executive summary should acquaint prospective lenders with all aspects of the proposed project.

Not all feasibility studies require the full range of investigations and preparation described here. Local financing may be approached with a simpler study, but it is not always possible to obtain local financing for large projects requiring great sums of money. Nationwide financing efforts usually require a full study; however, each study must be suited to the particular needs of the lender(s) for a given project.

CHAPTER 19
FINANCING PARKING FACILITIES

Michael P. Schaefer

The level of knowledge concerning the financing options available to prospective owners of new parking facilities is highly variable. The few firms that own and operate parking facilities as their primary business carefully guard their sources of borrowed or equity capital as well as their strategies for accumulating that capital. Further, with the growth in mixed-use structures, the financing of a parking facility is often but one component of a larger overall financing plan. Therefore, for some owners, financing a new parking garage is a bewildering prospect simply because they so infrequently deal with the debt and equity markets.

The capital markets use a language all their own. That language includes terms that can best be described as arcane, archaic, or cryptic—REITs, COPs, debt service, and coverage ratio, to name a few. Not surprisingly, the novice owner/developer is easily intimidated. This chapter provides an overview of the process of financing new parking facilities and acquaints the reader with some common financing terms. In fact, the discussion is simplified by employing the generic term lender, which can refer to a bank, investors, a syndicate, a real estate investment trust (REIT), and the provider of capital to fund construction of a new facility. The terms owner and developer are used interchangeably even though they may represent two separate and distinct parties.

Regardless of what is to be financed, some basic financial questions need to be addressed (see Figure 19-1). These questions are often answered sequentially and thus provide the basic bounds of the financing process.

FIGURE 19-1

BASIC FINANCIAL QUESTIONS

What do I want to acquire?

When do I want to acquire it?

How much does it cost?

Should I pay cash or borrow funds?

If I must borrow, what is my source of repayment?

How do I evaluate the potential revenue stream?

What financing structures are available to the private sector?

What financing structures are available to the public sector?

Are there ways to improve the credit quality?

Is there someone who can help me with the financing process?

Should I Pay Cash or Borrow?

The first major decision point in the financing process is whether to pay cash or borrow funds to finance a project. The expenditure of cash (pay-as-you-use) suggests that the owner has accumulated sufficient resources to finance the cost of a new facility. In most instances, however, an owner lacks the financial wherewithal to pay the costs upfront and therefore must borrow funds. Three areas of concern come into play: equity, efficiency, and effectiveness (see Figure 19-2).

FIGURE 19-2

FINANCING CONSIDERATIONS

Equity	Are the beneficiaries of the project paying for the project?
Efficiency	What financing method is most cost-effective?
Effectiveness	Will the funding be sufficient and received in a timely fashion?

If I Must Borrow, What Is My Source of Repayment?

With the how-to-finance question resolved, the owner next considers the source of repayment. Possible revenue sources fall into three broad categories: parking-related, other, and taxes.

Parking-Related Revenue Sources

Revenues generated by the operation of a facility (see Figure 19-3) are the most common source of payment to debt or equity holders. Municipal jurisdictions may supplement facility revenues with revenues from on-street meters. A limited number of jurisdictions impose impact fees or in-lieu fees. In such a case, owners may have the option of satisfying the code requirement for parking spaces or make a payment in

FIGURE 19-3

PARKING-RELATED REVENUES

User fees and charges	Fines
On-street meters	In-lieu fees
Impact fees	

lieu of providing code-required parking. This one-time fee is designed to cover the construction of the necessary parking infrastructure off site. Similarly, failure to provide code-required parking might result in the payment of an impact fee. Again, this one-time fee is designed to cover the cost of parking not provided with the developed property. In either case, the jurisdiction receives a lump-sum payment ostensibly dedicated to the provision of "public" parking space at some future date.

Other Parking-Related Revenue Sources

As more owners/developers engage in "urban camouflage" (building parking structures that look like something other than a parking garage), they should consider the numerous opportunities for capturing ancillary sources of revenue. For example, owners/developers may incorporate retail/commercial space into the lower levels of their facilities, integrate for-rent marquees into facility walls, or lease or sell space to third parties. In some instances where land values are particularly high, owners may even be able to sell development rights to the extent that their parking facility fails to take full advantage of permissible development rights.

Tax Revenues

The public sector has a clear advantage over the private sector when it comes to revenue generation capabilities. In addition to the revenues generated by a facility and its related enterprises, the public sector can potentially tap various tax revenue sources. From a lender's perspective, the preferred source of tax revenue is the ad valorem property tax, which is levied on all properties within the corporate boundaries of a jurisdiction. The pledge of property tax revenues may be limited or unlimited in amount, although investors prefer an unlimited pledge. For any given issuer of debt, the property tax is the strongest financial pledge an issuer can make in the absence of a credit enhancement.

Special assessments are often a limited form of the ad valorem tax. In cases where specific parties benefit from a particular public improvement, the public jurisdiction can sometimes charge the benefited parties for the cost of that improvement. That is, whereas ad valorem taxes are levied across an entire community, special assessments are usually imposed on a smaller number of taxpayers within a given location in a given jurisdiction. In the eyes of investors, the narrowed tax base associated with a special assessment marginally decreases the value of the revenue stream. Sources of tax revenue include ad valorem (property); special assessment; tax increment; and sales (general, gross receipts, hotel/motel, lodging, amusement, and so forth).

A popular revenue source for financing a parking facility built in support of an economic development project is tax increment(s). In fact, the public sector often works with the private sector to foster economic development. Thus, a successful economic development venture can increase the public sector's underlying tax base such that the marginal increase of future tax receipts over current tax receipts constitutes an "incremental" increase in tax revenues. Some states allow public jurisdictions to use the incremental increase as a pledged revenue source. The value of a tax increment stream is a function of the type of tax pledged. A general property tax is more stable than an entertainment tax. A sales tax on all goods and services is more stable than a tax imposed solely on a discretionary purchase such as cigarettes or hotel rooms.

Frequently, there is a nexus between the type of tax and the facility to be financed. For example, an entertainment tax may be used to support construction of a garage adjacent to a stadium or arena. By its nature, however, an entertainment tax is less secure than a sales tax imposed on all purchases within a community. A hotel/lodging tax is a popular tax because it is imposed on visitors to a community and thus represents new money to the community. The breadth of a sales tax determines its relative worth in the eyes of a lender. The broader the base, the more stable is the tax.

How Do I Evaluate the Value of a Revenue Stream?

Key Revenue Pledge Considerations

Four key factors should be considered in determining the merits of a particular revenue source: amount, stability, ability to increase, and ability to pledge legally.

Amount. Lenders are concerned about the absolute amount of pledged revenues. If a loan requires payments of $20,000 per month, the proposed revenue source must obviously generate at least that amount of capital. At a minimum, lenders want pledged revenues to cover the cost of operations and maintenance plus debt service. Ideally, monies should also be available to finance ongoing capital repairs to the facility and to provide the owner with a return on investment. When a facility's revenue is the primary source of pledged revenue, lenders want the facility to generate a high level of excess revenues (coverage requirement).

Stability. Lenders are also concerned about the stability of the pledged revenue stream and thus hedge themselves against revenue stream volatility by discounting the value of the pledged revenue. The most common form of discounting is the debt service coverage ratio or coverage requirement.

The ratio compares the amount of revenue available to pay debt service with the debt service itself. A ratio of 1:1 means that a dollar of revenue is available to pay a dollar of debt service. The higher the debt service coverage ratio, the greater protection the lender enjoys should the revenue stream experience some volatility. Coverage ratios have the added benefit of generating capital for reinvestment in a facility's physical plant.

Figure 19-4 illustrates the concept of stability. Assume for a moment $500,000 of pledged revenue to support a project. Further assume that operating costs are $200,000 while debt service is also $200,000. To preserve the revenue-generating capacity of the facility, the owner pays operating costs before debt service, leaving $300,000 of pledged revenues available for debt service payments. Stated another way, the ratio of $300,000 of revenue available to pay debt service to a required debt service of $200,000 (3:2) translates into a debt service coverage ratio of 1.5:1 or 150 percent.

FIGURE 19-4

ILLUSTRATIVE NET REVENUE DEBT SERVICE COVERAGE RATIO CALCULATION

Pledged revenue	$500,000
Operating expenses	($200,000)
Revenues available for debt service	$300,000
Debt service	($200,000)
Net income	$100,000
Debt service coverage ratio	150% (3:2)

Single parking facilities without revenue support beyond facility-generated revenues must frequently meet a stability test. To reduce the demand on cash flow, owners pledge additional sources of revenue that drive the debt service coverage ratio lower. For example, the debt service coverage ratio for a single facility might be 150 percent while that of a parking system consisting of multiple facilities and on-street meters might be only 125 percent. Owners sometimes create rate stabilization funds to hedge against a rate increase should the coverage ratio approach the legally required minimum.

Ability to Increase. Lenders want to know about the developer's legal and practical ability to increase revenues. In the case of a public owner/developer, the lender needs assurance that statutory authority will permit an increase in rates, fees, or charges so that the required debt service coverage ratio can be maintained. Moreover, even if a developer is authorized to increase a rate, fee, or charge, the amount of money generated by such an increase may be in question. For example, when the parking rates within a particular garage are already the highest in the city and the facility has surplus capacity, an increase in rates might push patrons to look for alternative parking arrangements. The developer may seek the counsel of an independent party as to the possible economic impact of potential increases in rates, fees, and charges.

Ability to Pledge Legally. After determining that revenues are sufficient, stable, and eligible for increases, lenders want to be assured of the developer's legal authority to pledge such revenues. This point seems self-evident; a pledged revenue stream has value only if the borrower has the legal right to make such a pledge. Another important consideration is the developer's position relative to the claim others might have on a particular revenue stream. A lender prefers a superior or parity claim on a revenue stream over a subordinate claim. If the claim is subordinate, the lender will safeguard its investment by discounting the value of the pledged revenue stream (by imposing a higher coverage ratio) and seeking a greater return on investment (a higher interest rate) as compensation for assuming greater default risk.

Feasibility Studies

A parking feasibility study determines the projected functional and financial feasibility of a proposed development and provides the basic evidence with which to attract investor interest and public support. The study is often essential just for gaining access to the capital markets. The obvious exception occurs when historic revenue numbers are sufficient to cover any proposed new debt service or the proposed debt service is to be paid from ad valorem tax receipts.

What Financing Structures Are Available to the Private Sector?

Taxable Financing Structures

The financing options available to private parking operating companies or private developers of parking facilities are more numerous than those available to local governments. Usually, private developers are restricted in their financing options only by the economics of the project and the prevailing appetite of the investor market. In contrast, public developers are constrained by the statutory authorizations that govern various debt instruments.

In the event that a large, creditworthy parking company or development company elects to place its corporate credit behind a standalone parking project, it increases the range of possible financing options. The choice of one option over another depends on a thorough economic analysis of the proposed project, the interest rates charged in the market, and the company's overall fiscal policies.

The ownership of private parking facilities has been characterized as another aspect of the real estate business. Indeed, the acquisition, financing, and ownership considera-

tions of the private parking industry largely mirror those of the real estate business, although parking facility operation is a business unlike any other.

Private Developer Financing

If a proposed parking facility is part of a new development, the level of occupancy by potential tenants will influence the project's financial feasibility. For example, the developer of a project with significant amounts of retail space may seek one or more major anchor tenants that will contribute toward amortizing the project's permanent loan. For large office projects, the developer may seek one or more major tenants (that will finance a large share of the facility) and then prelease a large portion of the space before seeking project financing. Developers of less speculative developments may already have entered into an operating and/or management agreement or may even have executed a lease with the major tenant that provided the basis for the project concept and that guarantees a minimum level of parking revenues. Regardless of the method of financing selected by a private developer, a well-prepared economic feasibility study is necessary for seeking financing for a proposed parking facility. In addition, a lender may require a study of the underlying commercial venture. The projected cash flow of the overall private development is significantly affected by the analysis presented in the parking feasibility study.

Conventional Debt/Equity

A distinguishing feature of publicly versus privately financed projects is the need for equity in the transaction. Whereas the public sector may be able to obtain 100 percent debt financing, a private developer most often must provide anywhere from 20 to 40 percent of project costs in equity. In other words, no more than 60 to 80 percent of a project can be financed. The required debt service coverage ratio is then a function of the equity contribution: the higher the equity, the lower the ratio. Loan terms are usually for seven, ten, 15, or 20 years with 20-, 25-, or 30-year amortizations. The most common private deal is a ten-year loan with a 20-year amortization of the debt. Interest rates are frequently indexed from U.S. Treasuries.

The private developer's choice of financial structure for a new parking facility is an integral part of the development decision-making process and can have a major effect on profitability. Developers may choose among a variety of financing alternatives that differ markedly from both a cash flow and legal perspective. It may be assumed that the developer will seek affordable financing that maximizes the expected rate of return on equity. In the process of obtaining financing, a private developer may also seek equity investors, perhaps through a limited-partnership investment group or through the project's major tenants. The private sector financing instruments for an income property that are available in today's marketplace are commercial mortgage—

backed securities (CMBOs); so-called thrift deals that feature negative amortization plus participations; pension participation deals with developer or lender priorities; real estate investment trusts (REITs); and land sale/leasebacks.

Despite the infinite variation on each type of financing instrument, the basic structures are applicable to most categories of income-property development.

Selecting the Best Alternative

Unfortunately, the process of selecting a financial instrument is more complicated than merely choosing the option that is expected to yield the greatest after-tax cash flow. In particular, cash flow must be adjusted to reflect both timing and relative risk. An investment decision rule that explicitly adjusts for the timing of the expected cash flow is net present value (NPV) in which future payments are discounted to a current value by using an assumed interest rate. Evaluating the risk that a future payment will in fact occur is a more complicated process necessitating the evaluation of the source of the revenue stream.

One facet of the risk assessment process is simplified to some extent because operating cash revenues do not vary with the method of debt financing. The method and amount of debt financing do, however, affect both before- and after-tax cash flows as well as their variability (risk). For example, while a higher loan-to-value ratio may increase the expected return on a project, the increased leverage heightens the sensitivity of after-tax returns to variations in expected operating cash flows and potential sales prices. Therefore, what should be the expected return on a more heavily leveraged financing alternative to compensate for the increased risk of the developer's equity position? The answer depends directly on the developer's perception of how likely the project will achieve projected income levels.

Although some methods of financing may appear to be more attractive, no financial structure is invariably the best. Available terms change on a weekly and even daily basis. Furthermore, lenders who prefer a specific financial structure may not be interested in a particular project. For example, a thrift deal may be available for an office building but not for a parking garage. Thus, the developer may have limited choices for a particular project type or location.

Negotiation Points

The increasing complexity of financing structures means that many different deal points must be negotiated. Figure 19-5 lists the most common negotiation points associated with the financing alternatives considered above.

A developer who is able to estimate the lender's expected yield can predict which negotiations are most likely to succeed. For instance, under some assumptions, a bullet loan may appear to be the least attractive alternative for both the developer and the lender; thus, it is unlikely that negotiations will produce a bullet loan agreement that is satisfactory to both parties. Which deal is best for the parking devel-

FIGURE 19-5

NEGOTIATION POINTS— PRIVATE SECTOR OFFERINGS

Loan amount

Interest rate

Origination fee

Loan term

Years of interest-only payments

Amortization term

Prepayment penalty

Annual cash flow participation to lender

Annual cash flow threshold priority to borrower (or lender)

Reversion participation to lender

Preferred return to lender (or borrowers)

Whether unpaid preferred returns are cumulative

Terms of land sale/leaseback

oper can best be determined by a comparative analysis of cash flows and careful consideration of the different risks presented under each financing structure.

What Financing Structures Are Available to the Public Sector?

Bond financing of public facilities by local government is governed by state statutes in all states and frequently by charters and/or local laws as well. As an example, some states do not permit local municipalities to issue revenue bonds for parking facilities. Other states are more flexible and permit parking facilities to be financed with revenue bonds, special-district bonds, tax-increment bonds, and a variety of lease-purchase obligations.

It is generally presumed that if a public developer is issuing debt, the bonds are tax-exempt. The public developer must, however, meet highly specific tests in order to receive an exemption from federal income taxation. The chief advantage of a tax-exempt designation, other things being equal, is a reduction in interest rates of about 1.5 percent (for example, from a 6.5 to a 5 percent interest rate) or, in the language of the industry, a savings of 150 basis points. The amount of the spread varies over time as market conditions and tax laws change.

The financing structures that a public developer may use to fund the capital cost of new parking facilities can be grouped into four categories that relate to the proposed source of debt repayment. The first category is tax-backed obligations, the most common of which are general obligation bonds. The second category is revenue bonds, with parking revenue bonds the most common type. The third category is "double-barreled" obligations that are backed by a defined revenue source in the first instance and, in the second instance, an ad valorem or general fund pledge if the revenue source is insufficient to cover debt service. The final category is lease obligations. Finally, there may be selected opportunities for government grants.

Tax-Backed Obligations

In 1812, New York City reportedly became the first U.S. city to issue bonds secured by property taxes. Bonds pledged against property taxes are regarded by many as the most secure investment next to U.S. Treasury bonds. Historically, the sale of general obligation bonds has been the principal method used by localities to fund infrastructure improvements, although the use of such bonds to finance publicly owned parking garages has become increasingly problematic. Competition for scarce property tax dollars coupled with an "antiproperty-tax-increase" environment has caused many municipalities to tap other sources of tax (and nontax) revenue to fund the construction of new parking facilities.

General Obligation Bonds. Statutes in all states govern municipalities' issuance of general obligation bonds for financing parking facilities or any other capital project. Many such statutes govern the specific terms of general obligation bond issues with respect to the bonds' maximum term, annual principal requirements, redemption provisions, and method of sale. In addition, most states authorize municipalities to issue bond anticipation notes in expectation of permanent funding, thus permitting municipalities to ascertain the final costs of construction of a capital project before they issue long-term bonds. Many states require general obligation bonds to be offered through a competitive public bid process. Some states even mandate a majority vote of the electorate before the affected governing body enacts the required authorizing bond resolution. The laws of the particular state in which the general obligation bonds are to be issued should be reviewed with knowledgeable bond counsel early in the financing process to ensure compliance with all applicable statutes.

For any given municipality, general obligation bonds carry the lowest possible interest rate or cost of borrowing. With the full faith and credit of the municipality pledged to the repayment of bonds, the interest rate reflects the best a municipality has to offer. The only way for a municipality to improve on its own full-faith-and-credit pledge is to purchase a credit enhancement device such as municipal bond insurance. Insurance achieves an AAA credit rating for a given bond issue; few municipalities in the United States possess a comparable rating.

Municipalities must, however, take care when issuing general obligation bonds intended to finance parking facilities. Not only must the issuer adhere to the public-purpose provisions of the 1986 Tax Reform Act and subsequent amendments in order to preserve the tax-exempt status of its issue, but a local government must also consider the implications of adding the new bonded indebtedness to its already outstanding statutory debt. Furthermore, the municipality must comply with its own fiscal policies with respect to other, nonrevenue-producing capital improvements.

Special-Assessment Bonds. In some states, municipalities have the ability under some statutes to issue special-assessment obligations; in other states, such obligations bear the full faith and credit of the issuing municipality. A special-assessment bond is payable primarily from a special assessment levied within a specific benefit district. The special assessment is imposed over and above the regular property tax. Special-assessment districts created by a governing body to finance a parking facility usually encompass a downtown area whose property owners will benefit from the presence of the facility. Special-assessment financing is more prevalent in the far western and midwestern states. In the East, for example, the statutory authority to issue special-assessment bonds only recently became available in the states of Maryland and Virginia.

The credit implications of special-assessment financing largely depend on the size and extent of the special-assessment district and the district's ability to levy an unlimited tax assessment on property owners. If, as is the case in some states, the general obligation of the municipality is pledged in addition to the special assessment, then the credit enhancements mentioned above are moot. Frequently, property owner opposition to the formation of a special-assessment district relegates special-district financing to oblivion.

Tax-Increment Bonds. Tax-increment financing has been used primarily in Arizona, California, Florida, Illinois, and Minnesota but, where authorized pursuant to implementing state statutes, may be used in many other states as well. Tax-increment bonds are payable from a highly segregated form of ad valorem property tax usually levied on properties within a specified area of a municipality. The bonds are used in conjunction with major urban renewal or development projects of usually not less than one square city block and frequently much larger.

By ordinance, a municipality establishes a base-year property assessment within the tax-increment area. Any increase in the property assessment over the base-year assessment as a result of planned urban development becomes the basis for segregating tax collections (at the regular tax millage) for the payment of tax-increment bonds. In some states, the legislation authorizing tax-increment bonds requires the full faith and credit of the municipality to be pledged against such bonds in the event that the tax-increment receipts are insufficient to meet bond debt service. Tax-increment bonds secured by a municipality's full faith and credit should carry the same credit rating as the community's general obligation bonds.

Tax-increment bonds not enhanced by the full faith and credit of the municipality may have a distinctly different credit standing. The following problems could arise:

- If tax-increment bonds are issued too early in a new project's development schedule, the investor bears the risk that the developer may fail to construct the scheduled development as planned.
- If the area designated for imposition of the incremental property tax is limited to a single developer's single development project, the security of the tax-increment bonds becomes an obligation of the developer, good or bad, and may jeopardize the tax exemption of such bonds under the 1986 Tax Reform Act as amended.

A new parking facility to be financed by a municipality's tax-increment bonds should be of a size and in a location that will serve an area larger than one development project. Before issuing tax-increment bonds, the issuer of the bonds should wait until the primary development project is well under construction, with financing commitments sufficient for project completion.

Other Tax-Backed Obligations. A variety of other tax-backed obligations could be issued to fund the public sector's construction of a public parking facility. Obligations include sales tax bonds, lodger's tax bonds, gross receipts tax bonds, and amusement tax bonds, to name a few. The characteristics of the various obligations' revenue stream make their issuance more analogous to revenue bonds.

Revenue Bonds

Revenue bond financing for public purposes began in the United States in 1897 when Spokane, Washington, issued $350,000 of waterworks revenue bonds. Spokane's motivation for pioneering a new type of public financing was identical to the impetus for the subsequent expansion of revenue bond financing throughout the country, namely, the evasion of legal restrictions governing the issuance of general obligation tax bonds or the necessity of imposing ad valorem property taxes to pay for such bonds. During the 1930s, the Great Depression was instrumental in significantly expanding the use of revenue bond financing. Cities and states with severely depressed tax budgets turned to self-supporting, user-charge methods of financing capital expenditures for public works. Currently, revenue bond financing of all types constitutes about 70 percent of the nation's total annual volume of new tax-exempt bond issues.

Today's market generally does not accept parking revenue bonds secured by the revenues from a single, stand-alone, publicly owned parking facility. Instead, parking revenue bonds are marketable only if clear, irrefutable evidence indicates the existence of an adjacent traffic generator of such magnitude to produce debt service coverage from net revenues of close to 1.5 times current market rates for parking. Lacking a traffic generator, parking revenue bonds require some other form of host public subsidy or guarantee to garner market acceptance.

Parking system revenue bonds (payable solely from parking revenues) are usually secured by a variety of parking facilities within a municipality, including off-street garages and lots and on-street meters. Given a reasonable history of efficient operation, sound enforcement practices, adequate market rates for parking, and reasonably protective covenants in the bond resolution or trust indenture, pure system parking revenue bonds for a system of facilities can be marketed at acceptable rates. A facility's revenue history should show coverage of annual debt service (including debt service for the proposed new financing) from net revenues of at least 1.3 times the debt service in each of the preceding three years. Revenue projections, including projections for the new facility to be financed, should show annual net revenue of between 1.25 and 1.5 times the annual debt service over the projected life of the new bonds.

In any type of public revenue bond financing for parking projects, a well-prepared economic feasibility study is a prerequisite to the bond sale. The study may be required to prove the economic viability of a parking revenue bond issued for a system of facilities and thereby ensure an investment-grade credit rating.

For public projects with benefits not directly measurable in dollars, a cost-benefit analysis that is part of the feasibility study is essential for evaluating project worth above costs. Certain public-involved parking projects may specifically require a cost-benefit analysis to identify direct benefits to the community in exchange for any public subsidy. Even when a municipality issues general obligation bonds for a new parking facility, it should perform a cost-benefit analysis to demonstrate the extent of likely public benefits.

Double-Barreled Obligations

In several states, state law permits the issuance of bonds backed by a pledge of specific revenues complemented by an issuer's full faith and credit and unlimited taxing power; thus, the bonds are termed double-barreled obligations and are commonly referred to as general obligation revenue bonds. Their interest rate corresponds to an issuer's general obligation credit rating despite the pledge of repayment from a "revenue" stream. Owing to the pledged revenue source, the debt does not affect the issuer's tax rate or its general obligation credit rating unless the pledged revenue stream proves inadequate. In many states, tax-increment bonds often have the double-barreled backing of both revenues and unlimited taxing power.

Lease or Appropriation Obligations

An increasingly popular method of acquiring public parking facilities is through lease agreements, certificates of participation (COP) in a lease, installment purchase contracts, annual appropriation obligations, and, in some cases, lease revenue

FIGURE 19-6

CONDITIONS PRECEDENT FOR A SPECIFIC SALE METHOD

Competitive	Negotiated	Private Placement
Known credit	New issuer	Either issuer type
A or better credit rating	A or lower credit rating	Noninvestment grade
Conventional structure	Innovative structure	Innovative structure
Conventional security	Unusual security	Unusual security
Simple tax opinion	Complex tax opinion	Complex tax opinion
Strong market demand	Weak market demand	Limited market demand
Stable, predictable market	Volatile market	Market conditions irrelevant
Public financial information	Public financial information	Confidential financial information

bonds (hereafter referred to collectively as appropriation obligations). The popularity of appropriation obligations has grown as more public jurisdictions face debt limits or are required by their respective state laws to obtain voter approval of debt issues. The fundamental distinction between a debt and an appropriation obligation is the public body's term of commitment. With a debt issue, the developer enters into an irrevocable contractual arrangement, much like a mortgage, to make debt service payments for the full term of the contract. In contrast, appropriation obligations are often subject to a governing body's annual recommitment to appropriate funds. In the event the governing body fails to appropriate money to make the required payments, the investor can reclaim the leased item or other pledged collateral. Investors earn relatively higher interest as compensation for bearing the additional risk of nonappropriation. To protect themselves against the risk of nonappropriation, some investors invest only in projects that provide an essential public service or are overcollateralized.

Grants

It is difficult to generalize about grant programs other than to say that they are currently a diminishing source of funding for new parking facilities. The Transportation Equity Act for the 21st Century (TEA21) is about the only source of federal grant money. Several states operate isolated grant programs that must be approached from the perspective that they represent supplemental rather than primary funding sources.

Method of Sale

Public sector obligations are marketed in one of three ways: a competitive public sale, a negotiated public sale, or a private placement. Figure 19-6 shows the different aspects of these approaches. A competitive public sale involves publishing a notice of sale and accepting bids at a defined time and place. The notice of sale explicitly states the terms of sale. The more an investment vehicle resembles a commod-

ity, the more likely it will be sold competitively. Investment vehicles such as general obligation bonds or those backed by municipal bond insurance require little explanation by salespersons and thus are likely candidates for competitive sales. A chief benefit of a competitive offering is that it provides the developer with the highest degree of comfort that the offered securities received a "market rate" and that the greatest number of market participants had an opportunity to purchase the issuer's bonds. Occasionally, developers benefit from underwriters' overly aggressive bids for bonds. Such an event never occurs with a negotiated sale or a private placement.

A negotiated sale requires the developer to select an underwriter and to "negotiate" the obligation's terms and conditions of sale. The method is most frequently used in the case of a first-time market participant or a complex transaction that requires the salesperson to communicate a story to a prospective investor. Unlike a competitive offering, a negotiated sale permits the investment banking firm(s) to engage in a substantial presale effort. The more successful the presale effort, the lower is the borrowing cost to the developer. For both a competitive sale and a negotiated sale, essential materials about the developer are made available to the general public.

One of the challenges faced by most issuers of negotiated bonds is the successful negotiation of sale terms and conditions. By its very nature, a negotiated sale places most issuers at a competitive disadvantage because they are infrequent participants in the capital markets relative to their investment banker counterparts (the investment banker has better access to information). An issuer can, however, level the playing field by retaining the services of a financial adviser who possesses the industry knowledge to represent the issuer's interests effectively in the negotiation process.

For developers who wish to keep their financial information confidential or whose transactions are so complex that only the most sophisticated investors are suitable candidates for purchasing an offering, there is the private placement method of marketing securities. The private placement method is similar to a negotiated sale in every respect except that the pool of prospective investors is greatly reduced both in the initial (primary) and after-sale (secondary) markets. Reflective of the more limited dissemination of information to the market, the offering document is referred to as a private placement memorandum and is distributed selectively to a few investors. The reduced exposure to investors often results in above-market yields.

Negotiation Points

It is not uncommon for developers to focus on the borrowing rate and neglect the terms and conditions of sale. As the adage goes, "The devil is in the details." Depending on the sale method, the developer may need to negotiate the underwriter's compensation. In any event, the developer must agree to a host of covenants that will affect the daily operation of the facility, the ability to incur future debt, and the financial attractiveness of the project's cash flow. Figure 19-7 lists some of the terms, conditions, and covenants a developer is required to consider when contemplating the sale of a municipal security.

Selecting the Best Alternative

As with taxable financing alternatives, selecting the best method of tax-exempt financing is a complicated endeavor. The process of arriving at the best alternative begins when the developer clearly defines the project's objectives and limits. These objectives and limits then become the benchmarks or reference points against which the developer evaluates all successive decisions. A successful sale achieves the desired end within acceptable bounds.

How Does Federal Tax Law Affect My Decision-Making Process?

The 1986 tax law, its subsequent amendments, and the attendant Internal Revenue Service interpretations have had a major effect on the attractiveness of different methods of financing public and private parking facilities. The revised federal tax code eliminated parking as an activity for which tax-exempt industrial development bonds could be issued, placed severe restrictions on what constitutes a public purpose for municipalities, and repealed many of the tax benefits previously available to real estate investors. The tax law's current criteria affecting both tax-exempt and taxable financing are described briefly below. It is advisable to consult an attorney who specializes in federal tax law (referred to as bond counsel).

Tax-Exempt Financing

With the changes introduced by the 1986 tax law and its subsequent amendments, the determination of a proposed

---

FIGURE 19-7

NEGOTIATION POINTS— PUBLIC SECTOR OFFERINGS

Loan amount

Underwriter's compensation (negotiated sale or private placement only)

Years of interest-only payments and amount of capitalized interest

Amortization schedule

Loan term

Interest rates (negotiated sale or private placement only)

Optional redemption dates and prepayment penalty

Capital replacements

Rate covenant/debt service coverage ratio

Additional bond test

Debt service reserve requirement

Insurance requirements

Maintenance covenant

Operating reserve requirement

Priority of debt

Continuing disclosure requirements (beyond federal mandates)

---

project's tax status must be contemplated early in the financing process. The law clearly distinguishes between what may be financed with tax-exempt bonds or leases and what must be funded with taxable financing. Developer ignorance of the law could affect a project's eligibility for tax-exempt financing. The terms and termination period are shown in Figure 19-8. In brief, the criteria for tax exemption from federal income taxes follow:

- *Public use.* Not less than 90 percent of the available spaces in a financed project must be available to the general public on a daily, monthly, or yearly basis exclusive of government or nonprofit institutional users.
- *Use of bond proceeds.* Not less than 95 percent of total bond proceeds must be spent solely for the construction of public parking spaces, including soft costs related thereto.
- *Corporate guarantees.* Not more than 10 percent of the annual debt service of the financing may be paid for or guaranteed by a corporate or nonpublic entity on a long-term contractual basis.
- *Management agreements.* Any management agreement for the operation of a parking facility must be of limited duration, must provide for either a periodic flat fee or fixed percent of gross revenues, and must give the owner of the facility the option to cancel at

FIGURE 19-8

SUMMARY OF FEDERAL TAX FOR QUALIFIED
MANAGEMENT AGREEMENTS

Compensation Method	Term Not to Exceed	Termination After
50 percent periodic fixed fee	5 years	3 years
Capitation fee	5 years	3 years
Per-unit fee	3 years	2 years
Percent of fees charged	2 years	1 year

the end of a specified period depending on the compensation method.

In addition, an issue may qualify for exemption from income taxes imposed by the state in which the investor resides. An attorney knowledgeable of the laws of the particular state should be consulted.

Taxable Private Financing

The primary effects of the 1986 tax law and its subsequent amendments on the private financing of parking garages follow:

- *Income tax rates.* After December 31, 1987, the tax rate on ordinary income and capital gains for individual taxpayers does not differ. As a result, in terms of tax rate, capital gains from a real estate investment provide no advantage over ordinary income.
- *Passive loss provisions.* Generally, the law disallows both the deduction of passive investment losses against portfolio income and any type of nonpassive investment income (no deduction is allowed against other income of the taxpayer) and the use of credits from passive investments against taxes, other than those allocable to passive investments. Passive investments are defined as those for a trade or business activity in which the taxpayer does not materially participate as well as those for all rental activities. The passive loss provisions generally apply to individuals, estates, trusts, and personal service corporations.
- *Alternative minimum tax.* The law added a new alternative minimum tax (AMT) of 20 percent for corporations and expanded to 21 percent the alternative minimum tax for individuals. Under the law, if AMT income is greater than one and one-third times regular taxable income, an individual taxpayer is subject to the AMT. However, the law broadened the scope of the AMT with respect to permissible preferences and adjustments. Some of the more significant changes in the law that affect real estate transactions and investments in real estate limited partnerships

include calculation of depreciation on real property on a straight-line basis over as long as 40 years, with varying terms for other types of property and equipment; a prohibition against the use of the installment method for the disposition of rental property where the purchase price exceeds $150,000 (thus, the taxpayer must recognize the entire realized gain on the sale in the year of sale for purposes of calculating the AMT); and the application of the new passive loss provisions when computing the AMT.

- *Depreciation.* The 1986 Tax Reform Act retains the ACRS (Accelerated Cost Recovery System), but with substantial modifications. First, residential real property must be depreciated on a straight-line basis over 27.5 years and nonresidential real property on a straight-line basis over 31.5 years. A taxpayer may elect irrevocably to apply an alternative depreciation system by using a straight-line method over 40 years, in which case the depreciation for regular income tax and the AMT would be the same.

Moreover, a lessee is now required to recover the cost of lessee leasehold improvements over the ACRS recovery period of the improvement rather than over the real property's basic ACRS recovery period or the period remaining on the lease, whichever is shorter. The changes in ACRS depreciation under the 1986 law generally provide more favorable depreciation allowances for certain personal property, but less favorable allowances for real property.

Do I Need Collateral?

The capital markets have undergone a radical transformation in recent years. Twenty years ago, market access often hinged on the quality of the collateral that secured a financing. Today, however, public regulations governing the divestiture of assets make it difficult for some public jurisdictions to grant a security interest in a facility. In some cases of default, investors can prohibit the use of a facility but cannot take actual possession of the property. An additional difficulty is associated with public facilities as collateral. Many publicly owned assets have little private sector value, although public parking facilities may be the exception. Nevertheless, while in some cases developers grant investors a security interest in a facility, they more commonly grant a security interest in the pledged revenue stream.

Are There Other Ways to Improve the Credit Quality of Financing?

To provide an adequate level of security for debt obligations, it may be necessary for the borrower to pay for a private credit enhancement in addition to whatever the issuer may be willing or able to provide directly. Today, the two predominant forms of outside credit enhancement are municipal

FIGURE 19-9

MUNICIPAL INSURERS

Municipal Insurance Companies	Moody's	Rating Source Standard & Poor's	Fitch
Ambac Indemnity Corporation	Aaa	AAA	AAA
Financial Guaranty Insurance Company	Aaa	AAA	AAA
Financial Security Assurance, Inc.	Aaa	AAA	AAA
Municipal Bond Investors Assurance Corp.	Aaa	AAA	AAA
American Capital Access Financial Guaranty	not rated	A	A
Asset Guaranty Insurance Co.	not rated	AA	not rated

bond insurance for tax-exempt bonds and bank letters of credit for both tax-exempt and taxable obligations. Municipal bond insurance provides the highest credit ratings for a proposed financing, although bond insurers are inherently conservative in their approach to analyzing and securing credits (i.e., high coverage ratios and onerous additional bond tests). Letters of credit from commercial banks are even more expensive and provide a rating for the proposed bonds only as good as that of the letter-of-credit bank.

Bond insurance is commonly purchased for the entire life of an issue. In contrast, letters of credit are frequently limited to no more than seven years in accordance with federal banking laws, although they often contain "evergreen" provisions that automatically extend or renew the guarantee on an annual basis. Consequently, letters of credit are usually associated with variable-rate financing or bullet loans rather than with long-term fixed-rate financing.

Municipal Bond Insurance

In the early 1970s, the insurance industry began providing irrevocable insurance to issuers of tax-exempt municipal bonds. Because of the advantages to issuers in reducing the cost of borrowing in the marketplace, the municipal bond industry has grown to the extent that it insured more than 50 percent of all new tax-exempt bonds issued in 1999. Generally, when parking revenue bonds attain an investment-grade rating on their merits, municipal bond insurance proves economically advantageous.

Bond insurance guarantees the bondholder timely payment of principal and interest. The policy is granted to the municipal issuer only after careful analysis by the insurance company and in exchange for a premium that is exacted only once. As a condition for underwriting the insurance policy, insurance companies carefully scrutinize the security provisions as evidenced by the bond covenants. This greater scrutiny must be factored into the cost-benefit analysis (a present value comparison of the cost of the premium versus the reduction in interest rates) when the developer decides

on the merits of bond insurance or any other credit enhancement.

All insurance companies that write bond policies charge a premium based on a fixed percent of the total principal and interest payments over the life of the bond issue, less such amounts of interest as may be capitalized from bond proceeds. An integral part of the insurance policy is the reimbursement agreement between insurer and insured. The agreement sets forth the rates charged and the repayment terms for any draws on the policy. Six insurance companies currently provide bond insurance (see Figure 19-9).

Letters of Credit

A letter of credit is an irrevocable obligation of a bank for a specific period of time to make payments upon the demand of the entity to which the letter of credit is drawn, up to the total amount stipulated therein. It specifies the procedure to be followed to effect a drawdown of funds and the bank's procedure in paying the funds to the holder of the letter of credit. As noted, letters of credit often contain automatic renewal provisions upon termination of the original term subject to the bank's option to terminate by affirmatively notifying the holder. The holder of the letter of credit usually assigns the letter to the trustee bank named on the borrower's debt obligation.

A letter of credit is always accompanied by and made a part of a reimbursement agreement between the issuing bank and the entity to which the letter is drawn. The reimbursement agreement sets forth the application of the entity or "borrower" for the letter of credit, the granting of the letter of credit by the bank for a specific amount and term, the rates charged by the bank, and the obligation of the borrower to repay any amounts drawn down pursuant to the letter.

In the event of a drawdown by the borrower, the reimbursement agreement classifies the amount as an "advance." It also sets forth the obligation of the borrower to repay the advance at the bank's lending rate over a specified period and out of any monies available to the borrower. In effect, any such advance made to the borrower by the bank becomes a bank loan to the borrower.

What Determines Interest Rates?

In purely economic terms, interest rates are a function of the competition for investment dollars. The greater the competition, the lower the rate; the converse is also true. The more immediate issue is the rate at which a developer can borrow funds. All other things equal, borrowing cost reflects the borrower's credit rating.

Credit Ratings

Every municipality or authority planning the issuance of bonds for new parking facilities should supply at least two of the three major credit rating agencies with complete and extensive information on the new financing as early as possible in the financing process. The rating agencies require a formal application to commence their analysis for rating purposes, and their fees are commensurate with the time and effort expended. All three agencies discuss their rating conclusions with the issuer before they publish them. If the issuer disagrees with the rating, the agencies are available for a hearing and to examine any additional information made available by the prospective issuer.

There is an inverse relationship between bond ratings and the interest rate of a new issue: the higher the rating, the lower is the rate of interest. Thus, it behooves any municipal or public authority issuer of parking bonds to back those bonds with the highest degree of security that is legally and economically available. Investors place a great deal of faith in the bond ratings of Moody's and Standard & Poor's. And the "name of the game" in marketing the financing of a proposed parking facility is to create the highest degree of investor interest in the new bonds both before *and* after the sale. The most effective way to stimulate that interest is to obtain the highest rating possible.

What Is the Financing Process?

Generally, any financing involves five phases. The first phase is financial planning, and it requires the developer to determine the financial feasibility of the project with an eye toward the ultimate financing mechanism. For this reason, one of the developer's most important Phase I tasks is to retain the services of all needed financial professionals. If the project is to be supported by user fees, a parking professional versed in projecting demand, revenues, and operating and capital expenses should be retained to prepare a financial feasibility study. In addition, it is often advisable to engage the services of an independent financial adviser so that the project's cash flow models can be tailored to reflect the plan of finance. The structuring of a financially feasible project is an iterative process that involves the developer, finance professionals, and the parking consultant (discussed later). Project assumptions must be tested and refined to arrive at the optimal financing structure. The independent financial adviser reviews the financing options in light of available revenue streams and other project parameters and provides direction regarding the appropriate method of sale. If tax-exempt financing is contemplated, the developer should retain bond counsel to ensure compliance with federal tax law.

The second phase of the financing process is documenting the plan of finance. The complexity of the financing mechanism, the source of capital, and the method of sale all determine the time required to prepare the needed documents. A simple commercial mortgage loan is a much simpler transaction to document than a public offering of municipal revenue bonds.

Phase III is the credit enhancement phase. The developer, in consultation with the finance professionals, determines the economic benefit, if any, accruing from the purchase of a credit enhancement device. If the developer decides in favor of a credit enhancement, the finance professionals must prepare solicitation packages for distribution to potential providers. The finance professionals are then responsible for evaluating any provider responses. In the case of a public offering of securities, the developer or the financial adviser must also prepare an application and submission materials for the rating agencies.

The sale of securities or funding of the mortgage occurs in the fourth phase. For a competitive solicitation of interest, the finance professionals need to solicit and evaluate a negotiated or private placement sale method; the developer must agree with the underwriter on the final interest rate. The final phase is the closing, whereby documents are finalized and the project funded.

Is There Someone Who Can Help Me with This Process?

The Role of the Parking Consultant

Many parking administrators or corporate service officers may be able to determine the need for local parking, and a local architect may be able to design a structure in which to park cars. But it is a skilled and experienced parking consultant who plans and designs efficient parking facilities that respond to clients' financial requirements. Moreover, a parking consultant's role in planning and designing parking facilities has major implications for project financing. In these days of increased Securities and Exchange Commission vigilance concerning the disclosure of material facts about any new public or corporate financing, underwriters are obligated to investigate beyond the obvious forms of security and look into the use to which borrowed funds will be put. Lenders also are much more aware of how their money is to be spent. In the case of new parking facilities, both underwriters and lenders accept the technical expertise of a qualified parking consultant who can demonstrate that a proposed project is planned and designed to perform as anticipated. Clearly, over the last 40 years, the functional and detailed design of parking facilities has become a highly specialized technical art.

What has all this to do with the financing of parking facilities? Regardless of the method of financing a public or private parking facility, the developer must propose the most cost-effective facility possible in order to present to lenders the most attractive financial position possible. Given that lenders are concerned with the security of their investment, a parking consultant's estimates of demand, rates, and capital cost—and thus economic feasibility—are the single most important factors in the lending decision. If the borrower is a private developer or industrial corporation, management has a responsibility to produce a well-designed, operationally efficient parking project while remaining accountable to partners or shareholders. If the borrower is a municipality, elected officials and staff are ultimately answerable to the taxpayers (and voters), whether a project is financed with revenue or general obligation bonds.

The Role of the Finance Professional

The capital needs and economic risks associated with new parking investments have grown dramatically over the past 20 years. Technological changes, inflation, and the pressure of increasing economies of scale mean that many new parking investment undertakings are beyond the means of traditional bank financing techniques. As a result, the role of the finance professional—who assists both public and private owners of new parking facilities—has taken on great importance.

The term finance professional includes a variety of professional functions or services provided by a firm or individuals specializing in the development of funding that satisfies lender requirements while minimizing the cost and degree of effective recourse to the developer. A finance professional can assume many roles depending on the type of client (public or private), the type of offering to be made (public bid or negotiated sale), and the relationship of the professional to the client (underwriting or advisory). These various relationships include a financial adviser or consultant; a mortgage broker; an investment banker or underwriter; a merchant banker or owner/participant; and venture capital finders.

The financial adviser and mortgage broker perform a fiduciary function and do not themselves act as principals in the financing on their own account. The financial adviser or mortgage broker represents the interests of developers, acting as a business agent in the analysis, negotiation, structuring, and placement of financial transactions and in long-term capital planning and budgeting. Financial advisers may be investment bankers offering financial advice or independent financial advisers. While either is competent, an investment banker's views may be limited by what the banker's particular firm can sell, by a desire to negotiate the financing, or by

an inherent bias toward representing the interests of investors. In contrast, given that neither an independent adviser nor a mortgage broker buys or sells securities or mortgages, each one adopts the developer's perspective. An independent financial adviser or mortgage broker funds the transaction by turning to any number of prospective firms; thus, each one's view of financing options can be expansive. Each selects the firm whose services best match the developer's needs.

The investment banker and merchant banker perform client services on their own account. That is, by acting as principals in arm's-length transactions, they frequently offer advice to their clients in the process of developing a specific financing package. The primary function of an investment banker is to create investment opportunities for the firm's clients (investors). Similarly, the primary responsibility of a merchant banker is to find investment opportunities for the firm's capital. Venture capital finders often participate, along with the investors from whom they obtain commitments, by purchasing equity in the financing.

CHAPTER 20

PARKING FACILITY CONSTRUCTION COST ESTIMATION

Michael P. Schaefer

One of the most frequently asked questions of any parking consultant is, What will my new facility cost to build? An initial response requires some concept of project design. This chapter therefore establishes a standardized range of dollar values for the various cost categories associated with the design and construction of a new parking facility.

The ranges cover obvious differential factors affecting new construction such as efficiency (the number of square feet per parking space), type of construction (cast-in-place concrete versus precast concrete or structural steel), architectural treatments, method of finance, ownership, and so forth.

One major impediment to establishing a standard process is the effect of differential cost accounting across the industry. No two projects account for their costs in the same manner while individual projects frequently do not include all the costs associated with a new facility. Furthermore, the level of specificity required by an owner increases as the project moves from concept to reality.

What the industry needs is an accepted method for providing reasonable estimates commensurate with the user's need for specificity. In particular, the notion of using different estimating methods for different stages of project development makes intuitive sense. The specificity of a cost estimate required at the preliminary or predesign stage of a project differs from the specificity of information needed by an owner who chooses to proceed with construction and must arrange for financing. Unless the owner has deep pockets, the financial markets often require construction contracts to be executed simultaneously with financing documents. Accordingly, this chapter presents a sequential approach to cost estimation that reflects the five sequential project phases recognized by the American Institute of Architects Document B141: schematic design, design development, construction documents, bidding or negotiation, and construction contract administration.

The purpose of this chapter then is threefold. First, it provides both consultants and those proposing to build new facilities with a means of generating order-of-magnitude estimates of construction costs at project inception. As discussed later, construction estimates are but one part of a project's total costs. Second, it presents a comprehensive checklist from which to prepare a project budget; that checklist in turn guides a project through completion. Finally, the chapter demonstrates that the project budget checklist may serve as the basis for developing a method for tracking new facility costs industrywide.

Preliminary Estimates

The most commonly used index budget estimates in new parking facility construction deal with cost per parking space. An economical structure at the time of this publication would fall in the range of $7,500 to $10,000 per space. Some facilities have reported a cost per space in excess of $25,000 because they are below grade or span an interstate freeway. If the cost per space for an above-ground structure exceeds $12,000, the structure would probably be considered expensive. The costs of subterranean structures increase at a geometric rate with the depth below grade. The second story below grade is much more expensive than the first, and the third is even more. Between the figures for above- and below-grade structures is a great deal of gray area; a structure could be either economical or uneconomical for its given site and constraints.

Cost per Space

While the cost-per-space index allows for a direct comparison of total costs, it provides little insight into how or why a facility's costs vary from average. It is generally more helpful to look at two separate indices that combine cost per space. The first is parking efficiency, and the second is cost per square foot. Parking efficiency is floor area per parking space.

It is easy to understand that a significant difference in cost per space results when a parking structure requires 50 more square feet of floor area per parking space than an otherwise identical structure in the same locality. If both cost $20 per square foot to construct, the less efficient design will cost $1,000 more per space than the more efficient design. Likewise, if one structure costs $20 per square foot and another $25, the cost per space will differ dramatically. If both structures have an efficiency of 320 square feet per space, the more economical structure will cost $6,400 per space while the more expensive structure will cost $8,000 per space. The aggregate cost differential is even more dramatic when the costs are calculated facilitywide. Assuming a

500-space facility, the $6,400-per-space facility's total cost is $3.2 million versus $4 million for the $8,000-per-space facility. Obviously, a schematic design of the facility is required to determine efficiency. For this reason, most feasibility studies include a schematic design of the proposed facility.

Area per Space

Parking geometrics (dimensions of stalls, aisles, and so forth) as well as the efficient use of the site are both reflected in parking efficiency. Differences in geometrics between the 1970s and today can account for a 10 to 100 percent difference in facility efficiency depending on long or short spans between columns in parking bays and, in turn, cost per space. Among the biggest "gobblers" of parking efficiency are single-loaded parking bays—i.e., an aisle with parking stalls only on one side. Further, the design of the floor-to-floor ramp system can have an enormous impact on efficiency.

At least five other factors influence the area per space, including the following: type of uses, width of site, shape of site, single purpose versus mixed use, and code requirements.

Recognizing the several ways of defining floor area (net floor area, gross floor area, gross leasable area, net rentable area, and so forth), this discussion defines parking efficiency as gross parking area (GPA) divided by total parking capacity (spaces). Gross parking area is further defined as the sum of the floor area on each tier. It is calculated by using out-to-out of exterior walls less enclosed areas devoted to auxiliary uses, such as stair towers, elevator shafts, lobbies, and storage and equipment rooms. Any other uses such as retail or office space should also be excluded from GPA. The refinement of gross parking area ensures that the gross measure truly reflects the efficiency of the parking layout rather than palatial stair/elevator lobbies or storage/mechanical space that responds to specific project requirements. In fact, most building codes and industry groups such as the Urban Land Institute and the Institute of Transportation Engineers now use the gross area measure—as opposed to the net area measure inside exterior walls—for all floor area calculations/relationships.

Parking efficiencies in new construction today range from about 200 to 350 square feet per space for long-span construction with self-park design and sloping parking ramps for vertical circulation; the average is about 315 square feet per space. The lower end of the range is generally achieved only with aggressive designs that rely on a significant percent of small-car-only stalls; the higher end is usually limited to small, awkward sites, subterranean structures, or mixed-use facilities whose superstructure is enhanced to accommodate commercial, residential, or office space constructed above the garage.

When express ramps (without parking) are used for some or all of the vertical circulation, the area of an individual parking space, excluding ramps, remains at about 200 to 350 square feet; however, when the ramp area is figured into the GPA calculation, as it is in most cases, efficiency can range from 325 to 450 square feet per space depending on facility size and the extent of the express ramping. About the only time that express ramps are not included in the efficiency calculation is when circular helixes are used. Circular helixes significantly skew the calculation of both cost per square foot and efficiency per space such that the estimated cost for the helixes is added before calculating cost per space.

Short-span construction, often required in mixed-use facilities, adds 15 to 25 percent to the square footage of each space, increasing the individual space to 310 to 400 square feet for self-park designs and 350 to 500 square feet for designs with express ramps. Long-span construction means that columns occupy less of the parking area.

In addition to the design, the manner in which the parking facility is operated can have a significant impact on the area per space. For example, office-employee parking spaces —because of low turnover—or long-term parking spaces can be designed with less generous parking stall widths than retail-customer parking spaces. A narrow site may dictate a shallow angle of parking by precluding 90-degree parking, which is generally more economical in consumption of space per stall as described in chapter 8. An irregularly shaped footprint creates wasted areas within parking structures. Mixed-use facilities make less efficient use of space because of the need for infrastructure that supports several other uses. Finally, code requirements vary greatly from jurisdiction to jurisdiction, often failing to reflect state-of-the-art space requirements (i.e., wider spaces or aisles than current use or vehicle size parameters would dictate).

Cost per Square Foot

The second critical index in understanding cost efficiency is cost per square foot, which is defined as construction cost divided by GPA. The construction cost is the total sum paid to the contractor(s) for construction of the facility, including change orders issued during construction but excluding design fees and testing services (although the latter may be difficult to separate in design-build projects). Cost per square foot is affected by geographic location, the facility's number of levels, the shape of the site, topography, soil conditions, architectural treatment, and supporting infrastructure needs.

Cost per square foot reflects the facility's architecture and engineering, including, for example, amenities, security systems, and parking access and revenue controls; foundations and structural and durability features; and electrical/mechanical and plumbing systems. It also reflects local construction costs and practices and other special conditions such as extensive excavation, dewatering, and so forth. Construction of a simple, above-ground, open parking structure generally costs between $20 and $30 per square foot depending on

locality; amenities and architecture can easily add $5 to $15 per square foot (in current dollars).

Cost per square foot may vary dramatically from the above ranges for underground parking as well as for low-rise (only one supported level) and high-rise (eight or more levels) structures. The traditional rule of thumb for the incremental cost of underground parking is that each level below grade costs another increment of the cost of the level immediately above it. For example, if an above-ground parking structure costs $5,000 per space, the first below-grade level would cost $10,000 per space, the second $15,000, the third $20,000. Subsurface conditions, however, have a major impact on cost; therefore, it is impossible to project reliably the cost per space of underground parking without geotechnical information and other project-specific information.

High-rise structures generally require stand pipes, sprinkler systems, ventilation, and sometimes other features associated with life safety that can add $1 to $5 per square foot. Elevator costs depend on user needs, architectural treatment, and the amount of visible façade. Above-grade sites may require expensive retaining walls. The location of a proposed facility may even necessitate the construction of extensions to existing infrastructure, the cost of which the new facility may have to bear. In addition, construction costs and needs vary considerably by region. Northern snow states and coastal states must protect against salt impregnation, a problem unheard of in desert states.

While the cost-per-square-foot measure does not include land, development, design, and financing costs or required reserves (discussed later), an initial budget should include 20 percent or more as an add-on to basic contractor construction cost budget estimates.

The various considerations noted above make it difficult for users to compare costs for a parking structure with any simple industry standard or even just with budget costs. Further, the cost estimation technique already described deals only with construction costs; several other component costs must be factored into the final cost analysis.

Detailed Checklist

The specificity of any cost estimates must be greatly refined by the time the owner begins to seek financing. Therefore, project costs may be divided into seven broad categories: land costs, development costs, design costs, construction costs, other owner costs, financing costs, and contingencies. Rather than address each line item, the discussion focuses on the most frequently overlooked items.

Land Costs

Figure 20-1A itemizes the six components of land costs. The two areas that can significantly increase the land cost budget are special assessments associated with the site and the cost of environmental remediation.

FIGURE 20-1

A. LAND COSTS

Acquisition
Special assessments/charges
Closing costs
Site improvements and demolition
Environmental remediation
Other

B. DEVELOPMENT COSTS

Site feasibility analysis
Appraisals
Title and recording
Real estate taxes during construction
Utilities during construction
Insurance during construction
Legal/real estate
Legal/general
Audit/cost certification
Financial feasibility study
Predevelopment fees
Development consultant(s)
Relocation expenses
Historic preservation
Governmental oversight
Special-district formation
Marketing
Startup expenses
   Initial equipment
   Real estate taxes
   Insurance
   Working capital
   Initial operating deficit
Other organizational costs

C. DESIGN COSTS

Design fee
   Architectural
   Civil engineering
   Structural engineering
   Mechanical engineering
   Electrical engineering
   Landscape
   Interior special material
   Traffic/parking consultant
   Other consultants
Surveys
Geotechnical investigation
Environmental assessment
Additional site representation
   during construction
Allowance for redesign

during construction
Testing services during construction
Zoning variance

D. CONSTRUCTION COSTS

General conditions
   Builder's overhead
   Builder's profit
   Permits/fees/plan checks
   Municipal service charges
   Builder's risk
   Bond premium
Site improvements and demolition
Off-site improvements
Earthwork
Foundations
Structural system
Architectural treatment
Masonry
Miscellaneous metals
Wood and plastics
Roofing/waterproofing
Doors, windows, and glass
Stairs
Finishes
Specialties
Access control equipment
Furnishings
Special construction
Elevators/escalators
HVAC/ventilation
Mechanical/plumbing/fire
protection
Electrical/lighting
Security
Signage/marking
Tests during construction

E. OTHER OWNER COSTS

Owners/representatives
Construction manager
Tests during construction
Quality control
Owner-furnished equipment
   and fixtures
Fixtures and equipment
   (not included above)

F. FINANCING COSTS

Public/private financing
Financial adviser
Bond counsel

Issuer's counsel
Special tax counsel
Underwriter(s) fee/origination fee
Underwriter(s)/bank counsel
Rating agency fee(s)
Credit enhancement fee
Credit enhancement counsel
Issuance fees (local government)
Appraisal
Trustee and counsel fees
Accountant verification
Escrow agent
Paying agent
Registration
Printing
Inspection engineer
Miscellaneous fees

G. GRANT PROGRAM COSTS

Grant program-specific fees
Federal
State
Local
Grant writer fees

H. DEVELOPMENT AND CONSTRUCTION PERIOD INTEREST

Capitalized interest (gross)
or
Capitalized interest (net)*

I. RESERVES

Capital replacement reserve
Operating deficit reserve
Debt service reserve fund
Other required reserves

J. CONTINGENCIES

Land acquisition
Design
Construction
Other owner costs
Development
Financing
Undesignated

*Gross interest expense less interest earnings.

Development Costs

While private developers are usually aware of development costs, government entities often overlook them. Development costs range anywhere from 5 to 15 percent of total project cost and include early costs such as site feasibility analysis, financial feasibility analysis, development consultants, and general legal advice or assistance as well as expenses related to real estate taxes, utilities, insurance, and interim financing during the construction period (see Figure 20-1B). Development costs also include items such as relocation expenses, historic preservation costs, various government oversight fees, and any fees associated with the creation of any special districts, not to mention the expense of marketing a project to prospective customers. The marketing expense can be significant if the project includes mixed uses such as residential, commercial, or office space. Startup expenses for initial equipment, real estate taxes, insurance, working capital, and an initial operating deficit must also be budgeted.

Design Costs

Figure 20-1C outlines the design costs associated with a new parking structure. The first several items are usually included as part of a single design contract. Funds for geotechnical investigation, environmental assessment, and zoning variances are often absent from most budgets, but they can add up and should be included.

Construction Costs

The construction budget is fairly typical of most building construction; however, Figure 20-1D lists a few items that are unique to parking, including access control equipment and, particularly in the case of underground facilities, ventilation equipment. Parking also generally requires special security and signage.

Other Owner Costs

Over the years, the method of constructing new facilities has changed dramatically. Therefore, more and more jurisdictions now retain the services of a construction manager or a construction manager/general contractor to ensure cost containment and timely project completion. At the same time, increasingly stringent regulations require an extended battery of tests during construction as well as various quality control reviews, which can be the province of an on-site manager. A construction manager, designated project representative, and inspection agencies can assist the owner in ensuring that furnished equipment and fixtures are in place and that the project is constructed to plans and specifications within project quality controls. Another function of the construction manager is to identify fixtures or equipment that has been overlooked (see Figure 20-1E).

Financing Costs

Financing a parking facility on a private basis through a bank is relatively straightforward and generally requires the payment of an origination fee, an appraisal fee, and certain legal expenses. In contrast, the complexity of a public financing, especially with respect to the large number of participants, can be overwhelming (see Figure 20-1F). The sale of public securities necessitates the retention of an underwriter. If the securities are tax-exempt, the owner must retain the services of bond counsel. The underwriter provides financing and receives payment for its services—usually a discounted price on the issuer's obligations that are subsequently reoffered to investors at par (100 percent). Bond counsel offers an opinion that the issuer has complied with all state requirements and federal laws and that the obligations are therefore lawful obligations of the issuer. Bond counsel also opines on the tax status of the bonds.

Given that the underwriter's primary (ongoing) client is the investor, a financial adviser frequently represents the issuer's interests. The issuer may have its own legal counsel in addition to bond counsel. A special tax counsel may be retained if particularly difficult tax issues are related to the issue. The underwriter also retains the services of underwriter's counsel to ensure compliance with federal disclosure laws.

If the obligations are rated, a fee is paid by the borrower to each rating agency that reviews the transaction. Given that parking garages are often viewed as a poor investment risk for investors, the purchase by the borrower of a credit enhancement can help improve the project's creditworthiness. The purchase price usually covers the fee for both enhancement and the credit enhancer's counsel.

Generally, local government carries out a public financing transaction and therefore must often pay local fees charged by the conduit issuer. To consummate the transaction, local government must also pay a host of other fees to various parties responsible for overseeing the receipt and payment of receivables (trustee fees).

At one time, an abundance of federal, state, and local programs provided funds for the construction of parking facilities. With tight budgetary times, programs are growing fewer in number. Figure 20-1G outlines the costs of procuring grant monies. The payment of fees to either a grant writer or for participation in a grant program for the purpose of determining grant eligibility is a cost that often goes overlooked in a project budget.

It is often necessary to budget funds during construction to pay the interest expense during construction. Unless another source of revenue is available, the owner often finds it necessary to capitalize the interest costs during construction as shown in Figure 20-1H. In other words, the owner needs to borrow more money on either a gross or net basis. On a gross basis, the owner calculates the anticipated interest expense and borrows a like amount of funds. On a net basis, the owner calculates the anticipated earnings on construction proceeds and various reserve funds and subtracts the earnings to reduce the amount of money to be borrowed.

As noted, parking is generally viewed by the investment community as a relatively vulnerable investment. For this reason, lenders attempt to protect their investment by establishing a variety of reserve funds that might include a capital replacement reserve, an operating deficit reserve, a debt service reserve fund, and any other required reserve fund (see Figure 20-1I). The capital replacement reserve can often be built up over time. The operating deficit reserve is usually funded in anticipation of the fact that a newly opened facility is unlikely to achieve full occupancy at the outset of operation. Therefore, a certain amount of money is set aside to cover the projected deficit between operating expenses and operating revenues during a facility's early years.

Contingencies

The amount of funds set aside for each of the first six budget categories is a function of the soundness of project budget estimates and where the owner falls along the design phase continuum. Land acquisition contingencies, for example, are usually related to unanticipated additional environmental remediation costs. Specifically, it is not uncommon to set aside at least 10 percent of design and construction costs for land acquisition contingencies during the schematic design phase and to reduce that amount to only 5 percent once the construction documents are completed. Other owner and development costs vary greatly with the stringency of the owner's cost accounting. Consequently, the amount of money set aside for contingent expenses in Figure 20-1J can likewise vary. The financing cost is generally estimated fairly closely such that a large contingency reserve for financing is usually not required. Finally, it is often prudent to set aside a certain amount of undesignated funds as a function of total project costs.

Conclusion

The cost estimation methodology described in this chapter offers a systematic approach to moving from rough estimates developed at project inception to an actual budget that is formulated as a project's design elements are solidified. The checklists provide a comprehensive guide to the development of that budget and may even offer a database from which to benchmark more accurately the construction costs of new facilities.

CHAPTER 21
BIDDING METHODS

Kenneth Kowall, James E. Staif, Norman L. Goldman, and Larry Church

When embarking on a new parking project, owners or developers generally ask a series of questions about factors affecting its feasibility, including the following:

- What are the project's specific needs and requirements?
- Where will the project be located?
- How will the project be financed?
- What is the budget and when do hard costs need to be known?
- What are the priorities with regard to aesthetics, cost, time, and quality?
- Who will design it?
- Who will construct it?
- Who will manage the project during design and construction?
- Who will manage/operate the completed facility?

The answers to the first five questions and the last question may determine who will design and construct the facility and who will manage project construction. Other factors, such as the experience and qualifications of a specific individual or firm, may also determine the selection of project participants and thus the answers to the remaining questions

The process of selecting a design firm, construction firm, and construction management firm is known as the procurement process. No matter how the selection is accomplished, bidding for some items will be complicated. By definition, bidding is a response to terms and conditions specified by the owner or agents of the owner.

The most common bidding method is the traditional design-bid-build project delivery method, or conventional bidding. Normally, the selection of an architect or engineering firm (design professional) is based on qualifications and experience and a consideration of price or fees. Ideally, the firm should be a parking consultant (PC) firm with demonstrated experience in the design of parking structures. The PC firm helps the owner define the project scope, prepares detailed plans and specifications, and assists the owner in soliciting bid proposals from contractors. The project is then constructed in accordance with the PC's plans and specifications.

Another approach, generally restricted to private projects, is termed the construction management or management-at-risk method. It involves the selection of a project management firm to coordinate project design and construction. The owner interviews management firms early on and makes a selection based on qualifications, similar project experience, overhead costs, profit percentage, and a preliminary estimate of the probable construction cost. Once the firm is selected, it participates in the final production of drawings and specifications by undertaking value-engineering reviews and, during the design process, providing the owner with updated construction cost estimates. Ultimately, the project management firm provides a guaranteed maximum price (GMP) when all drawings and specifications are completed. Variations on this construction management approach are discussed later.

Still another approach is the design/build project delivery method. The owner, often with the assistance of an independent designer or preselected designer/builder, assembles information that describes the scope and requirements of a project and then solicits construction proposals from design/build teams. The selected team prepares the final plans and specifications and constructs the project for a fixed price.

Other, more progressive approaches such as design-build-finance-operate go beyond project design and construction and extend to operations and financing. For completed projects, the use of leaseback and public/private lease purchase agreements is gaining prominence.

Conventional Bidding

Conventional bidding (design-bid-build), shown in Figure 21-1, remains the most common method of construction procurement. The owner identifies a need for a project and then selects a design professional to design the project. Often, however, the owner retains a PC before selecting the design professional. The PC undertakes various need and feasibility studies to determine or define more clearly the owner's needs or to investigate the financial feasibility of the proposed endeavor. The PC then completes the design, soliciting feedback from the owner at various intervals. The PC periodically estimates construction costs and works with the owner to define and maintain the project budget.

In its purest form, conventional bidding requires all drawings and specifications to be 100 percent complete

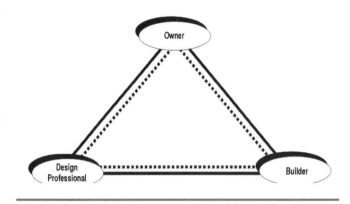

FIGURE 21-1

DESIGN-BID-BUILD OR NEGOTIATED SELECT TEAM

before they are made available to contractors for bidding on the construction phase of the project. The theory is that the owner selects the contractor that offers the lowest responsive price. With the help of the PC, the owner evaluates the bids and then selects and contracts directly with a contractor for construction of the project. Private owners are not required to accept the lowest bid, although various government regulations often require public owners to do so. At the least, public owners should prequalify contractors to eliminate firms that are ineligible based on experience, size, or financial considerations. The PC remains involved in the project to review shop drawings and monitor construction on behalf of the owner.

Conventional bidding has generally worked well, especially for public projects; in particular, it almost entirely eliminates the possibility of subjective evaluations during the selection process. The owner reviews and approves the final design before committing construction dollars and is secure in the knowledge that the PC will act as agent and adviser through completion of the project. Nonetheless, the several potential downsides related to conventional bidding have led to variations and alternative procurement methods. Design/build, for example, offers the possibility of cost savings as well as a faster schedule, with less hassle and financial risk to the owner as a result of separate design and construction contracts, which are standard in conventional bidding.

Negotiated Contracts

Even with prequalification, the low-bid contractor may not offer the owner the best quality or value. The contractor may try to "cut corners" or secure unjustified extras to compensate for the low bid. In some cases, negotiated contracts for construction, at least for private owners, have proven more successful.

With most negotiated contracts, the owner hires a designer, usually a PC. In this case, however, the PC prepares only schematic or preliminary drawings and outline specifications. The drawings, which describe the scope and quality of construction in general terms, are distributed to contractors invited to submit proposals, quote a price, and state the scope of their anticipated work.

The owner then selects a contractor based on several factors, including cost, completeness of the proposal, trust, and capability. Yet, the owner often reserves the right to call in another contractor if the size or complexity of the project warrants. The owner's designer then prepares detailed construction documents while the selected contractor often provides input to help control budget costs. Upon completion of the construction documents, the contractor reconfirms the earlier estimated construction cost. If all terms are acceptable to both the owner and contractor, the two parties execute a formal construction contract.

Fast Track

As the pace of society increases and project schedules compress, it is not always possible to wait until all drawings are 100 percent complete to award a construction contract. The fast-track method responds to the need for accelerated scheduling of project design and construction.

Fast track is a bidding method that lies somewhere between conventional bidding and design/build. Typically, as portions of the structure's design are completed, they go out separately for bid and are normally awarded to specialty contractors (foundation, superstructure, mechanical/electrical/plumbing, and so forth), thus speeding the start of construction. Fast tracking can, however, cause problems if the final design of later project components affects earlier components already awarded and possibly under construction. Moreover, if a large project involves several prime contracts, the owner might face additional administrative and coordination responsibilities. Thus, the construction manager was born (discussed later).

Issue for Pricing

Another variation on conventional bidding is called issue for pricing. It involves preparation of the design drawings to between 50 and 90 percent of completion before releasing them for bid. The drawings are then completed while the bidding, award, and shop drawing phases are underway. As with the fast-track approach, issue for pricing allows the schedule to be accelerated, but it also runs the risk that changes occurring after the award of the construction contract may cause the contractor to make a significant claim for additional compensation or construction time. Issue for pricing may work well on routine projects with contractors, design professionals, parking consultants, and owners who are familiar with each other and the type of project to be designed; however, it can lead to misinterpretation in the case of unique or complex projects or when the design pro-

fessional, contractor, or owner is unfamiliar with the type of structure under construction.

Construction Management

Construction management is about managing the entire building process, including planning and design, and should therefore be more appropriately called project management. For any project, the range of tasks to be accomplished extends to cost estimating and control, project scheduling, selecting appropriate systems, assessing market conditions, optimizing contractor and product selection, reviewing constructability concerns, and managing various other construction functions.

Traditionally, the design professional, the general contractor (GC), or both have performed the above tasks and continue to do so for many projects. But certain factors such as the development of fast tracking, ever-changing technology, and the specialization of private enterprise in general has led to the need for the independent construction manager (CM). Typically involved in larger or particularly complex projects, the construction manager brings together and coordinates design, construction, and administration so that the three functions work in harmony to produce the best result. To ensure the desired result, the CM must be brought on board early in the project.

Advantages and Disadvantages

When used correctly, construction management can reduce the owner's management burden, especially if multiple prime contracts are involved in a project. The CM can act as a liaison between the designer and contractor(s) to resolve differences and bring specialized knowledge to the team with respect to market conditions and any new technologies that may influence the selection of systems. The CM can also help avoid duplication of responsibilities, minimize the risk of project cost overruns, and accelerate the project schedule through the use of fast tracking, multiple prime contracts, and budget pricing. It should be noted, though, that unprofessional or poorly trained construction managers can become a bottleneck in communications, represent an unnecessary cost, or, at worst, supplant owners' interests with their own.

Contractual and Financial Relationships

The three basic CM relationships are CM as adviser, CM as agent, and CM as constructor. The CM as adviser in effect enters into an independent consulting contract with the owner to perform certain functions, some of which may be deleted from the PC, design professional, and contractor contracts. The CM is not, however, at financial risk for the overall cost of the project.

The CM as agent acts in a similar fashion to the CM as adviser except that the CM holds the contracts of the PC or design professional and contractor(s), thus insulating the owner and making decisions on the owner's behalf. In this role, the CM assumes some legal and possibly some financial risk related to the various pass-through contracts, but the risk is not related to the final cost of construction.

The CM as constructor is in effect the GC and therefore may subcontract for all or part of the usual GC services. While the construction manager (constructor) does not have direct contact with the design professional as is true in design/build arrangements, the CM does bear financial risk related to final construction cost. Among the possible financial arrangements are cost plus fee, guaranteed maximum price (GMP), partial GMP with exclusions, and a cost-plus-fee target price with incentives and penalties.

As both adviser and agent, the CM is contractually acting in the owner's interest but as a constructor. Contractually, the CM acts solely or partly in his or her own interest. The role differs from that of CM as adviser in that the constructor, as the owner's legal agent, has direct contact with and responsibility for the designer and builder as in a true design/build arrangement. This delivery method increases the risk to the contractor but also proportionately increases the financial reward. Independent construction management has succeeded and continues to work well in conjunction with fast tracking and the use of multiple prime contracts, especially in the case of complex or large projects. Figures 21-2 through 21-4 illustrate the various types of CM delivery methods for a project.

Traditionally, the construction manager as agent has been the most common construction management arrangement for parking garages, with the contractor as the lead firm. In part, the reason for the predominance of the arrangement is that the dollar value of construction services is much greater than design fees. Furthermore, some states require the designer/builder to have a contractor's license, thereby making it more difficult to subcontract the construction versus design portion of the work. In addition, some professional liability policies exclude coverage when the PC or design professional has an ownership interest in a project. Designer-led design/build is possible but has been slow to catch on.

Benefits

Design/build offers both the owner and the project several possible benefits. First, the owner negotiates and administers only a single contract and relies on only one source of responsibility for completion. A single source of responsibility can be particularly beneficial in preventing owner involvement in contract disputes between designer and builder, especially given that such disputes often lead to delays and additional costs. This does not mean, however, that the possibility of disputes between owner and designer/builder is eliminated.

Second, design/build can yield substantial time savings in that design and construction efforts can be overlapped. Depending on specific circumstances, such as level of owner involvement, time of year, building permit submission

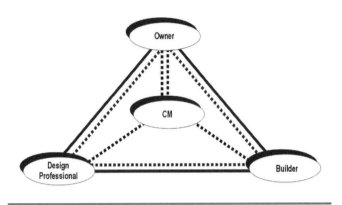

FIGURE 21-2

CONSTRUCTION MANAGER AS ADVISER

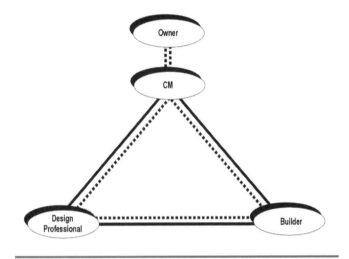

FIGURE 21-3

CONSTRUCTION MANAGER AS AGENT

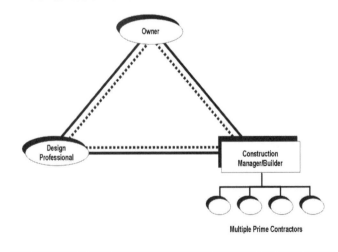

FIGURE 21-4

CONSTRUCTION MANAGER AS CONSTRUCTOR

requirements, and so forth, the savings in time can and does vary. Other building methods such as fast tracking may provide similar time savings.

Third, design/build can mean still additional cost savings if both designer and contractor, each with specialized knowledge that the other may not have, collaborate on innovative and cost-effective solutions to issues that arise during project development. Collaboration also eliminates some duplication of effort in cost estimating, administration, and so forth.

Risks

For all its advantages, design/build poses some potential risks. For example, because a design is not completed at the time the designer/builder is selected and the contract and price negotiated, the owner relinquishes some control in reviewing and commenting on the design as it progresses. In particular, the owner can request changes but risks additional charges for modifying portions of the project already constructed. Nonetheless, the owner can take steps to minimize the risk of additional construction costs. First, a thorough Request for Proposal (RFP) should be prepared, including preliminary design drawings and specifications. Second, the selected proposal should be thoroughly evaluated, particularly with respect to conformance with the stated criteria. Changes and clarifications can be requested at this time. Third, the owner can authorize the selected designer/builder to proceed with the design work only until such time that the affected parties agree on the design. If changes to the proposal are necessary, adjustments to the contracted price can be made without reworking any of the already completed construction.

With design/build, the designer no longer acts in the traditional role of owner's agent. As part of or as a subcontractor to the designer/builder, the designer is now obliged to advance the interests of the designer/builder. The designer is in the legal sense a vendor, not an agent, and thus has different rights and responsibilities. In this context, an owner should take appropriate measures to select a designer/builder based on qualifications and reputation as well as on price and then select a team headed by an eligible designer. If necessary, the owner should hire a consultant to initiate the preliminary design, to evaluate proposals, and later to monitor the designer/builder. Finally, the owner might consider construction inspection services provided by an independent firm or the consultant.

Need for Consultant

Depending on the owner's knowledge and available time, it may be advisable to retain a consultant experienced in the design of parking facilities, particularly with respect to the following:

- initial needs, feasibility, and site selection studies;
- assistance in obtaining project approvals and funding;
- preparation of RFP documents, including instructions

to bidders, design criteria, selection criteria, schematic design (optional), and guide specifications;
- evaluation of proposals; and
- advising the owner during design and construction.

Selection

Among the several methods for selecting a designer/builder, one method calls for making a selection based solely on qualifications and then negotiating a price and schedule or refining a budget price and schedule as the design evolves. The owner may negotiate with a designer/builder already known to him or her or with a firm recommended by a reliable source. On the other hand, the owner may issue a Request for Qualifications (RFQ) to find a qualified team. An RFQ should request name, background information, corporate and financial data, details of previous experience, and résumés of key personnel of the designer/builder and professional designer(s), if different, and references.

Another method is to issue an RFP and evaluate price, schedule, and other factors along with qualifications. An RFP should be sent only to a limited number of teams preselected by an RFQ or other process. The design criteria should be clearly stated, with as much background and supplemental information furnished as possible. Background information might include surveys, topographical surveys, a geotechnical soil report, aerial photographs, and hazardous materials information as well as other site-specific information. Schematic design drawings and guide specifications should be included to the extent necessary to communicate the design criteria. The more complete the RFP, the more complete and directly comparable will be the responses received from interested parties.

The requirements of the RFP submittal must be clearly stated. It is customary to ask for price, schedule, schematic plans and elevations, descriptions of major systems or components not shown on plans (structural, mechanical, and so forth), a staffing plan, and an organizational chart. A bid bond and certificate of insurance should be submitted as well.

The selection criteria must also be clearly stated. If price is the only criterion, the RFP requirements should so state, although a price-only criterion is not recommended. Even if all proposers have been prequalified by the RFQ or other means, some may reveal a thorough understanding of specific issues, demonstrate considerable commitment to the project, offer a desirable schedule, provide more "value," or simply offer a better design. The RFP should specify the percent or relative weights allocated to the various evaluation categories. Thus, each proposer knows what is most important to the owner.

Sufficient time must be allotted to the teams for preparation of their proposals. Turnaround time often ranges from two to eight weeks depending on the size and complexity of the project and the detail requested. Compressing this phase of the project will only cause problems later.

Some schematic design can be expected as part of a proposal, especially for the purpose of establishing value. If design is the predominant criterion, with less emphasis on price or schedule, the selection process will resemble a design competition. As an incentive to defray the high cost of proposal preparation for complex projects, an owner may offer an honorarium to each prequalified design team.

Public Design/Build

Design/build project delivery has been common in the private sector for years. Recently, many government laws and procedures have been amended to allow public design/build. For example, the U.S. Congress has adopted an amendment authorizing the use of and establishing procedures for a two-phase design/build procurement method. The Federal Acquisition Regulations Council is in the process of adopting specific regulations to implement the legislation (FAR Case #96-305). With the amendment, public sector owners and agencies now use design/build more often. They usually find it sufficient to structure the selection criteria to ensure a partial qualifications-based selection of the designer and therefore the design/build team and low-bid–based or "value-based" selection criteria for the project as a whole. The two-envelope method has been used when the technical and non-price-related items are reviewed in sequence before knowing the price in order not to distort the separate parts of the evaluation process. This makes it possible to select the most qualified team at a competitive price.

Additional Resources

Additional information on design/build is available through a variety of sources, including the following:

- American Consulting Engineers Council;
- American Institute of Design Professionals;
- Design-Build Institute of America;
- Design Professionals Insurance Co.; and
- Federal Acquisition Regulations Council.

Whereas design/build combines design and construction into a single contract, design-build-finance and/or -operate likewise combines financing and operation services into the same contract. Such construction is often referred to as turnkey construction.

Financial Opportunities

In the event that an owner has a need for a parking garage and for various reasons cannot or chooses not to raise the money for the facility through conventional processes, an outside funding source (equity partner) can be sought and secured. In most cases, the equity partner serves as the temporary or permanent owner and contracts with the user to furnish all or part of the facility under a variety of agreements, including free rental, lease, lease purchase, and so forth. In some cases, the user may possess and retain ownership of the land or lease the land to the financier/owner per the agreement.

In what is becoming a more common practice, however, the equity partner may remain separate from the design and construction process, tying all features into a single contract. Yet, equity partners often require a greater return on capital than conventional lending sources because of their "risk capital" funding status. The demand for a higher return translates into a higher-than-usual revenue stream (based on parking rates) or requires other aspects of the project to provide necessary funding levels. In many cases, the owner is well advised to consider some form of design-build-finance or operator leadership throughout the development process.

Operations Services

An owner may wish to contract with a parking management firm for operation of the facility. In fact, it is becoming more common to package the operations function with design, construction, and financing, thereby creating one package for all the services required by the owner. Several major parking management firms willingly consider any feasible project as a total development package. These firms use their own resources to fund the project or acquire funds from a financing partner with which they collaborate on a regular basis. It is a simple task for the operator to secure project design and construction services, in many cases from firms that the operator engages on a regular basis.

The operations services approach is reflected in a single development package and a single source of responsibility for the project that can extend for a period of 20 to 30 years or longer. The problem is that the owner relinquishes the right to modify conditions of any type without the consent of the operator or operator team.

CHAPTER 22
PARKING FACILITY OPERATIONS AND MANAGEMENT

Stephen J. Shannon

B y the time a facility is completed and opens to traffic, most aspects of its operation should have been addressed, including issues related to operations, internal traffic flow, vehicular and pedestrian safety, security, and operating expenses. Most important, procedures should have been established to ensure that revenues will be sufficient to repay the cost of construction debt service, cover the cost of operations, and yield an adequate return on investment. No matter how large or small a facility, many critical issues related to its operation must be carefully considered before the first patron pulls into the entry lane. This chapter familiarizes the reader with the primary issues associated with facility operations and emphasizes the importance of the early involvement of professionals experienced in parking management.

At first glance, the operation of a parking facility can appear simple. Given, however, that a parking facility can vary from a simple, uncontrolled, small surface lot to a complex, multilevel, multiuser structure with several entrances and exits, each facility is different and therefore requires careful consideration of its unique features. Accordingly, facility operations must be carefully planned months before opening and constantly monitored over the facility service life.

Method of Operation

The method of facility operation (attendant versus self-park) should have been fully examined early in the design and development process to determine the method's impact on facility operating costs. For two reasons, operating costs for a self-park facility are considerably lower than operating costs

FIGURE 22-1

ANNUAL GARAGE OPERATING COSTS DISTRIBUTION*

Based on 24-Hour Staffed Operation

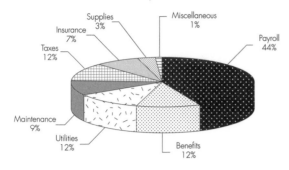

*Actual distribution can vary with size, location, age, and design of structure.
Source: Carl Walker Engineers.

for an attended facility. First, a self-park facility minimizes labor costs because there is no need to employ on-site attendants (valets) to park the vehicles. Second, because the operator does not take possession of patrons' vehicles, liability for damage is not an issue; thus, insurance costs are much lower.

Cost of Operations

Cost of operations is one of the most crucial issues to be considered. During the planning process, the owner makes certain assumptions related to operating costs. With the impending opening of the facility, however, the owner must reevaluate those costs and, if necessary, make any necessary adjustments to account for current market conditions. In any event, costs vary depending on several factors such as size, age, method of operation, type of user, and facility location (Figure 22-1). Expenses for a typical facility can include the following:

- wages and salaries;
- maintenance;
- payroll taxes;
- miscellaneous expenses;
- employee benefits;
- professional fees;
- insurance;
- accident claims;
- supplies;
- licenses and permits;
- telephones;
- taxes (sales, income, real estate);
- uniforms;
- management fees (or rent);
- corporate overhead;
- utilities; and

- operating equipment, service, and replacement costs.

The operation of a parking facility requires several types of insurance, including comprehensive liability, workers' compensation, business interruption, and garagekeeper's liability insurance. Workers' compensation rates vary from state to state and, in today's era of increased litigation, are rapidly becoming a major cost factor; therefore, parking operators must make every effort to minimize the associated costs by encouraging and maintaining a safe work environment for their employees. Likewise, due to the nature of the parking business and the volume of patrons served, the probability of damage to vehicles and injury to patrons is high. Vehicle damage is especially common at attendant-staffed and valet-type operations. While the various types of insurance provide liability coverage, the operator should also consider an annual allowance to cover the cost of deductibles. In fact, self-management of claims is critical to containing costs, particularly given that other miscellaneous and unexpected costs could arise. Thus, the operator should consider a contingency fund for unexpected operating costs. Finally, an important expense that requires careful itemization is the local parking tax, which varies from no tax to as high as 25 percent in some major cities. Maintenance cost is an important expense that can become extremely high if inadequate funds are appropriated and/or maintenance procedures are not properly carried out.

Personnel Management

The management and personnel who will staff the proposed facility are by far the most costly aspect of the operation, representing 40 to 60 percent of total expenses. For this reason, the duties and responsibilities of each employee must be clearly defined in a personnel handbook that addresses issues such as the following:

- job descriptions;
- employee benefits;
- operational procedures;
- daily housekeeping responsibilities;
- customer service procedures;
- safety and security; and
- emergency procedures.

While much planning and thought are required in developing a new parking facility (or any other business), all facilities must go through a "shakedown" period to allow for some adjustments to their unique operational aspects. For any facility to succeed, the owner must hire an experienced manager who fully understands the local market. The manager must then undergo thorough training in the facility's operations and management procedures. The manager's primary duty is to strike a balance between the cost of operations and the level of service. More specifically, the manager is responsible for overseeing the various line employees and meeting with the public on critical issues such as complaints and accidents. The manager also trains employees and ensures that the facility conveys a favorable image. The public perception of a parking facility can make or break it. In addition, the manager carefully plans the staffing schedule according to the facility's hours of operation and projected demand while maintaining an acceptable level of service in the public's perception. At the same time, because parking rates for the facility must be competitive yet attractive to prospective customers, the manager must regularly monitor occupancy and market rates and recommend rate adjustments as needed.

Cash Handling and Revenue Control

The facility management system, often furnished as part of the revenue/access control equipment package, is an important tool for the manager in minimizing any loss of funds. It can provide reports that aid in identifying the current status of the parking operation and "red flag" problem areas in the cash-handling process. The management system's various checks and balances should be reviewed periodically and revised as necessary to respond to new or changing conditions.

Governmental Influences

During the planning and construction of a proposed facility, local building and zoning codes influence the project's ultimate design and layout. In addition, most municipalities require various types of licenses as a prerequisite to operating a parking facility. Facilities can also be subject to periodic inspections for conformance with local ordinances. A local government may even require an audit to substantiate that the proper amount of taxes has been collected in proportion to revenues received.

In terms of federal regulations, the manager must monitor compliance with the Americans with Disabilities Act (ADA). Specifically, the manager must ensure adequate accommodations with respect to the number and type of ADA-prescribed parking spaces and access to unobstructed pathways into and out of the facility. Further, the manager must consider provisions for accommodating employees with disabilities by ensuring barrier-free access to the facility office as well as to at least one of the cashier booths.

Financing Influences

The source of funds that finances a project may impose limits and restrictions on facility operations, including minimum debt coverage ratios, minimum insurance coverage, requirements for a reserve fund for maintenance and repair, and limits on reserved parking, especially in the case of tax-free financing.

Safety and Security

Because of the combination of vehicular and pedestrian traffic associated with all parking facilities, the possibility of seri-

Centralized payment reduces personnel costs.

ous injury to a patron or employee must be minimized and therefore addressed during the early planning stages. In addition, before opening for business, each facility should be carefully reviewed to identify potential safety or security concerns that might have gone overlooked during the planning effort. Periodic safety and security inspections must be made throughout the life of the facility to ensure that management remains responsive to changing conditions. For example, a facility that opens in a relatively safe and prosperous neighborhood may initially require minimal safety and security devices. If, however, that neighborhood changes a decade later such that the incidence of crime increases, the installation of both security screens and upgraded lighting will become a necessity, along with increased security patrols. In some instances, security concerns can force a facility to reduce its hours of operation to minimize liability.

Safety inspections are also required to account for the normal wear and tear that a facility experiences over its life. Settlement of grade-level surfaces and deterioration of supported structural slabs can result in tripping hazards that can cause personal injury to patrons and expose the owner and operator to litigious claims.

Maintenance and Repair

The three critical factors in the performance of a parking structure are quality design, quality construction, and quality maintenance. If just one of these factors is ignored, the facility will suffer from unnecessary maintenance and repair costs. Establishing a comprehensive maintenance program is critical to the success of any parking operation.

Types of Management

The major types of parking facility management follow:

- self-operation;
- lease agreement;
- contract agreement;
- concession agreement;
- management agreement (fixed fee); and
- management agreement (percent).

Self-Operation

When an owner of a parking facility operates the facility with personnel under the direct supervision of the owner, the arrangement is referred to as self-operation. The owner receives all the gross receipts from the parking operation and pays all expenses. The operating personnel may be employees of the owner or employees of a temporary help service. In some cases, a facility operates with a mix of permanent employees (of the owner) and temporary employees. The former provide management and supervisory services while the latter serve as cashiers.

Lease Agreement

Under a lease agreement, the owner leases (rents) a parking facility to a private or public parking operator for a fixed annual compensation. The compensation is usually paid in monthly installments due on the first day of the month. The operator receives all the gross receipts. The lease may or may not require the lessee to pay real estate taxes and/or all routine maintenance costs such as utilities, paving repairs, pavement sealing, striping, and all other operating expenses. If the lease has a term greater that one year, the annual compensation may include an escalation clause that approximates the rate of inflation. If so, the clause is usually tied to a widely accepted index such as the U.S. Department of Labor's Consumer Price Index.

Contract Agreement

Under a contract agreement, the owner signs an agreement with a parking operator. The operator provides the cashiering and revenue control function for a fixed annual compensation and assumes responsibility for hiring and managing all operating and supervisory personnel. In addition, the operator covers all parking-related expenses such as uniforms, parking tickets, telephone, and other similar expenses.

Under a contract agreement, the owner pays the real estate taxes as well as all maintenance and repair costs. The operator is usually required to deposit the gross receipts daily into a bank account in the name of the owner. The operator is usually paid at the end of the month for services rendered during that month.

Concession Agreement

Under a concession agreement, the concessionaire provides all necessary labor and services for the operation of the parking facility in return for mutually agreed-upon compensation. The rate of compensation may vary, although it is usually a sliding percent of gross receipts, excluding any local use taxes imposed on parking facilities. As gross receipts escalate, the percent paid to the concessionaire drops to a defined lower percent.

The owner usually pays the real estate taxes and covers major repairs such as resurfacing the pavement, providing new revenue control equipment and lighting, and other major expense items. The concessionaire pays all parking operating expenses, including labor, bookkeeping, operating supplies, restriping, housekeeping, and snow removal.

The concessionaire collects the gross receipts. About ten to 15 days after the end of the month, the concessionaire subtracts its percent of gross revenues and then remits payment to the owner.

Management Agreement (Fixed Fee)

Under a management agreement, an owner contracts with a parking operator to manage and operate a parking facility on behalf of the owner. In simplest terms, the operator provides cashiering, supervisory, accounting, and auditing functions for a parking facility.

Compensation to the operator takes the form of a fixed fee and reimbursement of all out-of-pocket site-related expenses. The fee covers compensation for assuming the risk of the management agreement, interest on borrowed funds for the manager's working capital, and off-site internal audit expenses as well as a portion of the staffing and overhead costs of the company's home office, annual CPA audit expenses, depreciation of furniture and fixtures, premiums for performance bonds, and the company's profit from the operation.

Under most management agreements, the operator deposits the gross receipts daily to a bank account held in the owner's name. The operator submits an invoice at the end of the month covering both the fixed fee and reimbursement of the expenses.

Management Agreement (Percent)

A percentage management agreement is similar to the above management agreement except for the management fee. Instead of a fixed fee, the fee is based on a percent of gross receipts.

Therefore, the manager has an incentive to generate more revenue for the parking facility and to be compensated commensurately. From an operator's standpoint, the preferred method of compensation is a small percent of gross revenue and higher percent of the net revenue such that the operator is compensated for increasing facility revenues. The operator can receive additional compensation if he or she reduces expenses and further increases net revenues. Sometimes, the agreement stipulates that if a manager attains a revenue threshold that represents a significant increase in revenues, he or she is compensated with a bonus or increased percent of the revenues.

Conclusion

In sum, the operation of any parking facility can be extremely complicated and is best left to an experienced manager or parking management company. To the average person, several of the nuances of facility management may seem insignificant; to the skilled practitioner of parking design and management, however, those nuances can make the difference between successful and unsuccessful facility operation.

CHAPTER 23
PARKING ACCESS AND REVENUE CONTROL

Richard S. Beebe

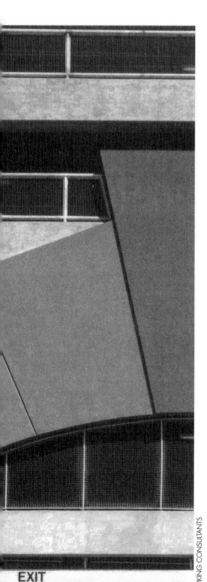

EXIT

Over the past 70 to 80 years, the evolution of parking revenue collection has generally followed the progress of the motor car, but at a significantly slower pace. From the earliest days, nickels and dimes collected by the founders of the parking industry represented the largest share of the revenue stream and subsequently created the need for revenue control systems as we know them today.

In those early days, the collection process was simple. Motorists paid a fee, often less than a quarter, and parked the car on a vacant lot usually rented by a local entrepreneur for a dollar or two a day. Given that the operator was likely the tenant (or perhaps the owner) and gross receipts might reach $6 on a good day, revenue protection and auditing were not considered important.

Even before World War I, however, parking in cities had become a major problem, and parking rates escalated in response to demand. The result was larger lots and construction of a few garages, higher parking fees in prime locations, valet parking operations, and a need to identify the vehicle and record the time of entry to establish the amount of the fee due. Thus was born the paper ticket that provided a claim check for the driver with a matching number on a stub that was placed on the windshield. Tickets later became more sophisticated, with a five-part ticket used by more advanced operators to ensure reasonable accounting practices.

Before World War II, facilities depended on a combination of ticket dispensers and registers. An attendant had to compare the entry time stamped on the ticket with the exit time on the clock located in the booth or office. But as revenue generation became more important, demand emerged for

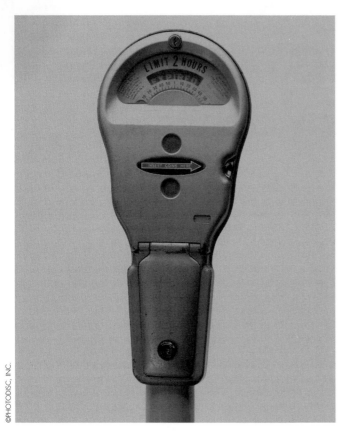

Parking meters are effective tools for fees collected by public agencies.

more sophisticated revenue control systems. Larger parking facilities with increasing revenue streams required unfailing revenue collection systems, leading to the development of many of the now-familiar systems that aid owners and operators in securing revenue.

Today, the accurate and efficient collection of parking fees is taken for granted and is obviously essential in the operation of any revenue-producing parking facility. In fact, revenue control systems (RCS) are catching up to the technology level of today's vehicles.

Accelerating costs of land, construction, and operations and maintenance and the required return on investment demand careful attention to all aspects of revenue collection and reporting. The goal of every revenue control system is the collection of 100 percent of the revenue due, although facilities seldom attain a perfect collection record.

Regardless of the type, size, location, or function of a parking facility, proper selection of parking revenue control equipment and use of appropriate procedures is vital to ensuring the collection of all parking revenues. This chapter discusses the range of revenue control equipment and systems currently on the market and the appropriateness of these systems for various categories of parking facilities. In overview, the level of sophistication of the revenue control system should equal the parking facility's level of sophistication and cash flow capability.

A new generation of more sophisticated revenue control systems has emerged to meet specific needs in large and small facilities and to serve varying user populations. The new systems are based on computer-based technologies ranging from basic to complex, including magnetic stripe, bar code, and punch-hole tickets; proximity readers; and credit and debit cards in online systems with the potential for controlling the RCS devices via a computer network. Major features of many of these new systems involve the capability to provide superior control of revenue, the ability to track all transactions from ticket issuance to ticket collection, redundancy of the entry/exit vehicle counting process, and the independent identification and coding of any exception (nonrevenue) ticket. Another essential item is speed of operation. The shorter the time involved for vehicles to negotiate entry and exit lanes, the more efficient and attractive the RCS appears to owners or operators. Accuracy, of course, must always remain the watchword of any system.

The selection of an appropriate revenue control system, including components and operating procedures, is based on the owner's need for one or more of the following functions:

- recording parking revenues by type, location, day, shift, lane, and so forth;
- maximizing revenue collections;
- accepting and recording card use (credit, debit, key, and pass cards) and other noncash payments;
- tracking ticket issuance/collection and matching transaction numbers to identify missing tickets;
- reducing theft or loss from any source;
- maintaining overnight License Plate Inventories (LPI) in overnight parking facilities such as at airports and hotels;
- providing high levels of customer service;
- simultaneously managing multiple facilities and coordinating revenue accounting for a system of facilities; and
- providing comprehensive revenue records and audits for subsequent management purposes.

Figure 23-1 presents the currently defined types of parking operations and the characteristics related to each. Each type of operation offers advantages and disadvantages for a given parking facility or system. In some cases, several operating types may be combined in a single facility during a single day. The owner or operator must therefore determine the effectiveness of each operating type as a means of managing revenue control before selecting the appropriate control system (or systems) for installation.

The specifics of a revenue control system planned for any particular facility or operation depend on the following factors:

- number of facilities in the system;
- size and type of operation or facility;
- size and volume of business, user characteristics, and transient/contract volumes;

FIGURE 23-1

TYPE OF PARKING OPERATION AND OPERATING CHARACTERISTICS

Operational and Revenue Type	Advantages	Disadvantages
Flat Rate	Payment on entry Single rate structure Periodic collection Minimal oversight Quick exit	Reduced revenue Potential for lost revenue Inappropriate for high turnover
Transient	Flexible rates Higher revenue yield per ticket than normal monthly parking Potential for higher turnover	Cash handling Competitive rates Possibility of no guarantee for maximum lot use
Contract (monthly) Nonreserved	Advance payment Predictable income Service provided to regular tenants Customer loyalty Facility use maximized by oversell opportunities	Need for close monitoring Need for equipment investment or manual audits Discounted rates No turnover during normal day hours unless space is available
Validation	Third-party promotion of facility	Abuse/theft by employees of issuing establishments Manual record keeping Discounted fee/revenue
Special Events	Facility use during maximized off-peak hours	High labor costs Reduced level of cash control
Valet	On- and off-site parking opportunities maximized High level of customer service	High labor costs Need for supervision Staffing difficulties during peak periods Damage risk to patrons' vehicles Risk of theft of vehicles or vehicle contents
Reserved Zones/Nests	Prime parking at premium rates Areas provided within higher levels of security Higher value	Possibility of additional equipment investment Need for monitoring for violations Loss of oversell opportunity for absent contract parkers Limited overselling

- dollar volume of revenue projected by type;
- need for security of revenue collected;
- availability and feasibility of the capital investment required to purchase, install, and maintain a system (relationship of investment to annual gross revenue);
- return-on-investment potential; and
- user acceptance of automated systems.

Standard RCS configurations, which are those described in sophistication levels 1 through 4 in Figure 23-2, are widely known throughout the parking industry and are in common

FIGURE 23-2

ALTERNATIVE REVENUE CONTROL EQUIPMENT OPTIONS: LEAST COMPLICATED TO MOST SOPHISTICATED*

Configuration/ Equipment Options	Level of Sophistication
"Apron" (special event)	1
Permits	1
Slot boxes	1
Pay and display	1
Mechanical meters	1
Tickets, cash drawer, time clock	2
Coin/token or key card with barrier gates	2
Ticket issue machines, cash register, key card, time clock with barrier gates	2
Electronic meters	3
Multispace meters	3
Ticket issue machine, fee computer/ manual entry with barrier gates	3
Ticket issue machine, fee computer/ machine readable (various upgrades of components) with barrier gates	4
Ticket issue machine, machine readable online, real time with barrier gates; pay-on-foot stations	5
AVI–Automatic Vehicle Identification Systems	6
LPR–License Plate Recognition Systems	6

*Based on activity level and features of revenue generation.

use throughout the world. Many of the higher-end systems rely on the latest technology in the field—magnetic stripe tickets; fully automated terminals; real-time, online reporting; and fully networked linkages whereby a central computer monitors every device. Hardware and software are matched to provide total transaction accountability, identifying exception tickets and noncashiered transactions—the two aspects of revenue collection still associated with some potential for fraud and/or laxity in reporting/auditing the revenue stream.

Among the new devices providing improved flexibility and revenue security for parking systems of all types and sizes are electronic multispace parking meters and pay-on-foot stations. Figures 23-1 and 23-2 provide some assistance in gauging the suitability of alternative RCS devices in varied circumstances.

To meet the needs of ever-increasing parking system capacity and revenue production, advanced transportation management technologies have been applied to the field of revenue collection and reporting. Two of these systems involve Automatic Vehicle Identification (AVI) and License Plate Recognition (LPR), both of which provide superior methods for controlling the flow of vehicle entry and exit and ensuring the collection of revenue. Indeed, these systems represent the direction of large-scale revenue control strategies in the new millennium: "No ticket, no ticket dispensers, no cashier terminals, and no cash." Each system, however, offers its own advantages and disadvantages that must be carefully weighed for installations in any given facility.

AVI uses transponders (tags) placed in vehicles that are "read" by antennae appropriately placed at entry and exit lanes or other control points. The antennae record the date and time of vehicle entry and exit. Parking charges, along with roadway tolls and similar motor vehicle–generated charges, can be billed directly to vehicle owners each month based on actual use of a parking facility as recorded at any AVI-equipped location.

AVI first gained wide acceptance as a control and billing system for railroad cars and then for revenue control of commercial vehicles operating on the nation's toll roads. Now used in locations such as airports with large volumes of repetitive parking, AVI offers a fast, cost-effective, and highly accurate means of collecting revenue. As evidenced by their growing use on toll roads and toll bridges, AVI systems can be used in any location with standard entry/exit lane or other access control configurations where the number of vehicle uses is sufficient to justify installation of the system and purchase of transponders for user vehicles. Any parking facility with several hundred or more monthly or regular users can use AVI to considerable advantage. In larger parking systems, AVI can perform the dual functions of revenue control and vehicle access control to designated locations.

License Plate Recognition is based on the initial photographic recording of license plates (or vehicle rear areas, including the plate) at the point of entry. Plate numbers are recorded (along with the parking ticket identification number if a ticket is issued) as are facility identification and the date, time, and lane of entry. License plate recognition data are stored in the computer, much like a License Plate Inventory file, for use at the time of exit.

Upon a vehicle's approach to an exit lane, the license plate number is again recorded photographically and "matched" in the computer to find the entry data for the same plate number. In one or two seconds, the computer finds the match, summarizes the transaction, and posts the amount due on the cashier terminal screen and fee display unit or in a central activity record file. Recording of the activity and assignment of the fee due are instantaneous, requiring no exit lane devices or cashiers and therefore significantly increasing the exit lane throughput (or capacity).

In the event that the exit read does not match an exact plate number from the entry data files, the computer can immediately scan all plate numbers with a similar mix of numbers and/or letters to find the most reasonable match. A cashier or supervisor can then verify entry and exit data from the ticket or by visual inspection and promptly process the transaction.

LPR systems are now in operation at several of the nation's largest airports and in hotel and other commercial locations. Accuracy read rates exceed 95 percent and are expected to reach 99 percent before the end of 2000. This rate is superior to virtually all other revenue control systems in terms of transaction speed, revenue collection, and accuracy of reporting/auditing functions. While AVI and LPR may be preferred for parking control systems in large facilities in the immediate future, more conventional systems may continue to prove satisfactory in many standard situations.

The most important criterion in evaluating the applicability and effectiveness of any revenue control system is not cost of installation or maintenance but rather the production and protection of revenue.

CHAPTER 24
MAINTENANCE

Mark Hoffman and James E. Staif

The term "maintenance" involves several components when applied to parking facilities, including sweeping, cleaning windows, plowing snow, servicing equipment such as elevators and fans, structural repair and preventive maintenance, repainting stall markings, and repair of asphalt pavement in parking lots. These and other maintenance tasks are needed for a variety of reasons, such as appearance, safety, and the fact that "an ounce of prevention is worth a pound of cure." Preventive maintenance, however, often goes ignored, particularly in regard to the basic concrete or steel structural system in multilevel parking facilities.

The service environment of a parking garage is more severe than that for most other buildings and more nearly approximates the service environment of highway bridges. In some areas of the country, extensive winter-time use of deicing salt often contaminates the concrete with chlorides, resulting in corrosion of reinforcing and structural steel and damage to the concrete. In all regions, exposure to temperature changes, coastal salt spray, and moisture poses a more severe service environment for parking garages than for other buildings.

Delayed repairs are usually more costly than preventive maintenance. Much of a good preventive maintenance program for structural elements starts with proper design of the facility to minimize later problems. However, all aspects of maintenance are important to the continued well-being of a parking facility. This chapter examines some of the more important aspects of parking facility maintenance.

Maintenance Program

Every parking facility requires a comprehensive, regular maintenance program. A good maintenance program not only protects the investment in

Good maintenance protects the investment and makes the facility more pleasant to users.

the parking facility but also makes the facility attractive and easy to use. The maintenance requirements for some elements of a parking garage, such as elevators and ventilation equipment, are similar to those for their counterparts in other building types. However, the frequency of maintenance may differ because of variations in climate and the garage's exposure to weather conditions.

A comprehensive maintenance program includes the following three basic elements:

- a schedule of what needs to be done and how often, supplemented by how it should be done;
- a budget to cover the costs of the program; and
- control or follow-up procedures by management to verify that the program is functioning.

A typical maintenance program might be divided into three categories:

- housekeeping;
- equipment maintenance; and
- maintenance of the structural system.

Housekeeping

Cleaning and other housekeeping activities maintain the facility's appearance and protect the structure's elements from damage. For example, if dirt and debris are not removed from the parking floors, they can clog floor drains and result in water ponding, which in turn creates a hazard if the water freezes. Ponded water can also cause damage to the structural system over a period of time.

Users of a parking facility prefer a bright, clean, well-kept facility. And patrons tend to litter less in a clean facility. Housekeeping tasks include but are not limited to the following:

- sweeping and washing floors in the pedestrian and vehicular areas;
- washing windows;
- cleaning stairs, including handrails;
- cleaning elevator cabs;

- emptying trash cans;
- picking up trash;
- cleaning floor drains;
- cleaning signs;
- removing grease drippings or snow and ice;
- replacing burned-out light bulbs;
- removing graffiti; and
- repainting stall stripes and other pavement markings.

The frequency of these tasks varies with the situation. Heavily used public areas require more frequent attention than little-used areas. Picking up trash on floors without sweeping also has some benefit. Floors should be washed at least once a year. In areas where salt is used to melt snow and ice or is present in the air, all floors should be washed down in early spring.

Equipment Maintenance

A parking facility might include many different types of equipment, all of which must function properly to ensure the safe, smooth operation of the facility. The maintenance program should require inspection of all equipment to verify that it is functioning properly. Equipment with moving parts usually needs to be inspected and lubricated at regular intervals.

It is desirable to maintain a file containing the manufacturer's manual for operation and maintenance of each piece of equipment as well as a log of the maintenance and repair work performed on that equipment. The manufacturer's recommendations for operation and preventive maintenance should be followed. When an inspection indicates that a piece of equipment is not functioning properly, the equipment should be repaired or replaced immediately.

Equipment in a parking facility that requires regular inspections, lubrication, or other preventive maintenance includes but is not limited to the following:

- parking and revenue control equipment;
- elevators, escalators, and manlifts;
- electrical equipment, including lights and emergency lights;
- doors, including hinges, closers, and latch sets;
- mechanically operated doors;
- security systems;
- heating, ventilation, and air-conditioning equipment;
- carbon monoxide monitors;
- sanitary facilities;
- sump pumps;
- fire protection system; and
- floor and roof drainage system.

Some of these elements, such as carbon monoxide monitors, should be checked daily for proper operation. Other equipment may need less frequent inspection or attention. Some of the equipment, such as elevators and parking control equipment, should probably be maintained under a service contract that calls for regular inspection, lubrication, and other routine service as well as for emergency repair service.

Nearly all of the equipment listed above is subject to corrosion, which can shorten the life of the equipment. All inspections should include observations for corrosion. Where corrosion is observed, the element should be cleaned and properly painted to maintain its appearance and integrity.

Maintenance of the Structural System

The structural system is one of the most frequently neglected elements in a parking garage. From the time a facility first opens, it requires regular inspection, preventive maintenance, and repair. The results of neglect may not show up for many years. In the extreme, partial collapse of the structure can occur. Delayed repair and catch-up maintenance expenditures can be costly and mean lost revenue while repairs are underway.

The most common causes of deterioration in a parking structure are salt-induced corrosion of internal reinforcing, freezing and thawing, corrosion of exposed metals, and movement of the structure due to changes in temperature and other factors. These several causes can interact and compound the rate of deterioration. Water is a causative agent in both freeze/thaw and corrosion damage. Cracks caused by movement of the structure often leak water that damage the structure as well as annoy users.

The maintenance program for the structural elements of a parking garage should start with an annual inspection of the entire facility. The inspection should note areas of deterioration, water leakage, or corrosion of exposed metals. The following elements require special attention:

- top surfaces of all floors and bottoms of parking floors;
- columns;
- beams;
- guardrails and handrails (to verify that they are rigid and safe);
- stairways;
- walls;
- connections and bearing pads in a precast concrete system; and
- wheelstops.

A qualified engineer experienced in parking should perform the inspection and provide the necessary consultation if the concrete portion of a structure is found to be cracked or deteriorated. The cause of the problem must be identified as a prerequisite to selecting the proper repair method. For example, a crack that is going to continue to undergo movement should be filled with a flexible rather than rigid material.

When leaks, deteriorated concrete, corrosion of exposed metals, or other stresses in the structural elements are noted, corrective measures should be taken immediately. The specific methods will vary with the situation, but the following general guidelines apply:

- Almost all concrete develops cracks, but many small cracks are of no consequence and need not be

Failure to maintain surfaces in this helix required the removal of concrete in preparation for repairs.

repaired. However, cracks requiring attention are usually those that allow water to leak into the interior of the concrete through the floor. Such leaks can corrode the reinforcing steel and cause other damage.

- When exposed metal corrodes, it needs to be thoroughly cleaned and painted with a protective coat or other appropriate compound. The painting can take place as part of isolated touch-up work or in the course of general repainting.

- Any water leakage through the concrete structural system should be stopped. The assistance of a qualified engineer is recommended to ensure that the solution fits the problem.

- When the deterioration of the concrete is evident, appropriate repairs and preventive maintenance are required. It is not enough simply to use asphalt to patch potholes or spalled areas in concrete floors. Because asphalt is porous, water will collect in the bottom of the patched hole and in turn accelerate further deterioration of that area. Many repair materials and methods are on the market, most of which work reasonably well for specific but not all types of repairs. Again, consultation with a qualified engineer is recommended before undertaking concrete repair work.

- Concrete structural elements are best maintained by preventing moisture from penetrating the concrete, particularly the top surface of each parking structural slab. Three material types can help prevent moisture penetration: a protective concrete sealer, a thin (traffic-bearing) membrane, and a membrane with a wearing course of protection. Many of these products are on the market; however, not all perform as promised.

- Preventive maintenance can take many forms for a concrete garage suffering from salt-induced corrosion of its internal reinforcing steel. Recent years have

Before: Deteriorated beams being prepared for repair.

After: Concrete has been replaced in beams.

seen the use of cathodic protection, realkalization, chloride ion extraction, corrosion inhibitor absorption, and oxygen starvation.

Surface Lots

Parking lots require many of the same maintenance procedures as garages; a facility must be cleaned and repainted, equipment must be maintained, and so forth. Given that most parking lots are surfaced with an asphalt mix, repair of potholes and periodic applications of seal coats to the surface should be a regular part of a maintenance program.

Budget

Budgets for maintenance vary. Some of the costs, such as those for cleaning and maintaining certain equipment, are incurred every month or at other regular intervals. Other maintenance tasks, such as repainting or applying protective coatings to concrete surfaces, are performed only once every several years. It may be desirable to build a reserve fund for items that need maintenance at long intervals as well as for unanticipated needs. Older facilities usually have higher repair and maintenance costs than newer facilities. Management must take an active interest in the maintenance program. The cleanliness, appearance, and condition of a parking facility generally reflect the attitude of management toward a maintenance program.

Summary

Maintenance of parking facilities is a multifaceted problem. A detailed maintenance program is required for each parking garage and parking lot. To implement the program requires an ongoing budget and the interest of management. Much of a maintenance program consists of regular observations to verify that all elements are clean and in proper working order. Any problems should receive immediate attention. Preventive maintenance is generally more cost-effective than

repair maintenance. Where parking facilities are operated by a different party from the owner, it is in the interest of both the owner and the manager to define clearly the maintenance responsibilities of each party.

Reference

National Parking Association. *Parking Garage Maintenance Manual.* Washington, D.C.: NPA, 1996.

APPENDIX
GLOSSARY

Thomas Feagins, Jr.

ADA—Americans with Disabilities Act.

Above-grade facility—an elevated parking structure with one or more levels above street or surface grade.

Access—the street system providing access to a parking facility, sometimes involving several streets.

Adequate rate covenant—an agreement often required in revenue bond–financed programs that guarantees that the operator will charge adequate rates to produce revenue necessary to cover principal and interest payments.

Air Quality Nonattainment Areas—Metropolitan areas that do not meet the air quality standards of the U.S. Environmental Protection Agency. Depending on the severity of the problem, sanctions may be imposed to improve air quality and discourage single-occupancy vehicle use.

Aisle, driving—the traveled path through a parking facility, providing access to the parking spaces.

Alarm devices—Part of the overall security system in a parking facility to warn of excessive hazardous fume concentrations or other customer dangers.

All-day parking—parking for the day, usually from early morning to late afternoon or longer.

Allocation model—a mathematical model used to determine the percent of parking space to be used by all-day, short-term, and other parkers.

Ambient light—spill from existing light sources.

Anchor point—a reference point used to retain and mentally structure environmental information; landmarks can be anchor points.

Angle parking—the angle at which the parking stall extends from the edge of the bay, usually ranging from 30 to 80 degrees.

Angle, stall—see Angle, parking.

Angular distortion—deleterious effect (on an image) caused by viewing obliquely or at a high angle of incidence.

Approach traffic—traffic using approach streets to a parking facility.

Arrow—concept-related symbol representing movement.

At-grade facility—parking facility built only at street or surface level.

Attendant parking—a system that relies on attendants (or valets) rather than on customers to park and retrieve vehicles.

Audible communication—information that is perceived through one's sense of hearing.

Audit procedures—methods used by a parking facility owner or operator to verify transactions and receipts.

Audit trail—information stored in the memory unit of a central computer or on the journal tape of a cash register that includes the number and type of transactions through each lane or cashier terminal, the dollar value of all transactions, the number of lost tickets or other exceptions, and a series of fiscal checks on the revenue control system and its operation.

Auto-free zone—an area, usually in or near a downtown, where vehicular traffic is severely limited or restricted.

Automated cashiering—upon entry, patrons are issued tickets in a standard format at ticket-issuing machines located at the parking facility's entrance. When exiting from a facility, patrons use a machine that calculates their parking fee based on time of use. When the patron pays the parking fee, the automated pay station accepts cash or a credit card, returns change when appropriate, and issues an exit verifier ticket and receipt to the patron. The exit verifier ticket is used at the exit lane's lag reader to signal the barrier (a gate arm) to raise to the open position.

Automated parking facility—facility operated by automatic parking equipment rather than by employees.

Automatic controls—equipment such as ticket dispensers, card dispensers, card readers, and parking gates used in an automated facility.

Automatic exit lanes—designated exit lanes containing a timed exit ticket reader, a device that is designed to accept exit tickets issued by a prepayment machine terminal and that reads the ticket and operates the exit gate automatically.

Automatic precashiering machines—automatic prepayment machines usually located in or near a parking facility's elevator lobby for the purpose of permitting the payment of parking fees before patrons retrieve their vehicle from the parking stall; sometimes called pay-on-foot.

Automatic Vehicle Identification (AVI)—electronic sensors, antennae, and transponders that detect a vehicle's presence for identification, resulting in some subsequent action such as access control and/or revenue collection.

Average length of stay—average length of time a vehicle is parked in a particular facility.

Average ticket cost—total revenue collected, divided by the total number of tickets issued.

Btu (British thermal unit)—the amount of energy required to raise the temperature of one pound of water by one degree Fahrenheit.

Back-in stalls—parking spaces into which the vehicle is backed from the driving aisle; a normal practice in valet parking to reduce the time required to deliver a car.

Barrel—a measure of petroleum or petroleum products equivalent to 31.5 U.S. gallons.

Bay, parking—a parking facility unit that has two rows of parking stalls and a central aisle (i.e., double-loaded aisle, aisle with vehicles on both sides).

Beam—the major horizontal support, resting on vertical columns, of a parking structure floor to which the floor slab is attached.

Below-grade facility—a parking facility constructed underground or below the surface grade.

Blind—descriptive of persons with no useful vision.

Bond counsel—usually an attorney who assists in the sale of bonds (in this instance, bonds to finance parking facilities).

Braille cells—the original (1829) definition was a "method of writing words . . . by means of dots, for use of the blind"; each cell is an arrangement of dots within a six-dot matrix and represents a word or sound.

Brightness differential—means whereby the suitability of the two colors comprising a sign (one for the background, the other for the message) may be determined.

Buildable area—that portion of a lot or land parcel on which a building can be constructed.

Building code—local ordinances controlling the building methods and component requirements for various types of construction.

Building directory—information, usually typographic in nature, that provides the names and locations of tenants in a building.

Bumper stop—a stop placed at the front of a parking stall to keep the vehicle from striking walls or extending beyond the specified parking area; usually mounted to a wall as opposed to a wheelstop, which is attached to the parking surface.

CBD—the central business district or downtown area of a community.

Candle power—a measure of light intensity in any location where artificial lighting is used.

Cantilever—in construction, a portion of a floor or deck extending beyond the vertical column; an overhang.

Capacity, facility—the number of vehicles that can be accommodated in any given parking facility under a particular type of operation.

Capacity, roadway—the capacity, in terms of vehicles, that can be accommodated per day or per hour on any given street or roadway.

Carpool—two or more people who share their automobile transportation to designated destinations on a regular basis.

Car size classifications—designation of vehicles by size: subcompacts, compacts, intermediate, standard, and luxury.

Car width—width of car in relation to a parking stall; most U.S. cars now range from 60 to 80 inches in width.

Carbon monoxide (CO)—a colorless, odorless, poisonous gas emitted from vehicle exhaust systems.

Carbon monoxide detectors—devices used to measure the concentration of CO and emit warnings if harmful levels are reached.

Card reader—an access control device, located in the entry and exit lanes of a parking facility, to permit controlled entry and/or exit via use of an authorized, encoded card issued by the owner or operator.

Cash drawer—a removable, usually lockable cash box located in each staffed cashier terminal for the storage of coins and bills.

Cashier terminal keyboard—a multikey pad for the entry of numeric data, such as fee amounts, to record functions such as lost tickets or gate override and to obtain license plate inventory information.

Cast in place—method of pouring concrete during construction whereby concrete is poured into a form fabricated on site.

Catalytic converter—device required on vehicles to increase the fuel combustion process and reduce exhaust emissions.

Central computer—control center location of microprocessor computer units that connect all components of the revenue control system and monitoring systems in the operations office of a parking facility.

Channelization—construction of islands or barriers, usually on roadways, to assist in control of traffic flow patterns.

Circular ramp—a ramp between floors of a parking facility whose centerline is circular.

Circulation—traffic flow pattern, such as two-way or one-way, for an on-street system or off-street parking facility.

Circulation system—the overall horizontal and vertical pedestrian paths of a setting; circulation systems can be organized on a linear, central, composite, or network basis.

Clean Air Act of 1970—law that empowers the U.S. Environmental Protection Agency to establish controls for improving air quality, particularly in areas with poor air quality.

Clear height—clear vertical height inside a parking structure; usually, seven feet is a desirable standard-space minimum and 8 feet, 3 inches for handicapped spaces.

Clear-span facility—a parking structure with vertical columns on the outside edges of the structure and a clear span between columns, making it unnecessary for vehicles to maneuver between columns.

Closed circuit television system (CCTV)—a means of providing security in parking facilities through the use of TV cameras that cover portions of the facility.

Code requirements—the parking facility requirements contained in a community's codes that affect zoning and construction as well as plumbing, electrical, and similar specialties.

Cognition—understanding; a generic term that includes retaining, structuring, and manipulating information.

Cognitive map—an overall mental representation of a setting that cannot be grasped from a single viewpoint but has to be integrated from different vistas.

Cognitive mapping—the mental structuring process leading to a cognitive map.

Coin changer—a device for changing dollar bills into silver for use in parking meters or other control devices.

Color coding—the use of a limited number of namable colors for the purpose of visual orientation or direction.

Color deficiency—inability to distinguish between certain colors.

Column—vertical support of a structure on which beams rest to support succeeding stories.

Column-free facility—see Clear-span facility.

Column spacing—the spacing pattern between columns or rows of columns in any structure.

Communication systems—telephone or voice-actuated systems providing communication with police or security agencies or internal communication within a parking facility.

Commuter parking—parking areas, usually specially designated, for users of mass transportation or car pool operations.

Compact car—a small car, usually less than 15 feet in overall length and 72 inches in width.

Composite construction system—system in which steel beams are fixed to the concrete slab above so that the slab acts with the beams as a single unit to resist bending.

Computer control equipment—see Automatic controls.

Construction cost data—information that includes current costs for individual construction components that form the basis for the preparation of project cost estimates.

Construction management—construction supervision by a qualified manager.

Contract construction documents—the design plans and specifications for construction of a facility.

Contract parking—long-term or specified-term parking arranged in advance, usually on a fixed-fee basis.

Corrosion in a parking structure—usually the gradual destruction of reinforcing steel or concrete by the chemical action of salt, water, and other substances carried by vehicles or in the atmosphere.

Cost, operations and maintenance—the cost of operating and maintaining a facility, including staff charges, utilities, insurance, supplies, and repairs; such costs are listed as expense items of the parking operator.

Cost per square foot—the cost of a facility divided by the number of square feet in the facility; usually applies to hard construction costs.

Cost per stall—the operating costs of a facility divided by the number of parking stalls.

Cost, project—the total cost of a facility, including land, construction, engineering fees, contingency costs, and any other hard or soft cost.

Cost, soft—costs associated with architectural, engineering, legal, financial, testing, and other nonhard construction items.

Coverage, debt service—the ratio of revenue less all facility operations and maintenance costs, divided by the required annual payments for principal and interest; usually expressed as a percent.

Crossover—an area between levels in a parking structure where motorists can change direction or proceed to an exit.

Cruising—the practice of traveling along a street or facility in search of an available parking space.

Curb—a raised edge on the side of a street or pavement surface.

Curb distance—the straight-line distance required along a curb for a parking stall and varying in length depending on the stall angle.

Curb parking—parking permitted along a curb, usually on a street; may be parallel or angle depending on street width.

DHV—design hour volume (volume of traffic selected for design criteria of a facility).

Dead load—the permanent weight of the structural components of a garage.

Dead storage—long-term storage of a vehicle in a parking facility where the vehicle remains parked beyond 24 hours.

Deaf—descriptive of persons with a profound hearing loss.

Debit cards—A payment method whereby a "monetary value" is encoded onto a card's magnetic strip such that for each parking use, the particular parking charge is deducted from the value indicated on the magnetic strip. The new balance is then encoded onto the card. The balance can be stored either on the magnetic strip, as described, or on a host computer's memory.

Debt structure—the repayment structure of a debt, including interest rate, repayment period, and related features.

Demand—the number of potential customers for a parking facility or parking system.

Demand/supply—a ratio of parking demand (vehicles) to parking supply (spaces), indicating an excess or shortage of available space.

Demountable—a parking structure designed for easy removal to another location.

Depreciation—a percent of the value of an improvement deducted each year for wear and tear.

Design/build system—a system in which a single entity is responsible for both the design and construction of a facility, often involving the fast-track method of construction; also referred to as design/construct.

Design load—the total load for a structure, including dead load, wind load, live load of the vehicles, and snow load.

Design standards—a set of criteria established to define the design characteristics of a parking facility.

Destination—the end-point of a single trip, such as home, school, work, or church.

Detector loops—inductive loop wires embedded in the pavement adjacent to a ticket-issuing machine, an exit booth, or barrier gate.

Diameter, ramp—the measure from outside wall to outside wall across a circular ramp.

Differential counter—a counting system, usually activated by loops or treadles, to determine movements into and out of a parking facility and thus the number of available parking spaces.

Differential counters—devices that detect each vehicle's entry by subtracting a count of one from the number of parking spaces currently available and that detect each vehicle's exit by adding a count of one to the number of parking spaces currently available.

Dimension, stall—the length and width of a parking stall.

Directional signs—signs placed in a parking facility that direct motorists to entrances, exits, stairs, or elevators.

Disability—in the context of physical health, a disability is any restriction or lack (resulting from an impairment) of ability to perform an activity in the manner or within the range considered normal for a human being.

Discharge time—the time required to empty a parking facility of parked vehicles.

Double-double helix—a garage designed such that a car rises or drops four floors per each 360-degree revolution.

Double helix—a garage designed such that a car rises or drops two floors per each 360-degree revolution.

Double tee—a structural element of precast concrete used to form the beam of a parking structure; shaped like a pair of Ts.

Double-zero traffic flow pattern—a garage designed such that a car rises or drops one floor per each 360-degree revolution. The entering and exiting drive patterns are arranged in two concentric circles. Cars are permitted to change from the in pattern to the out pattern every 180 degrees or vice versa.

Down ramp—section of a ramp for traffic proceeding downward in a structure; for above-grade facilities, the exit ramp.

Driver visibility—the ability of a driver to see within a facility, for example, at intersecting aisles and ramps.

Driveway—an entrance or exit roadway from a street to a parking facility.

Duration—the length of time a vehicle is parked; average length of time all vehicles are parked in a particular facility.

EPA—the U.S. Environmental Protection Agency, charged by Congress with developing and enforcing environmental regulations.

Economic feasibility—a project's feasibility in terms of costs and revenue, with excess revenue establishing the degree of feasibility.

Emissions gases—any particulate matter passing through the exhaust system of a vehicle.

Emissions standards—a series of graduated standards established by the U.S. Environmental Protection Agency to be implemented over a period of years to control the level of exhaust emissions from vehicles.

Employee parking—parking areas specifically designated for use by employees.

Energy conservation—the use of measures such as restricted travel and smaller, more efficient engines to reduce energy consumption.

Entry drive—point at which vehicles enter a parking facility (ingress).

Environmental impact—the environmental consequences of a parking facility in terms of air, noise, and water pollution generated by the facility.

Exit—the point at which vehicles leave a parking facility (egress).

Expansion joint—a construction joint between sections of large concrete slabs to allow weather-induced expansion and contraction of the slabs.

Exposed aggregate surface—concrete surface with a rough finish (stones exposed), providing a special design treatment.

Exterior panels—concrete, metal, or similar panels forming the exterior wall or parapet surfaces of a parking facility.

Façade—the face or front surface of a building or parking structure.

Facility—a parking lot, garage, or deck; generally refers to off-street parking.

Feasibility study—an analysis of parking needs, costs of recommended improvements, and projected revenues and costs; establishes the basis for the construction of an individual improvement or a complete system.

Fee collection—collection of fees at a parking facility either by mechanical means such as meters or coin-operated control devices or by a cashier.

Fee computer—a hardware device that calculates the parking fee based on information contained on a ticket that is either keyed manually or read automatically by a reader/validator .

Fee computer shroud—a metal cover plate placed over the wiring connections at the rear of the fee computer; prevents unwanted tampering with wiring connections.

Fee display—an illuminated digital "readout" dial, usually activated by a cash register, that automatically displays the amount of fee due for each parking transaction and in some installations includes the amount of change due, if any, to the patron.

Financial feasibility study—determination of a project's potential economic success; see also Feasibility study.

Financing—means of providing funds for a parking facility from private capital, public sale of general obligation or rev-enue bonds, special-assessment or tax-district funds, leases, not-for-profit associations, or a combination of these sources.

Fireproofing—the use of special materials or systems to produce a fire-safe or fire-resistant building.

Fiscal (financial) consultant—a specialist in the underwriting and marketing of bond issues and other forms of financing for public purposes.

Flat floor—having flat floors as opposed to sloped or ramped floors.

Flat-rate fee—a set amount charged for parking for a specific period of time, such as an hour, day, or month.

Floor area—the area of a floor, usually measured by multiplying the out-to-out length times the width; in some cases, the total floor area of a facility.

Flow system—the traffic flow pattern in a parking facility, such as one-way, two-way, or reverse-flow.

Foot candle—a unit of luminance on a surface that is everywhere one foot from a uniform point source of light of one candle and equal to one lumen per square foot.

Foundation—the lowest part of a structure on which the remainder of the structure rests.

Functional design—design of a structure or facility that increases its overall efficiency and provides maximum user acceptance; a parking concept plan showing traffic flow, stall geometry, and other features that determine the interior design of parking facilities.

Garage—a building for the storage and/or repair of motor vehicles, generally closed on all sides.

Gate arm—a wooden, plastic, or metal barrier arm extending outward from a gate cabinet and controlling entry to or exit from parking areas.

Gates—control devices to which a gate arm is attached; usually installed at entrances and exits of parking facilities to regulate vehicles and implement fee collection.

General information—one of the three basic information types in environmental communications; concerns obligations and prohibitions, hours of service, and other information a visitor needs (or wishes) to know in a public building.

General obligation bonds—bonds that are sold by a public agency to finance public improvements and that guarantee the full faith and credit of the issuing agency regarding repayment.

Generators—parking uses that generate parking demand, such as stores, office buildings, hospitals, and recreational facilities.

Geometrics—the design criteria that are applied to laying out a roadway or parking facility and that control the flow pattern of vehicles.

Girder—a main horizontal supporting member or beam in a structure.

Glare—undesirable degree of sheen reflected off the surface (of a sign) causing deterioration of legibility.

Glyph—symbol; pictograph; pictorial representation of an object or a concept; may also be an abstraction representing an instruction.

Grade—the degree of incline or slope in a ramp or floor of a parking structure.

Graphics—directional, identification, and warning signs.

Gross area—the entire area of a building, usually measured in square feet or square meters.

HVAC—heating, ventilating, and air-conditioning equipment.

Half-bay—a parking facility unit that has only one row of car stalls and a central aisle.

Handicap—in the context of health, a handicap is a disadvantage for a given individual, resulting from an impairment or a disability that limits or prevents the fulfillment of a role that is normal (depending on age, sex, and social and cultural factors) for that individual.

Head-in parking—system whereby vehicles are parked front first in the parking stall.

Headroom—the vertical clearance in a parking structure, usually about seven feet.

Hearing impaired—descriptive of persons with a moderate to severe hearing loss.

Helical ramp—a spiral or circular ramp.

Herringbone pattern—for the layout of parking spaces with alternate rows set at oblique angles to one another.

High turnover—having a high rate of turnover or a higher number than usual of vehicles per space per day.

Hollow-core precast concrete—a slab that has a hollow center section to reduce weight.

Honor box—steel boxes used in metered unattended parking facilities. To pay parking fees, customers insert coins or bills in appropriately numbered slots corresponding to parking space identification. The fee is typically a fixed-day or half-day rate but could also be an hourly rate. Customers are on their honor to pay the parking fee.

Hydrocarbons—compounds containing hydrogen and carbon that result from the operation of an internal combustion engine.

Ice control measures—the control of snow and ice in parking facilities, often accomplished by plowing, applying salt or chemicals, or heating exposed surfaces.

Identification—one of the three main information types in environmental communication; concerns means whereby people know that they have arrived at their destination.

Image—a physical or mental representation; as a mental representation, it can refer to a particular view of an object or an overall view of a large setting (cognitive map).

Imageability—the ease with which the spatial layout of a setting can be understood and mapped.

Impairment—in the context of health, an impairment is any loss or abnormality of psychological, physiological, or anatomical structure or function.

In-and-out parking privileges—parking, usually on a rental basis, in which the vehicle can be taken in and out during the day without added cost.

Indenture—an agreement, often part of a bond issue, that sets forth the terms of debt.

Indirect Source Regulations—regulations proposed by the U.S. Environmental Protection Agency to control the number of new or added parking spaces in connection with emissions from motor vehicles.

Information processing—generic term comprising environmental perception and cognition.

Insert key card—a technology whereby a key card is inserted into a reader slot for reading and verifying key card information.

Interactive display—device used in environmental communication that can, on demand, produce information specific to a user's needs, generally through a presentation on a video screen and/or through a telephone connection.

Interest during construction—interest to be earned on borrowed money during the time of construction; usually calculated when establishing funding requirements.

Intermediate car—medium-sized car between a compact and a full-size car.

Inventory spaces—total number of parking spaces available in a facility or parking system.

Island—a raised area in a roadway, driveway, or parking facility that is used to control or direct traffic flow.

Joint—a division between sections of a floor or slab that permits expansion and contraction of the floor or slab.

Joint materials—fillers, sealers, and similar compounds for filling or covering joints; can be flexible or solid.

Joist—a portion of a floor system that rests on the beams and supports the floor surface.

Journal tape—a cash register or fee computer printout that details each transaction's stream of data, e.g., entry and exit information, sequence number, transaction amount, cash register or fee computer number, and/or cashier code.

Key card access—parking ingress/egress controlled by a key card unit that recognizes a valid card for access to the facility. Key cards can be swiped, inserted, or proximity-read. In general, the higher the level of card system sophistication, the more thorough the control of parking facility operation and revenue production. The key card may identify the patron, count the patron, and signal the barrier gate arm to raise to the open position.

LED—acronym for light-emitting diodes, used in smaller versions of electronic signs.

Lane—a central path or corridor through a parking facility or a lane of a street, such as two-lane or four-lane pavements.

Lane control signals—red/green illuminated signal lights positioned over exit lanes to indicate when the lane is open (green) or closed (red) to traffic.

Lane counter—a nonresettable counter that provides an independent count of vehicles exiting the parking facility through a specific lane.

Lane status lights—a light at an entry or exit lane that indicates "open" or "closed" status. Lane status lights can use color, symbol, or word to denote a lane's use. Color denotes a lane's open or closed status by either green or red, respectively. Symbol denotes a lane's open or closed status by a graphic character.

Lane width—width of a lane, expressed in feet; also called drive-aisle width.

Leased space—parking space leased on a monthly or similar basis.

Legal opinion—certification by recognized legal authority that a bond issue is a proper function of a particular public agency.

Legend—verbal message on a sign face; specifically relates also to cut-out vinyl letters or images.

Legibility—the ease with which a displayed message can be seen or discerned; see also Readability.

Legibility distance—distance at which a given letterform in a given size can be discerned and understood.

Letterform—form that a letter (or alphabet of letters) takes in a given design.

License plate inventory—periodic recording of all vehicle license plate numbers in a parking facility in order to determine length of stay and prevent fraud by patrons claiming lost tickets.

Life safety code—a recently developed code aimed at guaranteeing adequate requirements for new construction.

Light levels—the amount of light intensity, usually measured in candlepower or foot candles in parking facilities.

Literacy impaired—descriptive of persons who are functionally illiterate in any given language, with respect to that language.

Live load—the added weight of vehicles and people imposed on the dead load weight of a structure.

Loading zone—a specially marked area for the short-term use of delivery vehicles.

Lobby entrance—area of a structure that can house elevators, stairs, offices, and similar elements.

Locator signs—parking space signs or other means of helping motorists locate their vehicles when they return to a parking facility.

Lockbox—a heavy metal box used in some parking facilities for the payment of parking fees; see also Honor box.

Long-term parking—parking for at least a half-day.

Lot design—the layout of a parking lot in terms of physical features and parking space layout and flow.

Machine-readable data—data encoded magnetically or by other means on a parking ticket that can be "read" automatically by a machine.

Magnetically coded cards—cards that, when inserted into card readers, activate parking controls through the use of magnetic data imprinted on the cards.

Management fee—amount paid, usually a fixed fee or a percent of revenue, to the professional manager of a parking facility.

Manlift—a mechanical conveyor or belt device for transporting parking attendants between floors of a garage.

Mass transportation—transportation by bus, rail, boat, or other conveyance, either publicly or privately owned, that provides general or special service to the public on a regular and continuing basis (not including school bus, charter, or sightseeing services).

Mechanical garages—garages in which vehicles are raised, lowered, and moved about by means of elevators and conveyor systems.

Metered parking—parking controlled as to time and fee by numbers at each space (see also Slot boxes); also may refer to individual spaces on the street with individual meters.

Mobility—ability to move about or travel safely, comfortably, gracefully, and independently.

Mobility impaired in wheelchairs—persons who are permanently or temporarily restricted to wheelchairs.

Mobility impaired who can walk—persons who have impaired strength, endurance, dexterity, balance, or coordination; those using crutches or other walking aids; persons with strollers, carts, or other encumbrances.

Mode of travel—means of reaching a destination, including walking, cycling, riding transit, driving a car, and being a car passenger.

Modular width—the unit width, in feet, of a module.

Module—a drive aisle with cars parked on each side of the aisle.

Monitor systems—warning systems installed to monitor security and/or concentrations of harmful gases.

Municipal system—a parking system, often composed of both on- and off-street spaces and operated by a municipality.

NFPA—the National Fire Protection Association, a professional association involved in the promotion of fire safety.

Nesting—the procedure by which a vehicle is required to pass through two entrance gates located in different areas before exiting from a facility. The second area, usually farthest from the garage entrance, is considered the nesting area.

Nonverbal communication—those types of communication that rely on symbols, glyphs, or pictures rather than words for their meanings.

O and M—operations and maintenance; the costs, usually expressed on an annual basis, to operate, staff, and maintain a parking facility.

Occupancy rate—the rate at which a given parking facility or parking system is occupied on an hourly, daily, seasonal, or annual basis.

Off-street—beyond the right-of-way of a street or highway.

One-way—accommodating traffic that moves in only one direction.

Online systems—systems in which all principal parking equipment components are linked directly to a central computer.

On-street—curb parking on a street or highway.

Open-deck facility—a parking structure with one or more levels and partial or parapet walls as opposed to a fully enclosed structure.

Operator—firm or individual responsible for the operation of one or more parking facilities either through ownership, lease, contract, or other arrangements.

Oral—spoken.

Orientation—one of the three basic information types in environmental communications; concerns a person's ability to perceive an overview of a given environment and recognize where he or she is at any given time within that environment.

Out clock, time clock, or cashier's clock—a clock that prints the vehicle's exit time on the patron's ticket; upon the completion of each transaction, cashiers calculate the parking fee based on the difference between entry and exit times.

Panel—a portion of a wall or parapet often constructed of concrete, brick, metal, or decorative materials.

Pan joist system—a structural system that uses a combination of joists and form pairs; a cost-effective composite system suitable for use in parking structure design.

Parallel parking spaces—spaces designed parallel to the curb of a street, lot, or parking structure wall.

Parapet—a partial wall usually constructed as part of a parking structure.

Park and ride—system of parking facilities located near mass transit lanes to accommodate the vehicles of travelers who complete their trips on transit vehicles.

Park and shop—validated parking for customers usually provided by an association of merchants.

Parking angle—the angle formed by a parking stall and the wall or centerline of the facility, ranging from 90 degrees (perpendicular) to 30 degrees.

Parking bay—the section of a parking facility containing an aisle and one or two rows of parking spaces.

Parking deck—a structure for vehicle storage or parking usually with partial walls as opposed to a fully enclosed garage.

Parking design—the layout and design of a parking facility based on standard criteria.

Parking fee—the amount charged for parking a vehicle, often determined by the length of stay and/or the area in which the vehicle is parked.

Parking level—a floor or level within a multistory parking facility (also known as a parking tier).

Parking lot—a surface area for parking off the street or beyond the right-of-way.

Parking meter—a mechanical device for collecting coins in payment of parking fees.

Parking regulations—provisions of local ordinances that control curb or off-street parking.

Parking restrictions—provisions of local ordinances that fully or partially restrict curb or off-street parking.

Parking revenue control equipment—mechanical devices used in parking facilities, including gates, counters, cash registers, and detectors.

Parking space—an individual parking stall.

Parking standards—a set of defined criteria for the layout of parking facilities.

Parking structure—any building above grade, below grade, or both for parking motor vehicles.

Parking tax—a tax imposed on parking charges, usually by local government.

Parking ticket—a ticket issued by a ticket dispenser or a parking attendant at an entry lane, identifying the time and date (minute, hour, date, month, and year), lane number, parking area, and (ticket) transaction number in printed numeric and/or magnetically encoded format.

Parking ticket serial number—an identification number, unique to each ticket, printed or magnetically encoded on each ticket at the time a vehicle enters a parking system.

Parking tier—a floor or level within a multistory parking facility (also known as a parking level).

Patron characteristics—the average actions of those using a parking facility or system, generally relating to length of stay or hours of arrival/departure.

Patron fee display—a hardware device, usually external to the cashier booth, that displays the patron's fee due. The device should be permanently positioned. The fee display can be programmed either to display the current time when inactive or to indicate the patron's change due after payment.

Patron intercom system—communication system, button- or voice-activated, built into entrance and exit lanes to permit patrons to talk directly with staff.

Pay-and-display units—patrons insert parking fee into a lockbox and are issued a numbered parking ticket for a specified length of time. Printed instructions tell the customer to display the ticket on the vehicle's dashboard to identify payment of the appropriate parking fee.

Peak period—period of maximum parking activity; can be by the hour, day of week, or season.

Perception—the obtaining of information through the senses.

Perimeter parking—parking space located near the edge of a downtown or similar major generator; also may refer to parking located at the ends and sides of parking facilities.

Pictograph—glyph or symbol incorporated into a sign.

Precast concrete—concrete building components fabricated at a plant and shipped to the construction site.

Prefabricated parking facility—a facility constructed in sections off site and then shipped to the site for assembly.

Post-tensioned concrete—concrete strengthened by the tightening of cables extended through the slab.

Poured-in-place concrete—concrete poured into forms erected on the jobsite, as opposed to precast concrete.

Printer—to validate a parking ticket, the printer records the date, time of exit, sequence number, transaction amount, rate code, and fee computer number or cashier number; a receipt may be issued by the printer or a separate unit.

Proprietary building systems—building systems owned and patented by an outside firm that receives fees for use of the systems.

Proximity key card—key card that is presented to the "face" of the access reader for verification of the key card; no swiping or insertion needed.

Public address system—audible system consisting of microphone, amplifier, and loudspeaker.

Punch-hole autoread—a fee computer that calculates the parking fee based on the punch holes inserted by the ticket-issuing machine at the entry and the fee computer's internal clock date and time.

Punch-hole-read tickets—autoread ticket feature derived from strategically placed holes punched in parking tickets at the entry point.

Radio transmitter—a hardware device that activates barrier gates when a vehicle's driver activates a hand-held transmitter; the transmitter in turn sends a radio signal to the barrier gate controller to raise the gate arm to the open position.

Ramp—an inclined portion of a parking structure for vehicle travel purposes only or for accommodating parking spaces on one or both sides of the ramp.

Ramp, express—a ramp, usually extending several floors or levels, for direct exit from a facility.

Ramp, garage—a garage or deck composed entirely of ramped floors connected at various levels.

Ramp, spiral—see Helical ramp.

Rates—the charges imposed for parking in a parking facility or an entire system.

Rating agencies—the recognized agencies that rate municipal bond issues, notably Moody's and Standard and Poor's.

Readability—the ease with which a message can be understood; see also Legibility.

Recirculation—the reentry of drivers into the interior flow pattern of a parking facility to search for vacant spaces.

Redeal—the act of resetting the access card system to let out parking patrons who have forgotten to swipe their card at a nesting or other exit reader.

Rental payments—income to a parking system from monthly, quarterly, or other long-term renters.

Reserve accounts—special accounts established in a bond issue.

Reservoir space—storage space within a parking facility for vehicles entering or exiting (also called queue area).

Return on investment (ROI)—the annual rate of return or earnings on an amount invested.

Revenue bond—a bond issue, generally marketed by a public agency, that is retired from the revenues produced by an improvement, such as a parking structure.

Revenue control equipment—the individual component items of equipment, such as gates, ticket dispensers and readers, cashier terminals, and others, that constitute the total revenue control system.

Revenue control system—system for the handling of money and recording of transactions to ensure control of revenue.

Revenue, parking—the actual revenue generated by a parking facility or system by providing parking space for vehicular parking.

Revenue projections—forecast of revenue anticipated from a parking facility or system.

Running time—the length of time a vehicle remains in motion within a parking facility.

Scanning—visual sweeping intended to get an overall idea of a setting.

Scissor-ramp garage—a design format in which ramped floors are situated opposite one another like the blades of scissors; also called a double-helix garage.

Screen, decorative—a screen, often of metallic or masonry materials, used to cover open areas of parking structures.

Search pattern—the flow pattern through a parking facility of vehicles in search of available parking spaces.

Search time—the time required to find an available space.

Security system—protective system installed in parking facilities, including closed-circuit television, voice transmissions, patrol of the facility, or special materials that improve visibility.

Seepage—the leaking of water through components of a structure.

Self-park facility—one in which cars are parked by the driver rather than by attendants or mechanical systems.

Self-service—see Self-park facility.

Service traffic—traffic, such as emergency equipment, utility vehicles, and delivery vehicles, required to provide necessary services to a given area.

Shear wall—specially designed wall sections of a structure intended to transmit loads that might otherwise deform the members.

Shorelining—maintaining of meaningful contact, by a blind person using a cane, of a continuous and recognizable environmental component, such as a curb.

Short span—the span of a beam that is less than the total length of the parking bay or module; usually involves columns between the outer walls of the structure.

Short-term parking—parking for a short period of time, usually less than eight hours.

Shuttle bus—local bus used to transport passengers between parking facilities or other terminals and major generators.

Sight impaired—persons with poor eyesight, partial vision, or anomalies of vision such as color deficiency and reduced fields.

Sign face—reading area of a sign on which are displayed its legends.

Signs, directional—signs that control the flow of traffic within a parking facility.

Simulation model—a mathematical model developed to simulate the use of a given improvement, in this case, a parking facility.

Single tee—a precast concrete element used to form a beam of the parking structure and shaped like the letter T.

Site—the area on which a parking facility or other improvement is constructed.

Site characteristics—the physical features of a site, such as shape, area, topography, soil conditions, and access.

Site location—analysis and investigation of a given site and the determination of its usability for particular purposes.

Slab—the exposed wearing surface laid over the beams of a structure.

Sloped-floor garage—see Ramp garage.

Slot boxes—boxes with slots numbered to correspond to parking spaces for the payment of parking fees; also called slot meter boxes or honor boxes.

Soffit—the exposed undersurface of any overhead component of a building, such as an arch, balcony, beam, cornice, lintel, or vault.

Sound detection—see Security system.

Space count—total number of spaces in a facility or system.

Space-counting device—see Differential counter.

Span—the span or length of a beam; the unsupported distance between columns.

Spatial cognition—retaining, understanding, structuring, and manipulating information of a spatial nature.

Spatial orientation—having an adequate cognitive map of a setting and being able to situate oneself therein.

Spatial planning—design phase to determine the layout of the setting at an urban landscape and architectural scale.

Special-tax district—an area defined by ordinance in which unique taxes can be imposed to fund improvements such as parking.

Specular gloss—sheen reflected off a surface, measured from matte (lacking in gloss) to supergloss.

Speech impaired—persons with articulation or voice disorders or with a developmental disorder that adversely affects their speech.

Sprinkler system—a system of pipes that are affixed to the ceiling or roof of a building and whose valves open at predetermined temperatures to release water for extinguishing fires.

Stair tower—the enclosure surrounding a stairway.

Stall—the area, usually marked with distinguishing lines, in which one vehicle is to be parked; a parking space.

Stall depth—length of the parking space (stall).

Stall width—width of the parking space (stall).

Steel frame—a structure with a framework composed of steel columns and beams.

Storage capacity—see Reservoir space.

Street level—that portion of a facility that is located at the same level as the adjacent street.

Striping—painted lines delineating stalls and circulation patterns.

Structural system—the type of system used in any given structure, such as concrete, steel, or wood.

Subcompact car—a very small vehicle, smaller than a compact.

Superelevation—the banking of a curved roadway or ramp to improve vehicle handling.

Surcharge—a charge, such as a tax or fee, in addition to normal parking charges.

Surface parking—parking at grade.

Survey, soils—the analysis of soil conditions on a particular parcel of property.

Sweeper—a device for cleaning parking areas, often powered by a gasoline or electric motor.

Swipe key card—key card technology whereby an access card is swiped through a reader slot for reading and verifying the card.

Symbol of access—symbol that represents specifically that the access (entrance) next to which it is displayed is accessible to persons in wheelchairs and generally that the facilities of buildings on which it is displayed are as a whole similarly accessible.

Tactile signs—signs with raised letters that are interpreted or read by tracing with fingers over the surfaces.

Tactual communication—information perceived through the sense of touch.

Tax-exempt property—property that, through ownership by charitable or public bodies, does not pay property or other taxes.

Tenant parking—parking provided for the regular tenants of a building or other generator.

Texture—extent to which essential differences in the constituent parts of a material object can be discerned visually, audibly, or tactually.

Three-loop system—in gated systems, a series of three loops, two to arm a device, e.g., ticket-issuing machine or access reader, and a third to signal the barrier gate arm controller to lower the barrier gate arm to the closed position.

Ticket dispensers—ticket-issuing machine (TIM)—equipment component that issues a parking ticket automatically upon detection of a vehicle's presence or when a "ticket issue" button is pushed.

Tier—a floor or level within a multistory parking facility (also known as a parking level).

Token—item used in place of coins for the payment of parking fees.

Token units—payment made at exit by inserting the parking fee due in tokens into a component that causes the parking gate to raise to the open position.

Trade area—the area from which a community or business district draws its patrons.

Traffic flow—the pattern of traffic movement through an area or parking facility.

Transaction receipt—a receipt issued to a patron at the time of payment, designating the transaction, date, and amount of fee paid.

Transient parkers—short-term parkers who pay for the use of a parking space daily, as opposed to long-term (contract) users.

Turning radius—the pavement or ramp width necessary to permit a vehicle to complete a turning maneuver.

Turnover—the number of vehicles using a given space or facility each day, often expressed as a ratio of the total number of vehicles using the facility in a given period to the total number of parking spaces in the facility.

Two-loop system—in gated systems, a series of two loops, one to arm a device, e.g., ticket-issuing machine or access reader, and a second to signal the barrier gate arm controller to lower the barrier gate arm to the closed position.

Underground garage—garage constructed entirely underground or below grade.

Ungated—parking revenue control systems that exclude the use of entry or exit barrier gates to control ingress/egress.

Uninterruptible power supply (UPS)—hardware device that contains a battery to power the revenue control system, including the computer equipment, in the event of a power failure.

Unsatisfied demand—the number of vehicles that cannot be accommodated in a parking facility or system.

Up ramp—a directional ramp for traffic moving upward through a parking structure.

VMT—vehicle miles of travel; the total vehicle miles of travel within any specified area or any parking facility.

Valet parking—attendant parking, usually provided as a service to patrons of commercial establishments.

Validation—ticket procedure by which merchants or service providers encourage customer purchases by minimizing the patron's cost of parking.

Validator—hardware component of the fee computer or a standalone device of autoread systems that pulls the ticket into the hardware where the entry lane–encoded information is read and compared to the fee computer's internal clock for parking fee computation.

Vandalism—malicious damage to property or vehicles.

Vehicle counter—a device used to count vehicles entering and leaving a facility.

Vehicle detector—device that senses the presence of a vehicle in a traffic lane.

Ventilation systems—systems, either mechanical or structural, for providing fresh air to a parking facility.

Verbal—concerned with words; distinct from nonverbal (concerned with pictures); not to be confused with oral.

Vinyl—very thin plastic film, opaque or translucent, used for creating graphic messages or backgrounds on signs.

Visitor parking—usually short-term parking.

Visual communication—information perceived through the sense of sight.

Walking distance—the approximate distance patrons will walk between a parking facility and traffic generators.

Waterproofing—the application of chemicals or other compounds to seal a structure from water and injurious chemicals.

Wayfinding—finding one's way to a destination; spatial problem solving comprising three interdependent processes: decision making, decision executing, and information processing.

Wearing surface—the topmost layer of any pavement.

Wheel or live load—the added load in a parking structure created by the parked vehicle.

Wheelstop—a bumper or block placed at the head of a parking stall to restrain a vehicle from moving forward.

Zoning—the regulation of land use, on a parcel or area basis, by local ordinance.